AFRICAN AMERICAN BIOGRAPHY

AFRICAN AMERICAN REFERENCE LIBRARY

African American Biography

VOLUME 5

Judson Knight

Lawrence W. Baker, Editor

**South Huntington Pub. Lib.
145 Pidgeon Hill Rd.
Huntington Sta., N.Y. 11746**

AN IMPRINT OF GALE

African American Biography, volume 5

Judson Knight

Staff

Lawrence W. Baker, *U•X•L Senior Editor*
Carol DeKane Nagel, *U•X•L Managing Editor*
Thomas L. Romig, *U•X•L Publisher*

Margaret Chamberlain, *Permissions Specialist (Pictures)*

Deborah Milliken, *Production Assistant*
Evi Seoud, *Assistant Production Manager*
Mary Beth Trimper, *Production Director*

Cynthia Baldwin, *Product Design Manager*

Pamela Reed, *Imaging Coordinator*
Gary Leach, *Graphic Artist*
Robert Duncan, *Senior Imaging Specialist*
Randy A. Bassett, *Image Database Supervisor*
Barbara J. Yarrow, *Graphic Services Manager*

Marco Di Vita, Graphix Group, *Typesetting*

This publication is a creative work protected by all applicable copyright laws, as well as by misappropriation, trade secret, unfair competition, and other applicable laws. The editors of this work have added value to the underlying factual material herein through one or more of the following: unique and original selection, coordination, expression, arrangement, and classification of the information. All rights to this publication will be vigorously defended.

Copyright © 1999
U•X•L, an imprint of The Gale Group
27500 Drake Rd.
Farmington Hills, MI 48331-3535

All rights reserved, including the right of reproduction in whole or in part in any form.

ISBN 0-7876-3562-6
ISSN 1522-2934

Printed in the United States of America
10 9 8 7 6 5 4 3 2

*To Tyler, who was born along with this book;
and to Deidre, who labored with me.*

Contents

Tiger Woods

Entries by Field of Endeavor ix
Reader's Guide. xxiii
Timeline of African American Events xxvii
Words to Know. xliii

Volume 5

Benjamin Banneker 1
Marion Barry. 9
Halle Berry 13
Ron Brown 17
Cab Calloway 23
Alice Childress 27
Cinque. 31
Bill Cosby. 41
Dorothy Dandridge 47

Dominique Dawes 53
Delany Sisters 59
Ralph Ellison 67
Louis Farrakhan 71
Ella Fitzgerald 77
George Foreman 81
Arthur Gaston 89
Zelma Watson George 93
Charles Gordone 97
Florence Griffith Joyner 101
Greg Gumbel 109
Alexis Herman 115
Jesse Jackson, Jr. 121
Earvin "Magic" Johnson 127
Barbara Jordan 133
Michael Jordan 139
Alan Keyes 147
Terry McMillan 155
Ronald McNair 159
Thelma "Butterfly" McQueen 165
Colin Powell 171
Chris Rock 177
Wilma Rudolph 185
Betty Shabazz 189
Tupac Shakur 197
O. J. Simpson 207
Tina Turner 217
Tuskegee Airmen 225
Venus Williams 233
Eldrick "Tiger" Woods 239
Andrew Young 249

Bibliography lix

Picture Credits lxxix

Index lxxxi

Entries by Field of Endeavor

Alexis Herman

Includes African American Biography, volumes 1–5. **Boldface** *type indicates volume number; regular type indicates page numbers; (u) indicates update to original entry.*

Art

Clementine Hunter	**2:** 366
Jacob Lawrence	**3:** 464
Gordon Parks	**3:** 575
Henry Ossawa Tanner	**4:** 696

Business

Dave Bing	**1:** 65
Elleanor Eldridge	**2:** 225
Arthur Gaston	**2:** 258, **5:** 89 (u)
Berry Gordy, Jr.	**2:** 286
Alexis Herman	**5:** 115

John H. Johnson **2:** 405
Jesse Owens **3:** 570
Barbara Gardner Proctor **3:** 594
Dudley Randall **3:** 607
Naomi Sims **4:** 672
Madame C. J. Walker **4:** 750
Maggie L. Walker **4:** 752
Oprah Winfrey **4:** 792
Andrew Young **5:** 249

Dance
Alvin Ailey **1:** 8
Katherine Dunham **1:** 215
Gregory Hines **2:** 349
Bill T. Jones **2:** 411

Education
Molefi Kete Asante **1:** 23
Augusta Baker **1:** 31
Amiri Baraka **1:** 37
Marguerite Ross Barnett **1:** 43
Mary McLeod Bethune **1:** 63
Shirley Chisholm **1:** 138
Joe Clark **1:** 140
Jewel Plummer Cobb **1:** 148
Johnnetta Betsch Cole **1:** 151
Marva Collins **1:** 160
Anna J. Cooper **1:** 165
Ellen Craft **1:** 175
Angela Davis **1:** 180
Juliette Derricotte **1:** 193
Irene Diggs **1:** 196
William Edward Burghardt (W. E. B.) Du Bois **1:** 209
Mary Hatwood Futrell **2:** 250
Henry Louis Gates, Jr. **2:** 261
Anita Hill **2:** 344
Elma Lewis **3:** 473

Naomi Long Madgett	**3:** 484
George Marion McClellan	**3:** 512
Elsanda Goode Robeson	**3:** 618
Charlemae Hill Rollins	**3:** 627
Gloria Scott	**4:** 654
Betty Shabazz	**5:** 189
Shelby Steele	**4:** 686
Niara Sudarkasa	**4:** 693
Mary Church Terrell	**4:** 707
Booker T. Washington	**4:** 758
Carter G. Woodson	**4:** 798

Exploration and adventure

Bessie Coleman	**1:** 158
Matthew Henson	**2:** 338
Mae C. Jemison	**2:** 394
Ronald McNair	**5:** 159

Fashion

Naomi Campbell	**1:** 116
Whitney Houston	**2:** 359
Beverly Johnson	**2:** 397
Elizabeth Keckley	**3:** 441
Patrick Kelly	**3:** 443
Annie Turnbo Malone	**3:** 490
Naomi Sims	**4:** 672

Film

Harry Belafonte	**1:** 55
Halle Berry	**1:** 61, **5:** 13 (u)
Naomi Campbell	**1:** 116
Dorothy Dandridge	**5:** 47
Ossie Davis	**1:** 188
Sammy Davis, Jr.	**1:** 191
Robin Givens	**2:** 273
Danny Glover	**2:** 276
Whoopi Goldberg	**2:** 278

Dick Gregory **2:** 289
Arsenio Hall **2:** 304
Gregory Hines **2:** 349
Lena Horne **2:** 357
Whitney Houston **2:** 359
Ice-T **2:** 371
Janet Jackson **2:** 376
Beverly Johnson **2:** 397
James Earl Jones **2:** 413
Spike Lee **3:** 467
Hattie McDaniel **3:** 515
Thelma "Butterfly" McQueen . . . . **3:** 525, **5:** 165 (u)
Eddie Murphy **3:** 552
Gordon Parks **3:** 575
Sidney Poitier **3:** 580
Richard Pryor **3:** 597
Paul Robeson **3:** 621
Diana Ross **3:** 629
Tupac Shakur **5:** 197
O. J. Simpson **5:** 207
John Singleton **4:** 674
Wesley Snipes **4:** 680
Robert Townsend **4:** 721
Tina Turner **5:** 217
Mario Van Peebles **4:** 737
Denzel Washington **4:** 761
Keenen Ivory Wayans **4:** 769
Oprah Winfrey **4:** 792

Government and politics

Marion Barry . . . . **1:** 45, **5:** 9 (u)
Mary McLeod Bethune **1:** 63
Julian Bond **1:** 67
Carol Moseley Braun **1:** 80
Edward W. Brooke, III **1:** 83
Ron Brown . . . . **1:** 95, **5:** 17 (u)
Ralph Bunche **1:** 104

Yvonne Burke Brathwaite	**1:** 106
Shirley Chisholm	**1:** 138
David Dinkins	**1:** 198
Marcus Garvey	**2:** 255
Zelma Watson George	**2:** 263, **5:** 93 (u)
W. Wilson Goode	**2:** 281
Patricia Harris	**2:** 328
Alexis Herman	**5:** 115
Jesse Jackson	**2:** 378
Jesse Jackson, Jr.	**5:** 121
Barbara Jordan	**2:** 424, **5:** 133 (u)
Sharon Pratt Kelly	**3:** 445
Alan Keyes	**5:** 147
Jewel Stradford Lafontant	**3:** 462
Constance Baker Motley	**3:** 544
Hazel O'Leary	**3:** 565
Adam Clayton Powell, Jr.	**3:** 583
L. Douglas Wilder	**4:** 773
Andrew Young	**5:** 249
Coleman Young	**4:** 803

Law

Carol Moseley Braun	**1:** 80
Yvonne Braithwaite Burke	**1:** 106
Marian Wright Edelman	**2:** 223
Patricia Harris	**2:** 328
Anita Hill	**2:** 344
Benjamin L. Hooks	**2:** 354
Barbara Jordan	**2:** 424, **5:** 133 (u)
Vernon E. Jordan, Jr.	**2:** 430
Flo Kennedy	**2:** 448
Jewel Stradford Lafontant	**3:** 462
Thurgood Marshall	**3:** 504
Constance Baker Motley	**3:** 544
Pauli Murray	**3:** 555
Edith Sampson	**4:** 647
Althea T. L. Simmons	**4:** 667

Juanita Kidd Stout **4:** 691
Clarence Thomas **4:** 710

Literature and journalism

Maya Angelou **1:** 17
Molefi Kete Asante **1:** 23
James Baldwin **1:** 34
Amiri Baraka **1:** 37
Ida B. Wells Barnett **1:** 40
Daisy Bates **1:** 50
Arna Bontemps **1:** 73
Ed Bradley **1:** 78
Gwendolyn Brooks **1:** 86
Claude Brown **1:** 88
H. Rap Brown **1:** 91
Ed Bullins **1:** 99
Octavia E. Butler **1:** 109
Stokely Carmichael **1:** 118
Charles Waddell Chesnutt **1:** 132
Alice Childress . . . . **1:** 135, **5:** 27 (u)
Eldridge Cleaver **1:** 143
Anna J. Cooper **1:** 165
Countee Cullen **1:** 178
Delany Sisters **5:** 59
William Edward Burghardt (W. E. B.) Du Bois **1:** 209
Paul Laurence Dunbar **1:** 212
Ralph Ellison . . . . **2:** 232, **5:** 67 (u)
John Hope Franklin **2:** 247
Ernest J. Gaines **2:** 253
Henry Louis Gates, Jr. **2:** 261
Nikki Giovanni **2:** 271
Charles Gordone . . . . **2:** 284, **5:** 97 (u)
Angelina Weld Grimké **2:** 291
Alex Haley **2:** 301
Virginia Hamilton **2:** 309
Lorraine Hansberry **2:** 317
Robert Hayden **2:** 330

Chester Himes	**2:** 346
Langston Hughes	**2:** 362
Zora Neale Hurston	**2:** 368
James Weldon Johnson	**2:** 402
Alan Keyes	**5:** 147
Naomi Long Madgett	**3:** 464
Paule Marshall	**3:** 501
George Marion McClellan	**3:** 512
Claude McKay	**3:** 517
Terry McMillan	**3:** 522, **5:** 155 (u)
Ron Milner	**3:** 530
Toni Morrison	**3:** 541
Willard Motley	**3:** 546
Gloria Naylor	**3:** 557
Huey Newton	**3:** 560
Gordon Parks	**3:** 575
Dudley Randall	**3:** 607
William Raspberry	**3:** 613
Ishmael Reed	**3:** 616
Charlemae Hill Rollins	**3:** 627
Carl T. Rowan	**3:** 632
Sonia Sanchez	**4:** 649
Bobby Seale	**4:** 657
Ntozake Shange	**4:** 662
Carole Simpson	**4:** 670
Shelby Steele	**4:** 686
Mildred Taylor	**4:** 699
Susan Taylor	**4:** 702
Jean Toomer	**4:** 713
William Monroe Trotter	**4:** 724
Mario Van Peebles	**4:** 737
Alice Walker	**4:** 747
Phillis Wheatley	**4:** 771
John A. Williams	**4:** 782
Sherley Anne Williams	**4:** 787
August Wilson	**4:** 790
Carter G. Woodson	**4:** 798

Richard Wright **4:** 800
Whitney M. Young **4:** 806

Medicine

Benjamin Carson **1:** 121
Charles Richard Drew **1:** 207
Effie O'Neal Ellis. **2:** 230
Lucille C. Gunning **2:** 297
Mae C. Jemison. **2:** 394
Daniel Hale Williams **4:** 779

Military

Benjamin O. Davis, Sr. **1:** 183
Marcelite J. Harris **2:** 325
Daniel James, Jr. **2:** 392
Colin Powell . . . . **3:** 586, **5:** 171 (u)
Tuskegee Airmen **5:** 225

Music

Marian Anderson. **1:** 14
Louis Armstrong **1:** 20
Pearl Bailey **1:** 28
Josephine Baker **1:** 32
Count Basie **1:** 48
Kathleen Battle. **1:** 53
Harry Belafonte **1:** 55
Chuck Berry **1:** 58
James Brown. **1:** 93
Grace Bumbry **1:** 101
Cab Calloway . . . . **1:** 111, **5:** 23 (u)
Naomi Campbell **1:** 116
Ray Charles **1:** 130
Nat "King" Cole **1:** 153
Natalie Cole. **1:** 155
John Coltrane **1:** 163
Elizabeth Cotten **1:** 173
Miles Davis **1:** 186

Entries by Field of Endeavor

Sammy Davis, Jr.	**1:** 191
Thomas A. Dorsey	**1:** 201
Duke Ellington	**2:** 227
Ella Fitzgerald	**2:** 242, **5:** 77 (u)
Aretha Franklin	**2:** 245
Zelma Watson George	**2:** 263, **5:** 93 (u)
Dizzy Gillespie	**2:** 268
Berry Gordy, Jr.	**2:** 286
Hammer	**2:** 312
Lionel Hampton	**2:** 314
Jimi Hendrix	**2:** 336
Billie Holiday	**2:** 351
Lena Horne	**2:** 357
Whitney Houston	**2:** 359
Ice-T	**2:** 371
Janet Jackson	**2:** 376
Mahalia Jackson	**2:** 382
Michael Jackson	**2:** 384
Beverly Johnson	**2:** 397
Robert Johnson	**2:** 409
Quincy Jones	**2:** 416
Sissieretta Jones	**2:** 419
Scott Joplin	**2:** 421
B. B. King	**3:** 451
Coretta Scott King	**3:** 453
Little Richard	**3:** 476
Branford Marsalis	**3:** 495
Wynton Marsalis	**3:** 498
Hattie McDaniel	**3:** 515
Thelonious Monk	**3:** 533
Jessye Norman	**3:** 562
Leontyne Price	**3:** 589
Charley Pride	**3:** 592
Public Enemy	**3:** 599
Queen Latifah	**3:** 605
Paul Robeson	**3:** 621
Diana Ross	**3:** 629

Tupac Shakur	**5:** 197
Bessie Smith	**4:** 677
William Grant Still	**4:** 689
Tina Turner	**5:** 217
Sarah Vaughan	**4:** 739
Sippie Wallace	**4:** 755
André Watts	**4:** 766
Stevie Wonder	**4:** 795

Religion

Ralph David Abernathy	**1:** 5
George Clements	**1:** 146
Louis Farrakhan	**2:** 239, **5:** 71 (u)
Barbara Harris	**2:** 323
Benjamin L. Hooks	**2:** 354
Jesse Jackson	**2:** 378
Martin Luther King, Jr.	**3:** 456
Malcolm X	**3:** 487
Eugene A. Marino	**3:** 493
Elijah Muhammad	**3:** 549
Adam Clayton Powell, Jr.	**3:** 583
Al Sharpton	**4:** 664
George Stallings	**4:** 683

Science and technology

Benjamin Banneker	**5:** 1
George Washington Carver	**1:** 124
Jewel Plummer Cobb	**1:** 148
Shirley Ann Jackson	**2:** 387
Mae C. Jemison	**2:** 394
Ronald McNair	**5:** 159
Garrett Morgan	**3:** 538
Lloyd Albert Quarterman	**3:** 602
Eslanda Goode Robeson	**3:** 618
Daniel Hale Williams	**4:** 779

Social issues

Ralph Abernathy	**1:** 5
Arthur Ashe	**1:** 25
Amiri Baraka	**1:** 37
Ida B. Wells Barnett	**1:** 40
Daisy Bates	**1:** 50
Harry Belafonte	**1:** 55
Mary McLeod Bethune	**1:** 63
Julian Bond	**1:** 67
H. Rap Brown	**1:** 91
Stokely Carmichael	**1:** 118
Cinque	**5:** 31
Eldridge Cleaver	**1:** 143
George Clements	**1:** 146
Johnnetta Betsch Cole	**1:** 151
Bill Cosby	**1:** 170, **5:** 41 (u)
Ellen Craft	**1:** 175
Angela Davis	**1:** 180
Irene Diggs	**1:** 196
Frederick Douglass	**1:** 204
William Edward Burghardt (W. E. B.) Du Bois	**1:** 209
Katherine Dunham	**1:** 215
Marian Wright Edelman	**2:** 223
Medgar Evers	**2:** 234
James Farmer	**2:** 237
Marcus Garvey	**2:** 255
Zelma Watson George	**2:** 263, **5:** 93 (u)
Dick Gregory	**2:** 289
Clara Hale	**2:** 299
Fannie Lou Hamer	**2:** 307
Dorothy Height	**2:** 333
Aileen Hernandez	**2:** 341
Anita Hill	**2:** 344
Benjamin L. Hooks	**2:** 354
Roy Innis	**2:** 374
Jesse Jackson	**2:** 378

John Jacob	**2:** 389
James Weldon Johnson	**2:** 402
Vernon E. Jordan, Jr.	**2:** 430
Flo Kennedy	**3:** 448
Alan Keyes	**5:** 147
Coretta Scott King	**3:** 453
Martin Luther King, Jr.	**3:** 456
Yolanda King	**3:** 459
Joseph E. Lowery	**3:** 482
Malcolm X	**3:** 487
Biddy Mason	**3:** 507
Floyd B. McKissick	**3:** 520
James Meredith	**3:** 527
Audley Moore	**3:** 536
Elijah Muhammad	**3:** 549
Pauli Murray	**3:** 555
Huey Newton	**3:** 560
Rosa Parks	**3:** 578
A. Philip Randolph	**3:** 610
Eslanda Goode Robeson	**3:** 618
Paul Robeson	**3:** 621
Bayard Rustin	**3:** 639
Dred Scott	**4:** 652
Bobby Seale	**4:** 657
Attalah Shabazz	**4:** 659
Betty Shabazz	**5:** 189
Al Sharpton	**4:** 664
Althea T. L. Simmons	**4:** 667
Shelby Steele	**4:** 686
Susie Baker King Taylor	**4:** 704
Mary Church Terrell	**4:** 707
Toussaint-Louverture	**4:** 718
William Monroe Trotter	**4:** 724
Sojourner Truth	**4:** 727
Harriet Tubman	**4:** 730
Nat Turner	**4:** 733
Denmark Vesey	**4:** 742

Charleszetta Waddles **4:** 744
Madame C. J. Walker **4:** 750
Faye Wattleton **4:** 763
Roy Wilkins **4:** 776
Andrew Young **5:** 249
Whitney M. Young **4:** 806

Sports

Hank Aaron **1:** 1
Kareem Abdul-Jabbar **1:** 3
Muhammad Ali **1:** 11
Arthur Ashe **1:** 25
Dave Bing **1:** 65
Bobby Bonilla **1:** 71
Riddick Bowe **1:** 75
Roy Campanella **1:** 114
Wilt Chamberlain **1:** 127
Dominique Dawes **5:** 53
George Foreman **5:** 81
Althea Gibson **2:** 266
Florence Griffith Joyner **5:** 101
The Harlem Globetrotters **2:** 320
Earvin "Magic" Johnson . . . . **2:** 400, **5:** 127 (u)
Michael Jordan . . . . **2:** 427, **5:** 139 (u)
Jackie Joyner-Kersee **2:** 432
Carl Lewis **3:** 471
Joe Louis **3:** 479
Willie Mays **3:** 509
Shaquille O'Neal **3:** 567
Jesse Owens **3:** 570
Satchel Paige **3:** 573
Jackie Robinson **3:** 624
Wilma Rudolph . . . . **3:** 634, **5:** 185 (u)
Bill Russell **3:** 637
O. J. Simpson **5:** 207
Venus Williams **5:** 233
Eldrick "Tiger" Woods **5:** 239

Television

Ed Bradley	**1:** 78
Don Cornelius	**1:** 168
Bill Cosby	**1:** 170, **5:** 41 (u)
Whoopi Goldberg	**2:** 278
Dick Gregory	**2:** 289
Bryant Gumbel	**2:** 294
Greg Gumbel	**5:** 109
Arsenio Hall	**2:** 304
Carl T. Rowan	**3:** 632
Carole Simpson	**4:** 670
Susan Taylor	**4:** 702
Robert Townsend	**4:** 721
Keenen Ivory Wayans	**4:** 769
Montel Williams	**4:** 784
Oprah Winfrey	**4:** 792

Theater

Charles Gordone	**2:** 284, **5:** 97 (u)
Yolanda King	**3:** 459
Paul Robeson	**3:** 621
Attalah Shabazz	**4:** 659
Jackie Torrence	**4:** 716

Reader's Guide

Tuskegee Airmen

African American Biography, Volume 5, presents 21 new entries on African Americans from many different areas of endeavor. In addition, profiles for 19 people from Volumes 1 through 4 are updated with new information. All profiles include both historical and contemporary figures, and cover such fields as civil rights, athletics, politics, literature, entertainment, science, religion and the military. With this fifth volume, *African American Biography* becomes an annual publication. Included in each new volume will be updates from previous volumes.

In Volume 5, students will read about "comeback kid" boxer George Foreman, *Challenger* astronaut Ronald McNair, the pioneering Tuskegee Airmen, singer-actress Tina Turner, and more. Other entries provide updates on comedian Bill Cosby, writer Charles Gordone, former U.S. congresswoman Barbara Jordan, *Gone with the Wind* actress Butterfly McQueen, and more.

Other features in *African American Biography, Volume 5*, include the following:

Reader's Guide | xxiii

- A list of African Americans from all five volumes, arranged by their field of specialization
- A chronology of events documenting important facts relating to the 40 African Americans covered in Volume 5
- Sidebar boxes that highlight information of special interest to students
- A "Words to Know" section that provides definitions for difficult cultural and common terms
- Extensive cross references, making it easy to refer to other African Americans covered in all five volumes; cross references to other entries in volume 5 are bold-faced upon the first mention in an entry
- Sources for further reading so students know where to delve even deeper
- A cumulative subject index, which allows students to easily find the people, organizations, and concepts discussed in all five volumes
- Black-and-white photos for each entry

African American Reference Library

The *African American Biography* set is only one component of the five-part African American Reference Library. Other titles in this multicultural series include:

- *African American Almanac:* This three-volume set provides a comprehensive range of historical and current information on African American life and culture. Organized by subject, the volumes contain 270 black-and-white illustrations, a selected bibliography, and a cumulative subject index.
- *African American Breakthroughs:* This volume provides fascinating details on hundreds of "firsts" involving African Americans. Arranged in subject categories, the entries summarize events and include brief biographies of many pioneers in African American history. This volume features illustrations, a timeline of firsts, and a thorough subject index.

- *African American Chronology:* This two-volume set explores significant social, political, economic, cultural, and educational milestones in black history. Arranged by year and then by month and day, the volumes span from 1492 until June 30, 1993, and contain 106 illustrations, extensive cross references, and a cumulative subject index.

- *African American Voices:* This title presents 35 full or excerpted speeches and other notable spoken works of African Americans. Each entry is accompanied by an introduction and boxes explaining terms and events to which the speech refers. The two-volume set contains pertinent black-and-white illustrations, a timeline, and a subject index.

Acknowledgments

Special thanks are due to Marco Di Vita, of the Graphix Group, for his quick and creative typesetting; Margaret Chamberlain, for her smooth handling of the permissions process; Allison Jones, for her proofreading; and Beth Baker, for her quality-minded indexing work.

The following advisors provided valuable comments and suggestions to *African American Biography, Volume 5:* Lynne Hofflund, Cabrillo Middle School, Ventura, California; Ann Marie Laprise, Detroit Public Library, Elmwood Park Branch, Detroit, Michigan; and Janet Sarratt, Ewing Junior High School, Gaffney, South Carolina.

Comments and suggestions

We welcome your comments on *African American Biography* as well as your suggestions for biographies to be featured in future volumes. Please write: Editors, *African American Biography,* U•X•L, 27500 Drake Rd., Farmington Hills, Michigan, 48331-3535; call toll-free: 1-800-877-4253; or fax 248-699-8066.

Timeline of African American Events

Andrew Young

1731 Benjamin Banneker is born.

1792 Benjamin Banneker assists in surveying the future city of Washington, D.C; he also begins publishing his almanac.

1806 Benjamin Banneker dies.

1810s Cinque is born in Africa.

1838 Cinque leads the other slaves aboard the *Amistad* in a mutiny.

1841 The U.S. Supreme Court rules in favor of Cinque and other *Amistad* mutineers; Cinque later returns to Africa.

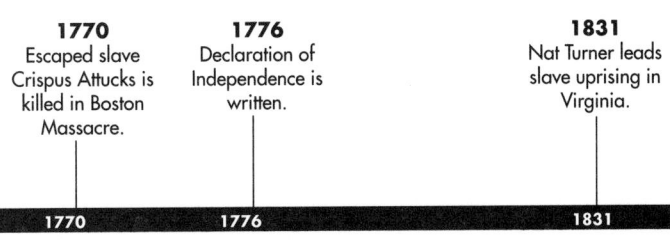

1770 Escaped slave Crispus Attucks is killed in Boston Massacre.

1776 Declaration of Independence is written.

1831 Nat Turner leads slave uprising in Virginia.

Timeline of African American Events

1861	The Civil War begins.
1863	The Emancipation Proclamation is signed by U.S. president Abraham Lincoln, freeing all slaves in the Confederate states.
1865	The Civil War ends; President Lincoln is assassinated.
1880s	Cinque dies.
1889	Sadie Delany is born.
1891	Bessie Delany is born.
1892	Arthur Gaston is born.
1903	Zelma Watson George is born.
1907	Cab Calloway is born.
1911	Thelma "Butterfly" McQueen is born.
1912	The luxury ocean liner *Titanic* sinks.
1912	Future Tuskegee Airmen leader Benjamin Davis is born.
1914	Ralph Ellison is born.
1914	World War I begins in Europe.
1915	*Birth of a Nation* is released; though an artistic success, the racist film leads to the resurgence of the Ku Klux Klan.
1917	The United States enters World War I; Arthur Gaston is among those who signs up to fight.
1918	Ella Fitzgerald is born.
1918	World War I ends.
1920	Alice Childress is born.
1922	Dorothy Dandridge is born.

Timeline of African American Events

1925	Charles Gordone is born.
1929	The Cab Calloway Orchestra begins playing at the Cotton Club in Harlem, New York.
1929	The stock market crashes, leading to the Depression.
1932	Andrew Young is born.
1933	Louis Farrakhan is born.
1936	Barbara Jordan is born.
1936	Marion Barry is born.
1936	Betty Shabazz is born.
1937	Colin Powell is born.
1937	Bill Cosby is born.
1939	Butterfly McQueen and Hattie McDaniel appear in *Gone with the Wind*.
1939	World War II begins in Europe with the German invasion of Poland.
1939	Tina Turner is born.
1940	Wilma Rudolph is born.
1941	The 66th Air Force Contract Flying School, home of the Tuskegee Airmen, opens.
1941	Ron Brown is born.
1941	The United States enters World War II after the Japanese bomb Pearl Harbor in Hawaii.
1942	The first class of Tuskegee Airmen graduates.
1943	Charles B. Hall of Indiana becomes the first Tuskegee flyer to shoot down a German aircraft.

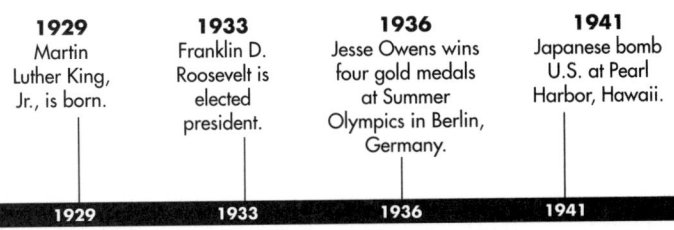

Timeline of African American Events

1944	In a five-minute span in January, Tuskegee pilots over Italy shoot down five German aircraft.
1944	The Normandy invasion (D-Day) takes place.
1944	The 99th Squadron—the most prominent group of the Tuskegee Airmen—combines with three other Tuskegee-trained squadrons.
1945	A group of Tuskegee-trained officers are denied entry to a white officers' club at Freeman Field in Indiana; when they protest, many are arrested and later court-martialed.
1945	German dictator Adolf Hitler commits suicide; a week later, Germany surrenders, ending the war in Europe.
1945	World War II ends when the Japanese surrender.
1946	Greg Gumbel is born.
1947	O. J. Simpson is born.
1947	Alexis Herman is born.
1949	George Foreman is born.
1949	U.S. president Harry S Truman integrates the armed forces.
1950	Zelma Watson George becomes the first African American woman to sing in a Broadway opera.
1950	Alan Keyes is born.
1950	Ronald McNair is born.
1951	Terry McMillan is born.
1952	Ralph Ellison publishes *Invisible Man*.
1953	Dorothy Dandridge appears opposite Harry Belafonte in *Bright Road*.

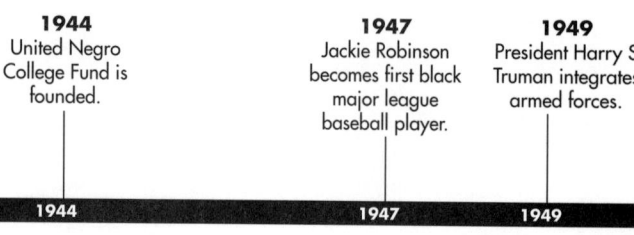

Timeline of African American Events

1954	Dorothy Dandridge appears in *Carmen Jones,* and later receives an Oscar nomination.
1954	The *Brown v. Board of Education* decision integrates public schools in the South.
1956	Alice Childress's play *Trouble in the Mind* wins an Obie Award.
1957	Dorothy Dandridge makes *Island in the Sun,* in which she plays a black woman romantically involved with a white man—a Hollywood first.
1957	The Soviet Union launches *Sputnik,* the first man-made satellite.
1958	The United States launches its first satellite, *Explorer.*
1959	Dorothy Dandridge stars in an all-black film production of *Porgy and Bess,* and wins a Golden Globe Award.
1959	Earvin "Magic" Johnson is born.
1959	Florence Griffith Joyner is born.
1960	Zelma Watson George becomes the first black female member of a U.S. delegation to the United Nations (UN).
1960	Wilma Rudolph wins three gold medals in track and field at the Summer Olympics.
1960	Ike and Tina Turner release their first single.
1961	The United States sends troops to Vietnam; the soldiers include Colin Powell and Tiger Woods father, Earl.

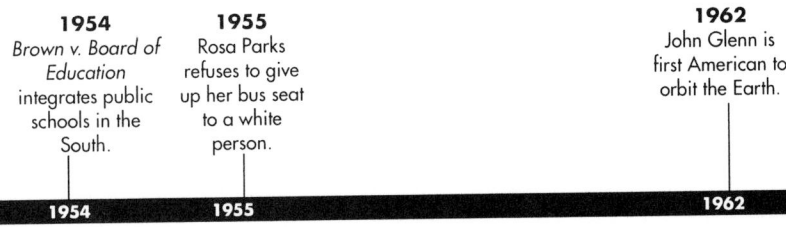

Timeline of African American Events

1961 Soviet Yuri Gagarin becomes the first man in space; later, Alan B. Shepard becomes the first American in space.

1963 Soviet Valentina Tereshkova becomes the first woman in space.

1963 Michael Jordan is born.

1963 Martin Luther King, Jr., leads the March on Washington.

1964 Malcolm X breaks with the Nation of Islam.

1965 *I Spy,* starring Bill Cosby, becomes the first prime-time TV program with an African American star.

1965 Malcolm X is assassinated.

1965 Jesse Jackson, Jr., is born.

1965 Dorothy Dandridge commits suicide.

1966 Tina Turner releases the single "River Deep, Mountain High."

1966 Chris Rock is born.

1966 Halle Berry is born.

1966 Barbara Jordan becomes the first woman elected to the Texas state senate.

1968 Martin Luther King, Jr., is assassinated.

1968 George Foreman wins a gold medal at the Summer Olympics.

1968 University of Southern California running back O. J. Simpson wins the Heisman Trophy.

1969 American Neil Armstrong becomes the first man to walk on the Moon.

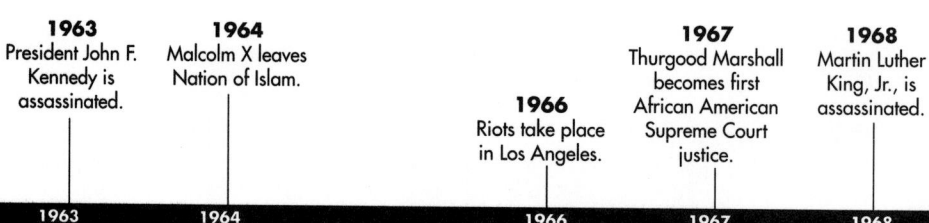

1963 President John F. Kennedy is assassinated.

1964 Malcolm X leaves Nation of Islam.

1966 Riots take place in Los Angeles.

1967 Thurgood Marshall becomes first African American Supreme Court justice.

1968 Martin Luther King, Jr., is assassinated.

Timeline of African American Events

1970 Charles Gordone wins a Pulitzer Prize for his play *No Place to Be Somebody*.

1971 Tupac Shakur is born.

1972 Bill Cosby launches the Saturday morning cartoon series *Fat Albert and the Cosby Kids*.

1972 A break-in at Democratic Party Headquarters begins the Watergate scandal.

1972 Barbara Jordan and Andrew Young are elected to the U.S. Congress.

1973 George Foreman defeats Joe Frazier to become the heavyweight boxing champion of the world.

1973 O. J. Simpson leads the Buffalo Bills, as they become the top-rushing team in the NFL.

1974 During the televised Watergate hearings, Barbara Jordan distinguishes herself as a member of the House Judiciary Committee; President Richard Nixon eventually resigns.

1974 George Foreman loses the world heavyweight boxing title to Muhammad Ali.

1975 Elijah Muhammad dies; Louis Farrakhan becomes Nation of Islam leader.

1975 The last U.S. forces leave Vietnam, Laos and Cambodia, all of which fall under Communist dictatorships.

1975 Eldrick "Tiger" Woods is born.

1976 Tina Turner leaves Ike, her husband and musical partner.

1976 Barbara Jordan is the keynote speaker at the Democratic National Convention.

Timeline of African American Events

1976 Dominique Dawes is born.

1977 Jimmy Carter of Georgia becomes president; soon, he appoints Andrew Young as ambassador to the United Nations.

1977 Alexis Herman becomes the highest-ranking woman in the Department of Labor.

1978 Ronald McNair is selected from 10,000 candidates to receive training as an astronaut.

1979 Barbara Jordan retires from politics.

1979 O. J. Simpson retires from football to become an actor and sports commentator.

1979 Magic Johnson and his Michigan State team win the NCAA basketball championship; Johnson is then drafted by the NBA's Los Angeles Lakers.

1979 Marion Barry becomes mayor of Washington, D.C.

1979 Andrew Young resigns from the United Nations after conducting an unauthorized meeting with representatives of the Palestine Liberation Organization (PLO).

1980 Cab Calloway appears in *The Blues Brothers* movie.

1980 Venus Williams is born.

1981 Andrew Young is elected mayor of Atlanta.

1982 O. J. Simpson marries Nicole Brown.

1983 Sally Ride becomes the first American woman in space.

1983 Colin Powell helps plan the U.S. invasion of Grenada.

1984 *The Cosby Show,* starring Bill Cosby, first airs.

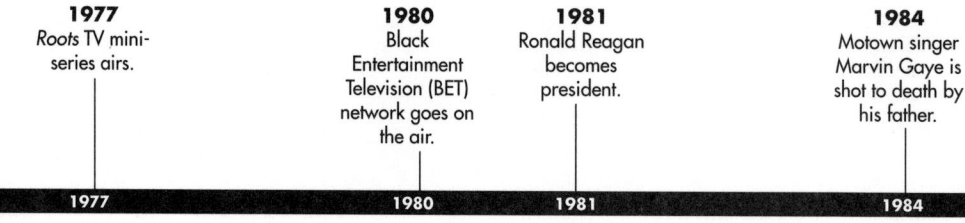

1977 *Roots* TV mini-series airs.

1980 Black Entertainment Television (BET) network goes on the air.

1981 Ronald Reagan becomes president.

1984 Motown singer Marvin Gaye is shot to death by his father.

1984 Democrat Jesse Jackson becomes the first significant African American presidential candidate in history.

1984 Louis Farrakhan gains national attention after he makes anti-Semitic remarks while campaigning for Jesse Jackson.

1984 Tina Turner releases *Private Dancer,* which will sell more than 11 million copies.

1984 Ronald McNair makes his first flight aboard the space shuttle *Challenger.*

1984 Michael Jordan and Florence Griffith Joyner appear in their first Olympics.

1985 Chris Rock gets his big break when Eddie Murphy sees his act at a New York comedy club.

1986 With the fiftieth anniversary of the 1936 novel *Gone with the Wind,* Butterfly McQueen, who appeared in the 1939 film, returns to the limelight; she also appears in the movie *Mosquito Coast.*

1986 Halley's Comet returns; the Delany sisters, who saw it in 1910, are alive to see it again.

1986 Colin Powell becomes director of the National Security Council (NSC).

1986 Ronald McNair dies with six others when the *Challenger* space shuttle explodes.

1987 George Foreman announces his return to the boxing ring.

1987 Alan Keyes becomes the highest-ranking African American in the U.S. State Department.

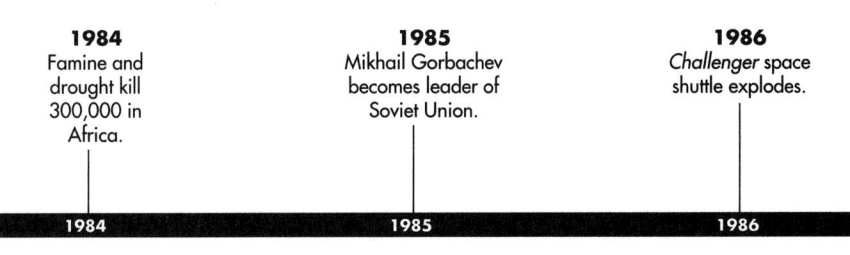

1984 Famine and drought kill 300,000 in Africa.

1985 Mikhail Gorbachev becomes leader of Soviet Union.

1986 *Challenger* space shuttle explodes.

Timeline of African American Events

1988	The Los Angeles Lakers win their fifth NBA championship with Magic Johnson.
1988	Ron Brown is Jesse Jackson's presidential campaign manager; Jesse Jackson, Jr., and his siblings introduce their father on national television.
1988	Florence Griffith Joyner wins three gold medals and one silver medal at the Summer Olympics.
1989	The first space shuttle flight after the 1986 *Challenger* disaster takes place.
1989	Ron Brown becomes chairman of the Democratic National Committee (DNC).
1990s	The U.S. Postal Service issues Benjamin Banneker commemorative stamps.
1990	Chris Rock becomes a featured player on *Saturday Night Live*.
1990	Tupac Shakur joins the rap group Digital Underground.
1990	Greg Gumbel becomes co-host of *The NFL Today* on CBS.
1990	Washington, D.C., mayor Marion Barry is videotaped smoking crack cocaine; later, he loses his bid for reelection.
1991	Chris Rock appears in *New Jack City*.
1991	*2Pacalypse Now* makes Tupac Shakur an overnight rap superstar.
1991	At fifteen, Tiger Woods becomes the youngest player—and the only African American—to win the U.S. Junior Amateur championship.

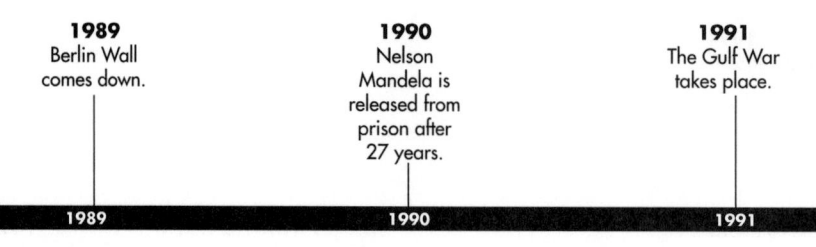

1989 Berlin Wall comes down.

1990 Nelson Mandela is released from prison after 27 years.

1991 The Gulf War takes place.

1991   The Gulf War (Operation Desert Storm) puts Gen. Colin Powell in the spotlight.

1991   Boxer George Foreman loses his match to Evander Holyfield, but makes an impressive showing.

1991   Magic Johnson announces that he has HIV; he retires from basketball and establishes a foundation that promotes AIDS awareness.

1992   Terry McMillan publishes *Waiting to Exhale*.

1992   The Spike Lee–directed film *Malcolm X* is released; Malcolm's widow Betty Shabazz serves as a consultant.

1992   Greg Gumbel hosts the CBS morning coverage during the Winter Olympic Games.

1992   A Texas state trooper is shot, and the man charged with the crime claims he was influenced by a Tupac Shakur song.

1992   Riots erupt in South Central Los Angeles after a jury acquits four white policemen for the 1991 beating of a black man, Rodney King.

1992   At the Summer Olympic Games, Dominique Dawes becomes the second black woman ever on the U.S. gymnastics team; Magic Johnson and Michael Jordan are members of the U.S. basketball "Dream Team."

1992   Barbara Jordan is the keynote speaker at the Democratic National Convention.

1992   With the help of DNC chairman Ron Brown, Bill Clinton is elected president.

1993   The Delany sisters, both more than 100 years old, become celebrities after they publish *Having Our Say*.

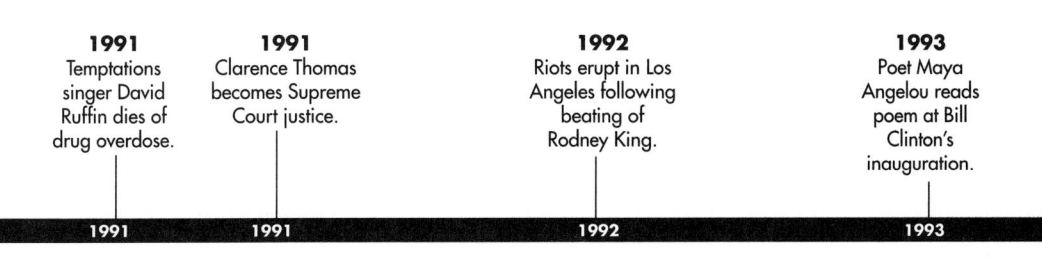

1991 Temptations singer David Ruffin dies of drug overdose.

1991 Clarence Thomas becomes Supreme Court justice.

1992 Riots erupt in Los Angeles following beating of Rodney King.

1993 Poet Maya Angelou reads poem at Bill Clinton's inauguration.

Timeline of African American Events

1993	Tina Turner's life is the subject of a motion picture, *What's Love Got to Do with It.*
1993	Tupac Shakur appears in the film *Poetic Justice.*
1993	Halle Berry and major league baseball player David Justice marry.
1993	Bill Clinton is sworn in as president; Ron Brown and Alexis Herman are key members of the administration, while Gen. Colin Powell steps down from the Joint Chiefs of Staff.
1993	President Clinton names Florence Griffith Joyner co-chairperson of the President's Council on Physical Fitness and Sports.
1993	Michael Jordan's father, James, is murdered.
1994	Betty Shabazz says she believes Nation of Islam leader Louis Farrakhan was behind the 1965 assassination of her husband, Malcolm X.
1994	Recently retired basketball star Michael Jordan becomes a minor-league baseball player.
1994	Tiger Williams becomes the first African American to win the U.S. Amateur Golf Championship.
1994	Greg Gumbel is CBS's sole anchor at the Winter Olympic Games.
1994	Ralph Ellison dies.
1994	Nicole Brown Simpson, former wife of O. J. Simpson, and Ronald Goldman are murdered; O. J. Simpson is charged with the crime, and attempts to flee from police.
1994	Zelma Watson George dies.
1994	Alice Childress dies.

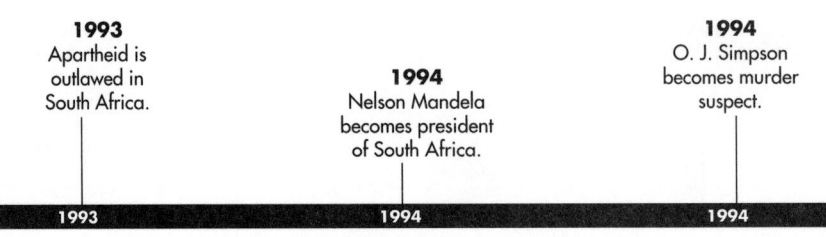

1993 Apartheid is outlawed in South Africa.

1994 Nelson Mandela becomes president of South Africa.

1994 O. J. Simpson becomes murder suspect.

1994	The O. J. Simpson murder trial begins.
1994	George Foreman defeats Michael Moorer to regain the world heavyweight boxing title.
1994	Marion Barry is reelected as mayor of Washington, D.C.
1994	Wilma Rudolph dies.
1994	Cab Calloway dies.
1995	HBO airs *The Tuskegee Airmen;* the Air Force removes all letters of reprimand from the files of Tuskegee officers punished for the 1945 Freeman Field incident.
1995	Michael Jordan returns to basketball.
1995	Betty Shabazz reconciles with Louis Farrakhan.
1995	Bessie Delany dies.
1995	O. J. Simpson is found not guilty of murder.
1995	Louis Farrakhan leads the Million Man March; among the speakers is Betty Shabazz.
1995	Jesse Jackson, Jr., is elected U.S. congressman from Illinois.
1995	Florence Griffith Joyner is inducted into the National Track and Field Hall of Fame.
1995	Charles Gordone dies.
1995	The film *Waiting to Exhale,* based on the book by Terry McMillan, is released.
1995	Butterfly McQueen dies.
1996	Random House publishes *Flying Home and Other Stories,* containing six previously unpublished pieces by Ralph Ellison.

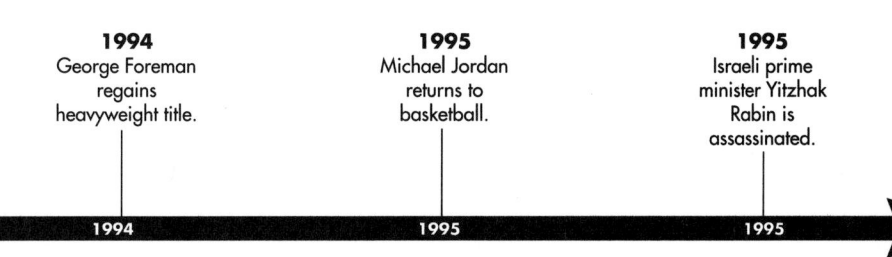

1994 George Foreman regains heavyweight title.

1995 Michael Jordan returns to basketball.

1995 Israeli prime minister Yitzhak Rabin is assassinated.

Timeline of African American Events

1996 Alan Keyes becomes the first African American presidential candidate in the Republican Party during the twentieth century.

1996 Terry McMillan publishes *How Stella Got Her Groove Back.*

1996 *When We Were Kings,* a documentary film about the 1974 Foreman-Ali fight, is released, and later wins an Academy Award.

1996 Chris Rock's HBO special *Bring the Pain* is a hit.

1996 Barbara Jordan dies.

1996 Arthur Gaston dies.

1996 Commerce secretary Ron Brown dies.

1996 After two comebacks, Magic Johnson retires from basketball for good.

1996 Ella Fitzgerald dies.

1996 The Atlanta Olympic Games open; Andrew Young is a primary organizer, and Greg Gumbel is daytime anchor for NBC.

1996 Dominique Dawes becomes the first African American to win a medal in gymnastics, and helps the women's team win a gold medal.

1996 Two journalists, responding to Louis Farrakhan's claim that slavery no longer exists in Sudan, purchase and free two black slaves.

1996 General Colin Powell makes the keynote address at the Republican National Convention.

1996 Tupac Shakur dies.

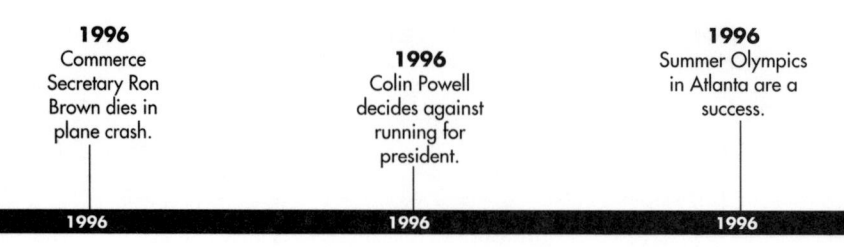

1996 Commerce Secretary Ron Brown dies in plane crash.

1996 Colin Powell decides against running for president.

1996 Summer Olympics in Atlanta are a success.

1997	The movie *Amistad,* commemorating the 1838 revolt led by Cinque, is released.
1997	Sadie Delany publishes *On My Own at 107.*
1997	Tiger Woods becomes the youngest golfer—and the only African American—to win the Masters tournament.
1997	Ennis Cosby, son of Bill and Camille Cosby, is murdered.
1997	O. J. Simpson is found liable for the murders of Nicole Brown Simpson and Ron Goldman in a civil case.
1997	Alexis Herman becomes secretary of labor.
1997	Betty Shabazz dies.
1997	Congress transfers authority over Washington, D.C., to the city control board, marking the beginning of the end of Mayor Marion Barry's power.
1997	Halle Berry and David Justice divorce.
1997	Venus Williams becomes the second female in history to reach the semifinals of the U.S. Open in her first appearance.
1997	George Foreman retires from boxing.
1998	Michael Jordan wins his sixth NBA championship with the Chicago Bulls.
1998	Marion Barry announces he will not seek a fifth term as mayor of Washington, D.C.
1998	Venus Williams wins her first Women's Tennis Association (WTA) tournament.
1998	Florence Griffith Joyner dies.

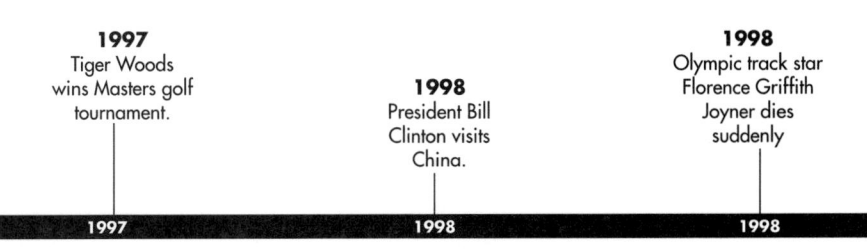

1997
Tiger Woods wins Masters golf tournament.

1998
President Bill Clinton visits China.

1998
Olympic track star Florence Griffith Joyner dies suddenly

Words to Know

Venus Williams

A

Abolitionists: A group of people, both white and black, who opposed slavery in America, especially during the years from 1830 to the Civil War (1861–65). They got their name because they called for the abolition, or the end, of slavery.

Acquired Immunodeficiency Syndrome (AIDS): A disease that removes the victim's immunities, or ability to resist other diseases. It is believed to be carried by the human immunodeficiency virus (HIV), and if a person who has HIV gets AIDS, it is likely to be fatal.

Anti-Semitism: Hatred and prejudice against Jews. Anti-Semitism has existed since the Middle Ages, when Jews were blamed for killing Christ and were resented because they were often successful businesspeople. The most extreme case of anti-Semitism occurred in Nazi Germany

(1933–45; *see* Nazism), when more than 6 million Jews were killed.

Apartheid: A system of enforced racial segregation and white supremacy that existed in the nation of South Africa from 1948 to the 1990s. (*See also* Segregation.)

Astronomer: Someone who studies the stars and other objects in the sky.

B
Black Muslims: *See* Nation of Islam.

C
Cabinet: A president's group of top advisors, who are usually heads of government departments such as the Department of Commerce or the Department of Labor.

Civil Rights Movement: Civil rights protect a person against discrimination because of their ethnicity, nationality, religion, or gender. The term "Civil Rights Movement" usually refers to the efforts led by the Rev. Martin Luther King, Jr., and others during the 1960s, which helped ensure that African Americans were not denied the vote and other basic rights as American citizens.

Civil War (1861–65): The Civil War was not "civil" in the sense of being polite; it got its name from the fact that part of the citizens or civilians took up arms against the government. Specifically, the eleven Southern states of the Confederacy rebelled against the federal government in an attempt to establish a separate nation. These states were united in their pursuit of an agricultural or farming economy, as opposed to the industrial or manufacturing economy of the Northern states. The Southern states' system was built on slavery, and because of that, the South lagged far behind the North economically and lost the Civil War. With the freeing of the slaves that followed the defeat of the Confederacy, African Americans enjoyed a brief period of political power. (*See also* Reconstruction.)

Cocaine/crack cocaine: Cocaine is a white powder derived from the coca plant, which grows in the mountains of South America. It makes people feel excited and energetic, but its use can lead to physical and mental problems, even death. Crack is a less expensive but even more powerful—and more dangerous—version of cocaine.

Cold War: The name for the conflict that existed between the United States and the Soviet Union (*see* Soviet Union) between the end of World War II in 1945 and the fall of Communism in the late 1980s and early 1990s (*see* Communism). It was called a "cold war" because it did not involve direct action between the two superpowers: mainly it was a war of words and ideas, though occasionally the two fought each other directly, as in the Vietnam War (*see* Vietnam War).

Communism: In theory, Communism is a system in which the people own everything in common; in practice, however, Communism means that the government—which is controlled by a very small group of people—owns everything. Communism in economics is the opposite of free-market capitalism; Communism in government is the opposite of democracy, which is practiced in the United States. Communism flourished from the time of its establishment in Russia in 1917 until its downfall in Eastern Europe in the late 1980s and 1990s. In the Vietnam War, the United States fought unsuccessfully against the establishment of a Communist system in Southeast Asia.

Congress: Congress is the main body of the U.S. legislative branch (*see* Constitution), which makes and passes laws. It is composed of the Senate and the House of Representatives, sometimes simply called "the House." Each state has two senators, who are elected to serve six-year terms; by contrast, the number of representatives (sometimes called congressmen or -women) from a state is determined by that state's population. Thus Alaska has very few representatives, whereas California and New York have a large number. Representatives are elected for two-year terms.

Constitution: The U.S. Constitution, which provides the framework for the U.S. government, was adopted in 1787. The Constitution is composed of a preamble, or introduction, six articles, or sections, and the amendments, which have been added over the years. The articles, among other things, establish the three branches of government: the executive (the president and those who work with the president, including Cabinet members), the legislative (Congress), and the judiciary (the courts). The first ten amendments, adopted in 1791, are called the Bill of Rights, and establish certain basic rights such as freedom of speech and the right to trial by jury. Among the most important amendments is the Fourteenth, which was passed in 1868 to guarantee the civil rights of newly freed slaves, and which forces state governments to abide by federal standards for protecting every citizens' rights.

D

Democracy: In practice, democracy is a form of government in which all citizens have a right to express their views, and potentially can influence government actions. The United States is a representative democracy, meaning that citizens elect others to help them exercise their democratic rights.

Democratic Party: One of the two main political parties in the American system. The Democratic Party dates back to President Thomas Jefferson at the beginning of the 1800s, and it has often combined a wide variety of groups. Thus the party experienced wide divisions over slavery in the years leading up to the Civil War. In the late twentieth century, the party comprised an even larger array of groups, many of whom—but not all—would be considered liberal politically.

Depression: The Depression, or Great Depression, followed the Stock Market Crash of 1929. A stock market is a place where people trade stocks, or units of value, in companies, and thus establish the value of those companies. Due to a complicated series of economic events, on October 29, 1929, the value of stocks suddenly dropped, and the United States was plunged into a financial crisis. Millions of people were out of work, and families suffered great hardship. President Franklin D. Roosevelt, inaugurated in 1933, introduced a number of welfare and public works programs (collectively called the New Deal) to counteract the effects of the Depression. The Depression also led to the rise of Adolf Hitler in Germany, as well as increased interest in Soviet Communism, which seemed to offer a solution to the crisis. Only with its entry into World War II in 1941 did the United States fully recover from the Depression.

E

Entrepreneur (pronounced ahn-truh-prin-OOR): Someone who starts and maintains a business. Unlike a person who works for somebody else, entrepreneurs take enormous financial risks—and can enjoy great rewards as well.

H

Halley's (pronounced HAL-eez) Comet: Discovered by astronomer Edmund Halley in 1682, Halley's Comet passes by Earth once every seventy-five to seventy-seven years. Its last appearance was in 1986.

I

Irony: When something happens in a way that it shouldn't, it is said to be ironic. Thus it was ironic, for instance, that the Tuskegee Airmen were fighting against racist Nazi Germany in World War II, but were themselves subjected to racism in America, a nation founded on the idea that "All men are created equal."

Islam: Sharing many common roots with Christianity, Islam—or the Muslim faith—is characterized by a belief in Allah as the one true god, and in Muhammad as his prophet. Muhammad lived in present-day Saudi Arabia in the 600s A.D., and his followers spread Islam throughout the Middle East, North Africa, and parts of southern and eastern Asia. Because Muhammad came from the city of Mecca, one of the traditions of Islam is to make a hajj, or pilgrimage, to the holy city. (*See also* Black Muslims.)

J

Jim Crow: *See* Segregation.

Joint Chiefs of Staff: The Joint Chiefs of Staff act as the principal military advisers to the secretary of defense, a member of the president's Cabinet (*see* Cabinet). The group is made up of the heads of the Army, Navy, Air Force, and Marines, along with a chairman. Their job is to help ensure that the country is not attacked by foreign powers. (*See also* National Security Council.)

K

Ku Klux Klan: A white racist organization founded after the end of the Civil War in 1865 in order to frighten African Americans and keep them from exercising their civil rights (*see* Civil Rights Movement). The organization died down in the late 1800s, but a new Klan—distinct from the first one—appeared in 1915. Again it died down, but experienced a brief resurgence in reaction to the Civil Rights Movement of the 1960s. By the end of the twentieth century, the Klan was a small organization, despised by most of society. Because of civil rights laws, it could no longer exercise terrorism, and confined its tactics to marches and rallies.

M

Muslim: *See* Islam.

N

Nation of Islam: Sometimes called the Black Muslims, the Nation of Islam is a sect, or relatively small group, tied to the Islamic faith (*see* Islam). Founded in 1930 and later led by Elijah Muhammad (1934–75), the group advocated a highly rigid, clean-cut lifestyle that involved giving up alcohol, tobacco, and pork. But in addition to Islamic ideas, the Black Muslims adopted racial beliefs that set them apart from mainstream Islam. Members were trained to think of blacks as superior to whites, who they called "blue-eyed" devils. After the death of Muhammad in 1975, his son, Warith Deen Mohammed, took the leadership. Thereafter the group abandoned racism, embraced mainstream Islam, and ultimately changed its name to the American Muslim Mission. A much smaller splinter group, led by Minister Louis Farrakhan, returned to the old "Nation of Islam" name, as well as the racist beliefs.

National Association for the Advancement of Colored People (NAACP): A civil rights organization (*see* Civil Rights Movement) founded by W. E. B. Du Bois in 1910. The NAACP played a key role in civil rights victories of the 1950s and 1960s, such as *Brown v. Board of Education,* a 1954 Supreme Court decision that integrated public schools.

National Security Council: A council of the federal government established in 1947 to oversee defense and foreign policy. Composed of the president, vice president, secretary of state, and secretary of defense, its advisers are the chairman of the Joint Chiefs of Staff (*see* Joint Chiefs of Staff) and the director of the Central Intelligence Agency (CIA). The head of the council's staff is the national security adviser, or the assistant to the president for national security affairs.

Natural rights: The belief that all human beings are born with certain basic rights; though a government may refuse to recognize these rights, it does not mean they don't exist. Natural rights involve basic human dignity and freedom, and are closely associated with the idea of "natural law."

These principles, which flourished during the 1700s, are the founding ideas behind the United States' Declaration of Independence and its Constitution. In the 1800s, natural law and natural rights came under attack; one result of this was the rise of the Nazi and Communist systems in the 1900s. (*See also* Communism and Nazism.)

Nazism: The system of government in Germany from 1933 to 1945, when Adolf Hitler was in control. The foundations of Nazism were racism, anti-Semitism (*see* Anti-Semitism; Racism), and nationalism, or the belief that one's own nation is superior to all others. These beliefs led Hitler to build up Germany's military and begin invading other countries in an attempt to expand the nation's borders, and this in turn led to the start of World War II in Europe.

O

Olympic Games: The Olympics are a set of amateur athletic competitions which bring together all the nations of the world every two years. They are based on the Olympic Games of Greece, which were played every four years from 776 B.C. to about 400 A.D. In 1896, the Olympics were revived, and 1924 saw the first Winter Olympics, featuring sports such as skiing and ice skating. Starting in 1994, the Winter and Summer Olympics took place in alternating even-number years.

P

Palestine Liberation Organization (PLO): A political group that represents the Arab people living on land claimed by the nation of Israel. For much of its history, the PLO has been led by Yassir Arafat (1929–), and at times it has used terrorism to achieve its objective of a separate Palestinian nation. At other times, Arafat and others have exercised diplomacy—that is, they have talked with Israeli leaders, and tried to work out a solution together.

Primary: Every even-numbered year, national elections are held in the United States, and people vote for candidates ranging from county commissioners to U.S. representatives to—every four years—the president of the United States. These elections usually occur in November, whereas primary elections, or primaries, take place earlier in the year. At the primaries, voters can choose between a variety of candidates for one political party, and from those they select the candidate they want to represent the party. The candidate chosen to represent the party in a given race (for instance, for Congress) will then face candidates from other parties in the general election in November.

Pulitzer Prize: An annual award recognizing achievement in literature, journalism, and music.

R

Racism: The word "racism" is often used to describe any belief that a certain race possesses specific characteristics. But a more precise definition is the belief that a person's race is the main factor in deciding who they are and what they can be. Coupled with this viewpoint is the idea that some races are "better" than others.

Reconstruction: The Reconstruction (1865–77) followed the Civil War (*see* Civil War). During this time, the federal government made an ultimately unsuccessful attempt to enforce rapid racial change in the South. Black candidates were elected to political office, and blacks were encouraged to vote. This caused bitter reaction on the part of Southern whites, including the establishment of the Ku Klux Klan (*see* Ku Klux Klan), and in 1877 the federal government withdrew its troops from the South. This was followed by a period of reaction against blacks, leading to the enforcement of segregation (*see* Segregation).

Republican Party: Sometimes called the GOP or Grand Old Party, the Republican Party dates back to President Abraham Lincoln and the Civil War (*see* Civil War). For many years, the party was associated with progressive ideas regarding racial issues, the economy, and other areas of political life; but from the 1930s, it came to be seen as the home of big business and conservatism. In the 1990s, it was certainly associated with conservative viewpoints, yet though it did not represent as wide a spectrum as the Democratic Party, there was disagreement within Republican ranks over issues such as abortion and "family values."

S

Segregation: The enforced separation of people by race. In the South, segregation was formally established around the end of the nineteenth century with the so-called Jim Crow laws. As a result of these laws, African Americans could not go to hospitals for whites, or even use the same bathrooms or drinking fountains as whites. The Civil Rights Movement of the 1960s overturned legal segregation.

Soviet Union: Sometimes referred to as the U.S.S.R. (Union of Soviet Socialist Republics), the Soviet Union was the name for the Communist country that combined present-day Russia and fourteen nations surrounding it in northeastern Europe, southwest Asia, and central Asia. Soviets were groups of workers' councils that predated the Russian Revolution of 1917, which established Communism in Russia. Under Communism, the Soviet Union built up its military, but economic problems associated with Communism ultimately led to the nation's downfall. The Soviet Union ceased to exist in December 1991.

Space program: The effort, starting in the 1950s, to explore outer space. The U.S. space program competed with that of the Soviet Union, and though the Soviets were the first to put a satellite (1957) and a human being (1961) in space, the United States put the first man on the moon (1969). The U.S. space program is directed by the National Aeronautics and Space Administration (NASA), and in the 1970s NASA turned its attention toward the development of the space shuttle, a sort of airplane that flies into outer space. The explosion of the shuttle *Chal-*

lenger in 1986, which killed all seven crew members on board, was a setback to the shuttle program, but starting in 1989, NASA resumed regular shuttle launches.

Supreme Court: The highest court in the United States, the Supreme Court is the final decision-making body regarding legal cases. Under the U.S. system, if a person disagrees with a lower court's decision, he or she can make an appeal to a higher court; if successful, the case can go all the way to the Supreme Court. The Court is composed of nine judges or justices, one of whom is the head, or chief justice.

T

Terrorism: The use of bombings and other forms of violence and intimidation to make a political point.

U

Union: An organized group of workers in a specific trade, such as truckers, auto workers, or mine workers. Unions engage in collective bargaining for such job-related issues as wages and working hours. The establishment of unions in the 1890s brought much-needed changes to the American workplace, where people often worked under almost inhuman conditions. At that time, unions faced severe and often brutal opposition from employers; by the 1990s, however, unions themselves were extremely powerful, and many had been linked to organized crime. In addition, union rules made it difficult for some businesses to operate profitably, and for this reason, many American jobs went to countries whose workers could produce goods more cheaply than unionized American factories.

United Nations (UN): An organization of almost all the world's countries, formed just after World War II (1939–45) to deal with international problems. The UN General Assembly meets in New York City, and a number of UN offices are located in Geneva, Switzerland. In the first years of its existence, the UN acted as a peacekeeping force, but differences between the United States and the Soviet Union led to a stalemate. After the fall of the Soviet Union, however, the UN was able to act effectively in situations such as the Gulf War of 1991.

United Service Organization (USO): A group, organized in 1941, which provides a variety of services for the armed forces, ranging from entertainment to spiritual ministry.

V

Vietnam War: The conflict between Communist and anti-Communist forces in the southeast Asian nation of Vietnam. Initially the French, who had held the area as a colony, fought against the Communists, led by Ho Chi Minh (1890–1969). But France was defeated at the Battle of Dien Bien Phu in 1954, and the U.S. became involved. Many American leaders believed in the "Domino Theory": that if they allowed Communism to take over in Vietnam, it would spread to other countries like dominoes falling. Initially the United States only sent advisors, who helped the non-Communist South Vietnamese; but by the 1960s, the United States was committing troops. The war became more and more unpopular, because it lacked a clear objective and was costing American lives in a cause that did not seem to directly affect the United States. In 1973, the United States signed a cease-fire agreement with Communist North Vietnam, and two years later, the North Vietnamese won the war.

W

Watergate scandal: The scandal known as Watergate began in July 1972, when men working for President Richard M. Nixon were caught attempting to break in to Democratic Party offices in Washington, D.C.'s Watergate Hotel. From there, the scandal snowballed, as it became more and more clear that the president himself had been behind the crime and—more importantly—the subsequent cover-up. A number of members of his administration resigned; others went to jail. In the summer of 1974, the House of Representatives began holding hearings to impeach Nixon—that is, to vote on the possible removal of him from office—but he resigned on August 9, 1974.

Will: A will is a legal document through which a person directs what should be done with their estate (that is, everything they possess) after they die.

World War I (1914–18): World War I was a conflict, chiefly fought in Europe, between the Allies (Britain, France, the United States, and many other countries) and the Central Powers (Germany, Austria, and nations aligned with them). Russia initially joined the war on the side of the Allies, but with the removal of the Russian czar (pronounced "ZAR") or emperor, and the later establishment of Communism in 1917, it withdrew from the conflict. Most of the fighting in western Europe took place on the border of France and Germany, where there was a series of bloody battles that did little to shift the borders. The war ended with the German surrender on November 11, 1918.

World War II (1939–45): World War II, which took place in Europe, Africa, and Asia, was much larger in scope than World War I. The cause of the war was the desire on the part of Nazi Germany (*see* Nazism) and Japan to gain territory. Germany, Japan, Italy, and the nations aligned with them were called the Axis; and they were opposed by the Allies, which included Britain, the United States, the Soviet Union (which had initially supported the Axis, but switched sides after Germany invaded Russia in 1941), China, and other nations. The war in Europe began with the Nazi invasion of Poland in 1939, and for almost two years, the only nation actively resisting German aggression was Britain. The focus of the war shifted to North Africa and Russia, and by 1943, with the invasion and surrender of Italy, the Allies were starting to win. A decisive event was D-Day, the Allied invasion of Normandy, France, on June 6, 1944. Germany surrendered on May 7, 1945. In Asia, Japan had long been conducting military actions against China, but on December

7, 1941, it struck out at a number of enemies, including the United States at Pearl Harbor, Hawaii. As in Europe, the tide began to turn in 1942 and 1943, particularly with the Battle of Midway. Allied forces took a series of islands near Japan, and then, rather than conduct a land invasion of Japan itself, the United States dropped two atomic bombs on the Japanese cities of Hiroshima and Nagasaki in August 1945. The Japanese surrendered on September 2, 1945.

Y

Yoga: Yoga is an ancient practice of both physical and spiritual discipline, which originated in India. It is usually associated with exercises and meditation.

Benjamin Banneker

*Born November 9, 1731
Baltimore County, Maryland*

*Died October 9, 1806
Baltimore County, Maryland*

Astronomer, mathematician, surveyor

Benjamin Banneker was an extremely gifted black man who lived at a time when almost all African Americans were slaves, and when many whites believed that blacks were inferior to them. Banneker proved the falsehood of this belief by distinguishing himself as an astronomer (a scientist who studies the movement of the stars and the heavenly bodies) and a mathematician. Among his many achievements were his work in laying out the present-day city of Washington, D.C.; the construction of a wooden clock by hand; and the writing of an almanac, a book containing information about the weather and other facts.

Banneker was never a slave himself, and enjoyed good relations with whites, many of whom supported him in his scientific endeavors. Yet, in spite of his genius, he was well aware that many whites would consider him a second-class citizen. In 1791 he sent a copy of his almanac to one of America's founding fathers, Thomas Jefferson (1743–1826). Jefferson was then

If your love for [the Declaration of Independence] was founded on sincerity, you could not but be solicitous, that every individual, of whatever rank or distinction, might with you equally enjoy the blessings thereof. . . .

—Letter from Banneker to Thomas Jefferson, August 19, 1791

the secretary of state, but would later become the country's third president.

In the letter that accompanied the almanac, Banneker urged Jefferson to recognize in his work evidence that African Americans were capable of great things. From this recognition, he suggested, it should be clear that blacks deserved the same "rights of human nature" that Jefferson himself had eloquently described in the Declaration of Independence in 1776. And if Jefferson was serious about his belief in those rights, Banneker indicated, he would be interested "in making sure that every individual, of whatever rank or distinction, might with you equally enjoy the blessings" of those rights.

Son of a freed slave and former "owner"

The family history behind Banneker was as unusual as Banneker himself. His mother's father was a black man, a slave from Africa, but his mother's mother, Molly, was a white woman from England. There she had been a servant girl. When she was caught stealing a pail of milk, she was told she could go to America as an indentured servant instead of going to prison. An indentured servant was someone who, in return for having their passage to America paid, had to work a set number of years for the person who had paid their way. They were the white equivalent of slaves, though there were two big differences: whites enjoyed greater rights than blacks and whites eventually would be set free.

Once Molly finished her indenture, she bought a farm in Maryland, and with it two slaves. She freed the slaves, which was unusual in itself. But then she did something *very* unusual—she married one of the slaves. His name was Banna Ka. He changed it to Bannaky, then Banneker. They had a daughter named Mary, who grew up and, like her mother, married a freed

The title page of Benjamin Banneker's Almanac.

slave named Robert. In 1737, the couple purchased a farm in Maryland, where their son Benjamin was born and raised.

Builds his own clock

Banneker learned to read from his grandmother Molly. Soon he became an avid reader of many books, especially the Bible. Later he went to school with both black and white children, something that would not become common in the North for many years—and in the South until the 1960s. The school was run by members of the Quaker religious sect. This group opposed slavery and would prove to be one of Banneker's strongest supporters in the future.

For the most part, however, Banneker taught himself. At the age of twenty-one, he became intrigued with the workings of a pocket watch that belonged to a white man named Josef Levi. Levi gave him the watch, and Banneker studied it until he figured out how to make one on his own. It was not a time when people could just buy anything they needed: watches were hand-made and hard to come by. Using the pocket watch as a model, Banneker carved pieces out of wood and built a clock. This started Banneker on the first of his many careers, repairing watches and clocks.

Surveys the city of Washington

In 1759, Banneker inherited the family farm after the death of his parents. Banneker, who never married, lived alone and devoted much of his time to studying the movement of the stars in the sky. A multi-talented man, he also learned to play the flute and violin.

Banneker lived this way for many years. In 1791, however, he sold the farm to a family named the Ellicotts. Not having to run the farm gave Banneker more time for work that truly interested him. He lived off of the proceeds from the sale for the rest of his life.

At the age of sixty, Banneker's life headed in a new direction. The U.S. Congress had just authorized the creation of a new national capital in an area next to Maryland and Virginia. The site would be named after the country's first president, George Washington (1732–89). In 1792, Major Andrew Ellicott (1754–1820), a cousin of the family that purchased Banneker's farm, asked Banneker to assist him in surveying the vast area set aside for the city.

Major Pierre Charles L'Enfant (pronounced Lawn-FAWN; 1754–1825) had designed the capital city, but after a dispute he returned to his native France. He took his plans with him, and the American surveyors had to proceed on their own. Although there is some dispute among historians, many believe that at this point Banneker reproduced L'Enfant's plans from memory, thus allowing the project to continue. Whether or not this is true, it is certainly a fact that a black man helped to lay out the design for the nation's capital.

Almanac and letter to Jefferson

For years Banneker produced an annual almanac, one of the most successful works of its kind in the American colonies. From 1792 to 1797, it was printed in several editions. Banneker received considerable support for his almanac, in the form of both encouragement and financial investment, from his Quaker friends. Many of them belonged to anti-slavery societies. These groups led to the Abolitionist movement, which opposed slavery in the years leading up to the Civil War (1861–65).

With encouragement from his friends, Banneker sent a copy of the almanac to Secretary of State Thomas Jefferson. In a letter to Jefferson, Banneker addressed "the almost general prejudice and prepossession, which is so prevalent in the world against those of my complexion . . . a race of beings, who have long labored under the abuse and censure of the world." Jefferson had written persuasively about the cause of freedom in the Declaration of Independence. Banneker wondered why he could not apply the same principles to black people.

Honored as nation's first black scientist

Jefferson wrote back to Banneker: "No body wishes more than I do, to see such proofs as you exhibit, that nature

The 1990 U.S. Postal Service commemorative stamp of Benjamin Banneker.

has given to our black brethren talents equal to those of the other colors of men." But despite Jefferson's opinions about blacks, the system of slavery would not change for many years. In fact, some progressive laws of the time were even reversed. For instance, when Banneker wrote to Jefferson, he was allowed to vote; but in 1802, Maryland revoked voting rights for African Americans.

In 1793, Banneker completed his surveying work, in which he was responsible for maintaining the survey expedition's astronomical clock (an elaborate device that mechanically shows the motion of the Sun, Moon, and planets).

Banneker continued publishing new almanacs until 1797. Author A. Silvio Bedini, who wrote a biography on Banneker, called the 1793 *Almanac* "one of the most important publications of its time." In addition to the letter Banneker wrote to Jefferson, that year's almanac included "A Plan of a Peace Officer for the United States," an anonymously written article that urged the U.S. government to establish a Department of Peace. Though it was eventually determined that the writer of the article was prominent physician and educator Benjamin Rush (1745–1813), the fact that it was published in Banneker's *Almanac* helped show that black people were not intellectually inferior. According to Bedini, Banneker's almanacs were among the first publications to successfully publicize the cause of abolitionism by presenting "tangible proof of the mental equality of the races."

During the next thirteen years, Banneker lived in obscurity, mostly studying and performing scientific experiments. On October 9, 1806, Banneker died. He is buried in Oella, Maryland.

In later years, several monuments were erected in Banneker's honor. In the 1990s, the United States Postal Service issued a Benjamin Banneker stamp, designed by African American artist Brian Pinckney, who also illustrated the children's book *Dear Benjamin Banneker*. In June 1998, the Benjamin Banneker Historical Park and Museum opened in June 1998 in Catonsville, Maryland.

Sources for further reading

Able, James A. "The Story of Benjamin Banneker." *Cricket,* February 1994, pp. 21–25.

"Bannekers Break Ground." *Jet,* September 30, 1996, p. 23.

Bedini, A. Silvio. *The Life of Benjamin Banneker.* New York: Scribner's, 1972.

"Benjamin Banneker to the Secretary of State." [Online] http://www.lib.virginia.edu/etext/readex/24073.html (accessed on October 8, 1998).

Ferris, Jerri. *What Are You Figuring Now? A Story About Benjamin Banneker.* New York: Scholastic, 1988.

Hudson, Wade, and Valerie Wilson Wesley. *Afro-Bets Book of Black Heroes From A to Z: An Introduction to Important Black Achievers for Young Readers.* East Orange, NJ: Just Us Books, 1997.

Maryland's African American Heritage. "Benjamin Banneker." [Online] http://tqd.advanced.org/3337/banneker.html (accessed on October 8, 1998).

Metcalf, Doris Hunter. *Portraits of Exceptional African American Scientists.* Carthage, IL: Good Apple, 1994.

Pinckney, Andrea Davis. *Dear Benjamin Banneker.* San Diego, CA: Harcourt Brace, 1994.

Potter, Joan, and Constance Claytor. *African Americans Who Were First: Illustrated with Photographs.* New York: Cobblehill Books, 1997.

Stamp on Black History Month. "Benjamin Banneker." [Online] http://library.advanced.org/10320/Banneker.htm (accessed on October 8, 1998).

Marion Barry

*Born March 6, 1936
Itta Bena, Mississippi
Mayor of Washington, D.C.,
1979–90; 1995–98*

UPDATE

When Washington, D.C., mayor Marion Barry left office in 1990, following convictions on drug charges, his return to power seemed unlikely. But after serving prison time, his career appeared to be on the rebound, and in 1994 he announced that he would run for a fourth term. His reelection later that year marked one of American political history's great comebacks—but the victory was to be short-lived. **(See original entry on Barry in volume 1.)**

Barry grew up poor in a single-parent home in Memphis, Tennessee. In college in the 1960s, he became involved in the civil rights movement. He moved to Washington, D.C., in 1965, where he helped establish a youth-training program called Pride, Inc. His election to the D.C. Board of Education in 1971 began his political career.

In 1974, Barry was elected to the D.C. city council. His popularity surged—among blacks *and* whites. The District of

I'm in recovery, and so is my city."

Columbia, the nation's capital, is an unusual place. It is not part of any state, and was controlled directly by the U.S. Congress until it began to enjoy a degree of home rule (self-government) in the early 1970s. Few places in America have a sharper contrast between black and white: the blacks, who comprise the majority of the District's population, are mostly poor; the whites, most of whom work for the federal government or the many foundations headquartered in Washington, tend to be highly successful. In this racially divided city, Barry seemed able to offer unity. So when he announced his candidacy for mayor in 1978, he received widespread support.

Barry's first term was successful, and the city experienced fast economic growth while crime declined. But after three years of careful money management, Barry began to expand the city's budget—partly by providing jobs to friends—and this cost him much of his white support. Also, there were rumors of scandals involving sex and drugs. In his second and third terms, the city's economy slowed down, crime increased, and Barry's administration began to acquire an increasing reputation for corruption.

On January 18, 1990, Barry was videotaped smoking crack cocaine with an ex-girlfriend. He was convicted on drug charges in August, and in October was sentenced to six months in prison. Meanwhile, he had opted not to run for reelection for mayor, but against the advice of friends, he ran for a city council seat. After having been mayor, the post would have been a step down—had he been elected. But Barry, who had never lost an election, finished third. It seemed his political career was at an end.

Stages an amazing comeback

Because of lengthy appeals, Barry did not enter the minimum-security federal prison in Petersburg, Virginia, until October 1991. He was released in April 1992, and immediately ran for a city council seat. Amazingly, he won by an overwhelming majority. In May 1994, he announced that he would run for mayor again. Rather than avoid discussion of his past misdeeds with regard to sex, alcohol, and drugs, he made a campaign issue of them. "I'm in recovery," he said when he announced his candidacy, "and so is my city."

Black voters responded to the campaign of redemption—Barry defeated then-Mayor Sharon Pratt Kelly (also an African American) without significant white support. Nationwide, the 1994 elections brought the first Republican majority to Congress since 1952. In the heavily liberal Washington, though, voters rejected conservative ideas.

Yet the reelected Barry's troubles were not over. By now, Washington, once financially sound, was $722 million in debt. The budget that Barry presented did little to address this problem. Despite the fact that D.C. has the largest per-capita municipal work force in America (the largest number of city government workers in proportion to the population), he refused to cut any jobs. Instead, he planned to ask Congress to pump hundreds of millions of dollars into the city.

"His plan sank like a stone on Capitol Hill," Vernon Loeb of the *Washington Post* wrote. "Barry's critics cited it as Exhibit A in making the case for establishment of an independent board to restore order to the city's finances." The Republican majority in Congress was not amused by Barry's mismanagement: it created a committee with control over D.C.'s budget. Without the ability to direct how money was spent, Barry's power was limited.

Adding to his problems, Barry underwent surgery for prostate cancer in early 1996. Soon thereafter, he began reversing his budgetary strategy. He announced that he would cut 10,000 jobs over the next four years in a bid to gain support from Congress. Things were looking up. But in May 1996, Barry went on a two-week vacation; he said he needed to recover from "the telltale signs of spiritual relapse and physical exhaustion." Many people took this as code language, and believed that Barry had experienced a drug or alcohol relapse. Given his problems with Congress, he didn't have room for any mistakes. He announced upon his return that he was "all right and ready to move forward," but his power over D.C. was almost at an end.

In the summer of 1997, Congress transferred authority over nine major city departments to a special board. A board chairperson, Camille C. Barnett, was elected in December 1997. She now holds effective control over D.C., and has a salary much higher than Barry's. Barry had become a figurehead (a leader who appears to have political power, but really doesn't). In May 1998, he announced that he would not seek election for a fifth term.

Barry's critics were pleased with his decision. One observer compared the Barry of the 1990s to a rusted-out automobile, and said that it was hard to reconcile what Barry had become with what he had once been. "Barry's critics," wrote Vernon Loeb in the *Washington Post*, say that despite his populist rhetoric, Washington's most needy people—public housing residents, foster children, inmates, the mentally ill—fared miserably during the mayor's time in office."

Sources for further reading

Carter, Janelle. "Barry Rails Against White House, Congress." Associated Press, August 6, 1997.

Goldberg, Jeffrey. "Marion Barry Confronts a Hostile Takeover." *New York Times,* October 29, 1995, Section 6, p. 39.

Janofsky, Michael. "Washington's Mayor Is Back and Says He's Going to Stay." *New York Times,* May 14, 1996, p. A-14.

Loeb, Vernon. "A Turbulent Era That Defined D.C. Comes to an End." *Washington Post,* May 22, 1998, p. A-1.

"Nation's Capital 'Getting Better,' According to Mayor Marion Barry." *Jet,* April 28, 1997, p. 25.

Powell, Michael. "Control Board Picks Management Chief: Appointee to Oversee Major D.C. Agencies." *Washington Post,* December 23, 1997, p. A-1.

Halle Berry

*Born August 14, 1966
Cleveland, Ohio
Actress, model*

UPDATE

The 1990s saw the rise of Halle Berry as a film star. She had acclaimed roles in films such as *Losing Isaiah* (1995) and *Bulworth* (1998), but she was not above a little good-natured silliness either, as she proved in *The Flintstones* (1994) and *B*A*P*S* (1997). In her personal life, Berry underwent a painful separation and divorce from major league baseball outfielder David Justice (1966–) in 1996 and 1997. **(See original entry on Berry in volume 1.)**

Born the child of a white mother and a black father in 1967, Berry was raised in Cleveland, Ohio. Her father was an abusive alcoholic who left when she was four years old, and she and her older sister, Heidi, were raised by their mother. Due to her biracial heritage, Berry often found herself the object of cruel taunts from other children. By the end of high school, though, the once-shy Berry had emerged as prom queen, cheerleader, and class president.

> "The range [Berry is] capable of is phenomenal. She can go from good girl to vamp like you and I shed socks. So few people can do comedy and drama. But that's Halle—beautiful, funny, the entire package."
>
> —Flintstones *director Brian Levant*

Berry competed in several beauty pageants in the 1980s. She was the first runner-up in the Miss USA pageant in 1985, and the first African American contestant in the Miss World pageant in 1986. For a time she studied journalism, but her real dream was acting. In 1987, she moved to Chicago, Illinois, to work as a model and study acting. During that time, she met acclaimed television producer Aaron Spelling (1925–), who helped launch her career. She performed with comedian Bob Hope (1902–) for the United Service Organization (USO), which entertains U.S. troops overseas. In 1991, director Spike Lee (1957– ; see entry in volume 3) cast her in his *Jungle Fever,* and during the same year she played radically different roles in *Strictly Business* and *The Last Boy Scout.*

Berry has been romantically linked with several celebrities. While filming *The Last Boy Scout,* her boyfriend at the time—she has refused to name him, referring to him only as "someone well-known in Hollywood"—hit her so hard that she lost 80 percent of the hearing in her left ear. She was briefly involved with actor Wesley Snipes (1962–), star of *Jungle Fever,* and later dated comedic actor Eddie Murphy (1961–), a mirror-image of their on-screen romance in *Boomerang* (1992). But when she met Justice in 1992, while filming the miniseries *Queen* for CBS, she thought she had found true love. The two were married on New Year's Day in 1993.

Divorce and a rising star

Berry has diabetes, a disease relating to the body's inability to process all-important blood sugar. In June 1994 she told *Jet* that Justice helped her keep her diabetes under control, as well as maintain stability in the unsettling world of Hollywood. By all appearances, they were a happy couple: in November of that year, they purchased a home in the fancy Hollywood Hills section of Los Angeles, California, near fellow stars Herbie Hancock (1940–), Sharon Stone (1958–), and Jerry Seinfeld (1954–). At the beginning of the following year, they made *Ebony*'s "10 Hottest Couples of 1995" list.

In early 1996, however, their marriage broke up. In February 1996, Justice was questioned by Riviera Beach, Florida, police when they saw him parked in an area known for drugs and prostitution. After the breakup, Justice told *People* magazine in May 1996, "I always felt I was walking on eggshells with her. Everything I did was wrong." In July, Justice sued Berry for alimony (support payments). In October, Berry filed a restraining order against Justice, demanding that he stay at least 500 yards from the house in Hollywood Hills, which belonged to her. In May 1997, Justice gave a tell-all interview with *Ebony Man,* and two months later, the divorce became final.

Even as she experienced losses in her personal life, Berry enjoyed a series of professional successes. "The range she's capable of," said *Flintstones* director Brian Levant, "is phenomenal. She can go from good girl to vamp like you and I shed socks. So few people can do comedy and drama. But that's Halle—beautiful, funny, the entire package." In *Losing Isaiah,* one of her most acclaimed films to date, she played a crack addict. The makeup people gave her fake pimples, crusty lips, and matted hair—a far cry from her usual beauty. While going through her divorce, she made the outrageous comedy *B*A*P*S,* directed by Robert Townsend (1957–). "I wasn't feeling very funny," she told *Jet.* "But it turned out to be therapeutic. I could laugh and be silly and let go of all that negative energy."

Berry, who along with fellow models Cindy Crawford (1966–) and Claudia Schiffer (1970–) was a spokeswoman for Revlon cosmetics, became more and more popular as the 1990s drew to an end. In 1998, she appeared in *Oprah Winfrey Presents: The Wedding* for HBO, and also began work on another HBO production, a film based on the life of starlet **Dorothy Dandridge** (1992–65; see p. 47). In *Bulworth,* a film acclaimed by many for its frank treatment of the racial divide between blacks and whites in America, she received praise from her co-star (and the film's writer/director), Warren Beatty (1937–). He told *Elle,* "Halle combines intelligence and strength and vulnerability and a good sense of humor.... And the fact that she's good to look at doesn't hurt."

Berry looks forward to a more solid personal relationship. "The next time around," she told *Jet* in March 1998, "I can't settle for what looks good on paper. I can't settle period.

I need someone who can really be there for me in an intimate way, someone who is available to me emotionally, someone who will allow me to be me and celebrate all that I am in my good and my bad parts."

Sources for further reading

"Actress Halle Berry Reveals How She Copes with Diabetes." *Jet,* June 20, 1994, p. 37.

"David Justice Seeks Alimony from Estranged Wife Halle Berry." *Jet,* July 29, 1996, p. 18.

"The 50 Most Beautiful People in the World." *People,* May 8, 1995, p. 68.

Halle Berry. [Online] http://www.geocities.com/Hollywood/Set/1592/ (accessed on October 8, 1998).

"Halle Berry, Mariah Carey, Vanessa L. Williams Talk About Their Careers After Marital Breakups." *Jet,* March 2, 1998, p. 58.

"Halle Berry Must Choose Between a Black Man and White Man in TV Movie 'The Wedding.'" *Jet,* February 16, 1998, p. 54.

"Halle Berry Portrays Georgia Hairdresser Who Moves to Beverly Hills to Make Her Dreams Come True in Comedy 'B.A.P.S.'" *Jet,* April 7, 1997, p. 22.

"Halle Berry Stars in Murder Mystery 'The Rich Man's Wife'." *Jet,* September 2, 1996, p. 32.

"Justice Is Served: As Their Divorce Turns Nasty, Halle Berry Plays Court-Order Hardball with Baseball's David Justice." *People,* October 21, 1996, p. 64.

Schneider, Karen S., Johnny Dodd, and Paula Yoo. "Hurts So Bad: Actress Halle Berry Planned Her Success Carefully, But She Didn't Foresee the End of Her Marriage." *People,* May 13, 1996, p. 102.

Scruby, Jennifer. "Halle's Comet." *Elle,* February 1998, pp. 78–80.

Smith, Jessie Carney, ed. *Notable Black American Women, Book 2.* Detroit: Gale, 1996, pp. 30–33.

Ron Brown

Born August 1, 1941
Washington, D.C.
Died April 3, 1996
Croatia
U.S. secretary of commerce

UPDATE

As leader of the Democratic National Committee (DNC), Ron Brown helped secure the 1992 election of President Bill Clinton (1946–). He later served as Clinton's secretary of commerce, and in this capacity traveled to many countries to encourage business development. It was on one such trip, to the eastern European country of Croatia, that Brown died on April 3, 1996. He and thirty-two others were on board a military aircraft when it crashed into a mountainside during a storm. **(See original entry on Brown in volume 1.)**

Brown's upbringing in New York's Harlem district was unlike most other African American children who grow up there. His parents sent him to exclusive preparatory schools, and after high school he attended Middlebury College, a distinguished institution in Vermont. He later served as an Army officer in West Germany, then earned his law degree.

In 1968, Brown became a lobbyist for the National Urban League, and later served in various capacities for U.S.

"Ron Brown was an exceptional bridge builder across racial lines, across economic lines, and across age lines."

—U.S. representative Sander Levin of Michigan

senator Edward Kennedy of Massachusetts (1932–). In 1981, Brown took a job with a prestigious law firm, where he became known for back-room dealings and a client list that included such controversial figures as former Haitian dictator Jean-Claude "Baby Doc" Duvalier (1951–).

From 1981 to 1985, Brown served as deputy director of the DNC, and in 1988 was campaign manager for presidential hopeful Jesse Jackson (1941– ; see entry in volume 2). Brown was credited with making peace between Jackson and Massachusetts governor Michael Dukakis (1933–), who became the Democratic Party's nominee. Soon Brown acquired a reputation as one who could unify both blacks and whites. In 1989, he was elected chairman of the DNC.

Brown helped black Democrats L. Douglas Wilder (1931– ; see entry in volume 4) and David Dinkins (1927– ; see entry in volume 1) gain victory in the Virginia gubernatorial and the New York City mayoral races respectively. But Brown's greatest success came during the 1992 presidential election. Despite high popularity ratings for President George Bush (1924–) following the 1991 Gulf War with Iraq, Brown believed that a Democrat could defeat Bush. The election of Clinton proved him right, and Clinton rewarded him with the commerce secretary position.

Death raises questions

When Brown died he was, as many journalists later pointed out, doing what he did best as commerce secretary: promoting American business. With the end of the Cold War, the Communist nation of Yugoslavia had broken into several countries, including Croatia, Bosnia, and Serbia, which were caught up in a bitter ethnic war. As the chief government representative for American business, Brown traveled to Croatia in April of 1996 in order to encourage U.S. investment in that country. But he never got to complete his mission: while en route, his plane crashed into a mountainside during a storm. Brown and thirty-two others, including a dozen business executives, were killed instantly.

Following Brown's death, U.S. trade ambassador Mickey Cantor was named interim commerce secretary; in December 1996, President Clinton appointed Chicago lawyer William Daley to take Brown's place. Meanwhile, many in the African American community—and many outside it—began to raise questions concerning the late commerce secretary's death (see accompanying sidebar).

In 1996, the Ronald H. Brown Foundation was established, the *Amsterdam News* reported, "as a way to transform the vision and accomplishments of the late Ron Brown into a practical legacy of achievement." A scholarship program for African American high schoolers, as well as a corporate leadership award have also been established. In September 1997, the U.S. House of Representatives voted to name a federal building after Brown. In 1998, *The Life and Times of Ron Brown*, written by Brown's daughter, Tracey, was published.

U.S. Army investigators walk past the wreckage of the airplane that crashed with Secretary of Commerce Ron Brown on board.

Was Ron Brown murdered?

The administration of President Bill Clinton, which began on January 20, 1993, was surrounded by scandal and allegations of scandal, and Ron Brown himself was not immune from these. He was accused of taking bribes (accepting money in exchange for favors) from foreign governments and from individuals. His name was linked with charges that Clinton and other top Democrats granted special favors to Asian businessmen in exchange for large financial contributions during the 1996 election. Thus, Brown's death on April 3, 1996, raised questions that he might have been killed.

While praising Brown's role as a leader in his party and a promoter of international commerce, several obituaries also questioned his financial dealings. *Time,* for instance, noted that "at the time of his death, an independent counsel was investigating his ties to a rich businesswoman who had allegedly paid Brown $400,000 for his share of a company in which he had invested no time or money." *U.S. News & World Report* commented that the publicity surrounding the investigation of Brown "had diminished his chances for reaching a long-sought goal: becoming Secretary of State."

According to the Gannett News Service, among the challenges faced by William Daley, Brown's successor as commerce secretary, were "a series of investigations about the controversial business relationships of the late Ron Brown." New questions were raised in a scandal surrounding former DNC vice chairman (and Commerce Department employee) John Huang. He was accused of helping to arrange special favors for Asian businessmen in return for campaign donations to prominent Democrats in the 1996 elections.

Amidst all these questions, a rumor circulated that the military doctor who conducted the autopsy (an examination of a body to determine the cause of death) of Brown had found a hole resembling a bullet wound in Brown's head. This claim was questioned by many, and another doctor said that the hole could not have been from a bullet,

Sources for further reading

"Black Caucus Asks U.S. to Check Reports that Secretary Ron Brown Died from Gunshot." *Jet,* January 12, 1998, pp. 39–40.

Brown, Tracey L. *The Life and Times of Ron Brown.* New York: William Morrow, 1998.

"Clinton Leads Final Tribute to Brown: 'This Man Loved Life and All Things in It.'" *Detroit News,* April 11, 1996.

because there was no exit wound (point at which the bullet leaves the body). But the controversy had begun.

An unlikely group of conservatives, liberals, and Muslims—represented respectively by 1996 presidential hopeful **Alan Keyes** (1950– ; p. 147), comedian Dick Gregory (1932– ; see entry in volume 2), and Nation of Islam leader **Louis Farrakhan** (1933– ; see entry in volume 2, and update on p. 71)—began to raise suspicions that Brown had been murdered. The scandal seemed to recall events surrounding the July 1993 suicide of White House aide Vincent Foster, who some claim was murdered.

In January 1998, Congressional Black Caucus chairwoman Maxine Waters (1938–) asked President Clinton and Attorney General Janet Reno (1938–) to authorize an investigation. The following month, a conservative legal civil rights group, Judicial Watch, petitioned a three-judge panel to conduct an investigation. The District of Columbia chapter of the National Association for the Advancement of Colored People (NAACP) supported the group's petition.

The Air Force, which published a twenty-two-volume report on the crash in June 1996, said that Brown was not murdered. Attorney General Reno and President Clinton agreed. So did the mainstream media—and, more surprisingly, the conservative magazine *American Spectator.* The *Spectator* had previously been in the forefront of the movement to investigate Clinton's ties to wrongdoing in the Whitewater scandal, which involved profits from a land deal in Arkansas during the 1980s. But the *Spectator* wrote that all that the evidence suggested that Brown had simply died from the plane crash. Nonetheless, it said questions still needed to be answered: "It is one thing for the President to call his Whitewater critics right-wing nuts, but quite another for him to cavalierly dismiss the concerns of black supporters."

Hosenball, Mark, and Gregory L. Vistica. "The Life and Times of a Rumor." *Newsweek.* January 9, 1998, p. 31.

Roberts, Steven V. "The Death of a Salesman." *U.S. News & World Report,* April 15, 1996, pp. 38–39.

White, Jack E. "An Empty Seat at the Table: Ronald Harmon Brown: 1941–1996." *Time,* April 15, 1996, p. 72.

"Year-End Culmination of Ron Brown Salutes." *Amsterdam News,* January 1, 1998, p. 4.

York, Byron. "Ron Brown's Body." *American Spectator,* February 1998, pp. 50–53.

Cab Calloway

*Born December 25, 1907
Rochester, New York
Died November 18, 1994
Hosckessin, Delaware
Singer, bandleader*

UPDATE

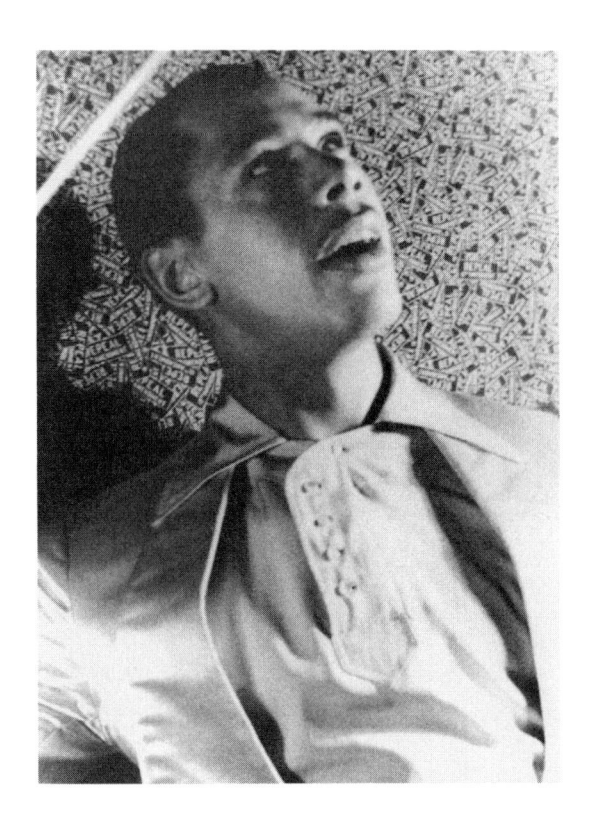

Famed singer and bandleader Cab Calloway, who became famous as much for his ultra-cool style as for songs such as "Minnie the Moocher," died on November 18, 1996, of complications resulting from a stroke. He was eighty-six years old. **(See original entry on Calloway in volume 1.)**

Born Cabell Calloway III in Rochester, New York, in 1907, Calloway came from a successful family. His father was a lawyer, and his parents assumed he would study law, too. But Calloway, already a talented performer who enjoyed singing solos at the Bethlehem Methodist Episcopal Church, had other plans. His sister, who worked as a jazz singer in Chicago, helped him get a job as a singer with a band.

By 1927, the twenty-year-old Calloway had organized his own band in Chicago. They called themselves "Cab Calloway and His Alabamians," and their fame soon spread to New York City. They went to New York to play a gig at a club, but discovered that the engagement had been cancelled. Cal-

*"Hi-de-hi-de-hi-de-hi,
Ho-de-ho-de-ho-de-ho,
He-de-he-de-he-de-he,
Hi-de-hi-de-hi-de-ho!"*

—from "Minnie the Moocher"

loway disbanded the group, and was about to return to Chicago in defeat when he received a part in a Broadway comedy, *Connie's Hot Chocolates*. In the show, his rendition of "Ain't Misbehavin'" made him a favorite with audiences.

Soon he formed the Cab Calloway Orchestra, which in 1929 began playing at the famed Cotton Club in New York's Harlem district. There Calloway developed a number of the elements that would characterize his style. This included scat—the random musical use of nonsense syllables. In the 1930s and 1940s, he became an international celebrity, with numerous film appearances and a list of hits that included "Minnie the Moocher," "Hi-De-Ho Man," "It Don't Mean a Thing If It Ain't Got That Swing," "Jumpin' Jive," and "It Ain't Necessarily So." Known as the Dean of American Jive, Calloway was the essence of what later generations might call "cool," "bad," or "phat." In his day, the word was "hep," and Calloway was the acknowledged authority on it. His book *Hepster's Dictionary* became a best-seller.

Calloway helped launch the careers of many performers who worked with his band at one time or another. These included singers Pearl Bailey (1918–90; see entry in volume 1) and Lena Horne (1917– ; see entry in volume 2); trumpeter Dizzy Gillespie (1917–93; see entry in volume 2); and saxophonists Chu Berry (1910–41) and Ben Webster (1909–73). Through his influence on Louis Jordan (1908–75), sometimes considered the founder of postwar R&B (rhythm and blues), Calloway in turn influenced a whole generation of performers that included Chuck Berry (1926– ; see entry in volume 1), Ray Charles (1930– ; see entry in volume 1), and Elvis Presley (1935–77).

Still going strong into the 1980s and 1990s

In his seventies and eighties, Calloway continued to perform. In 1980, Calloway appeared alongside Dan Aykroyd (1952–) and John Belushi (1950–82) in *The Blues Brothers*. Fittingly, Calloway played the Blues Brothers' mentor (teacher); and he did what *Newsday* called "a still-electric performance of 'Minnie the Moocher.'" During the late 1980s and early 1990s, echoes of his style began to appear on MTV and elsewhere in the hip-hop dance moves of Janet Jackson (1966– ; see entry in volume 2) and Hammer (1962– ; see entry in volume 2). Conscious of her debt to him, Jackson asked Calloway to appear in her 1990 video, "All Right." He also became known to an even younger generation through numerous appearances on *Sesame Street*.

On June 12, 1994, Calloway suffered a stroke at his White Plains, New York, home. He and Nuffie, his wife of forty-one years, decided that he should be placed in a Delaware nursing home. He died there on November 18, with family members beside him. "He had two separate lives," said Nuffie, "his life on stage and his life with his family. When he closed the door of his dressing room, he came home as a husband, father, and grandfather."

More than 2,000 people attended his memorial service in New York City on November 29. Many of Calloway's old band members performed. Actor-comedian **Bill Cosby** (1937– ; see entry in volume 1, and update in on p. 41) told mourners not to grieve for Calloway. "He'll be performing up there every night. He'll be the loudest one up there."

In September 1997, Nuffie Calloway was involved in a lawsuit against her husband's manager. She claimed that in the last months of Calloway's life, the manager had taken advantage of her husband's failing mental and physical health by convincing him to transfer the rights to his songs and his life story for less than their actual value.

Sources for further reading

O'Neill, Ann. "The Court Files." *Los Angeles Times,* September 14, 1997, p. B1.

Overbea, Luix Virgil. "'Hi-De-Ho' Man Cab Calloway Touched a World with His Music." *Bay State Banner,* November 24, 1994.

Price, Susan. "Cosby Leads Tribute for Calloway." *Newsday,* November 30, 1994, p. A52.

Seymour, Gene. "Cab Calloway Dies: 'Hi-De-Ho Man' a Pop Music Icon." *Newsday,* November 20, 1994, p. A7.

Alice Childress

Born October 12, 1920
Charleston, South Carolina
Died August 14, 1994
New York, New York
Playwright, novelist, actress

UPDATE

Alice Childress, author of numerous plays, screenplays, novels, and other works, died of cancer on August 14, 1994. Among her famous plays were *Trouble in the Mind* (1955), which won the Obie Award in 1956, and *Wedding Band: A Love/Hate Story in Black and White* (1966). Her most well-known novel was *A Hero Ain't Nothin' But a Sandwich* (1973), and other notable works include the screenplay *Wine in the Wilderness* (1969). Childress's writing often dealt with controversial subjects such as drug addiction and interracial marriage. **(See original entry on Childress in volume 1.)**

Though she was born in Charleston, South Carolina, Childress was raised in the Harlem section of New York City. She was an enthusiastic reader, but had to drop out of high school in her teens after her grandmother died. After a brief marriage that left her with a child, she supported herself through a number of jobs. In 1940, when she was twenty years old, she began her acting career with an appearance in the play

"Books, plays, telewriting, motion picture scenarios, etc., I seem caught up in a fragmentation of writing skills. But an idea comes to me in a certain form and, if it stays with me, must be written out. . . ."

On Strivers Row. Nine years later, she acted in, directed, and wrote *Florence,* and later attracted national attention with *Trouble in the Mind.*

Childress's work often dealt with sensitive subjects. *Trouble in the Mind* portrays a group of black actors trying to play roles written for them by whites. *Wedding Band* tells the story of an interracial love affair in South Carolina in 1918—a time and place in which intermarriage between blacks and whites was forbidden. *A Hero Ain't Nothin' But a Sandwich* looks at drug addiction, which resulted in the book being banned in a school library in Savannah, Georgia.

Her 1955 play still being performed

Childress wrote several musicals with her second husband, musician Nathan Woodward. She also worked with fellow playwright and friend Clarice Taylor (1927–) on a number of plays. But in the late 1980s, she and Taylor had a disagreement over the legal rights to a work concerning entertainer Jackie "Moms" Mabley (1897–1975). Childress took her former partner to court, and in 1991 she won the case.

In 1993, Childress received a Lifetime Achievement Award from the Association for Theatre in Higher Education. Around that time, she was writing a novel about her African great-grandmother, who was born a slave, and her Scottish-Irish great-grandmother; but before she could finish it, she died of cancer on August 14, 1994.

A group of artists and writers held a memorial for Childress in November 1994, on Roosevelt Island, New York, where she had last lived. The memorial, which included a local high school's performance from her play *Like One of the Family,* was sponsored in part by the Roosevelt Island Community Library, which had named a section of the library in Childress's honor.

During the 1990s, Childress's name continued to be discussed for a number of reasons. In 1997, for instance, the rock band Ben Folds Five released a song called "Alice Childress," raising questions from fans who wondered if it had anything to do with the playwright. (As it turned out, it did not.) Also, in a court battle involving the legal rights to the hit Broadway musical *Rent,* lawyers frequently mentioned the by-then famous case of *Childress v. Taylor.* And in April 1998, yet another revival of Childress's *Trouble in the Mind* began at the Samuel Beckett Theatre in New York City. By then her hit play was forty-three years old, and people were still coming to see it.

Childress once said: "Books, plays, telewriting, motion picture scenarios, etc., I seem caught up in a fragmentation of writing skills. But an idea comes to me in a certain form and, if it stays with me, must be written out...."

Sources for further reading

African-American Playwrights. "Alice Childress." [Online] http://www.scils.rutgers.edu/~cybers/child.html (accessed on October 8, 1998).

Bourne, Stephen. "Obituary: Alice Childress." *Independent,* April 30, 1994, p. 12.

"This Weekend." *Newsday,* April 10, 1998, p. B2.

Wright, Sarah E. "Celebrities Remember Alice Childress with Love." *New York Amsterdam News,* November 19, 1994.

Cinque

Born c. 1810
Present-day Sierra Leone, Africa
Died c. 1880
Sierra Leone
Slave revolt leader

Cinque, sometimes referred to as Joseph Cinque (pronounced "sink-AY"), led a slave revolt aboard the ship *Amistad*, which was carrying captured Africans in 1838. Tried for their part in the mutiny, Cinque was defended by former president John Quincy Adams (1767–1848). Adams won the case before the U.S. Supreme Court in 1841, and Cinque and the other mutineers were freed, making theirs the first and only successful mutiny in the history of the American slave trade.

The details of Cinque's early life in Africa are uncertain, and the facts of his death are likewise clouded in mystery. But in the years between his capture and his return to Africa in 1841, Cinque became a celebrated figure among both African American slaves and abolitionists. Abolitionists were white people, mostly in the northern United States, who supported an end to slavery. Cinque remained a powerful symbol of the eternal desire for freedom. In 1997 the movie *Amistad* told the story of the revolt and the subsequent trial.

"All we want is make us free!"

—Kale, child slave and Amistad *mutineer*

Sold into slavery

Historians know little about Cinque's early life. He was born in the 1810s in what is now the West African country of Sierra Leone. His name, in the Mende language of his tribe, was actually Sengbe Pieh (pronounced "sing-BAY pea-AH"). At the time of his capture by slave traders, he was in his twenties and had a wife and three children.

Unfortunately, he lived in a part of Africa with an active slave trade. Cinque was captured by members of an enemy tribe and sold to Spanish slave traders who owned a so-called "slave factory" on the island of Lomboko. They in turn sold him to a Portuguese slaver on his way to Cuba.

Human cargo

Thrown in with the human cargo aboard the Portuguese slave ship *Técora,* Cinque was subjected to extraordinarily cruel treatment. The slaves were crowded into the cargo hold and chained to one another and to the sides of the ship. Nutrition and medical care were so poor that half of them died before reaching their destination. Thus in their greed to transport as many slaves as possible, the slavers actually cheated themselves. They considered the human beings captured from Africa to be their property, and yet they did not treat this "property" as well as they would have treated horses or cattle. The fact that Cinque survived is a tribute to his strength, both physically and mentally.

In the Spanish colony of Cuba, the importation of slaves was illegal, but slavery itself was not. Therefore the slavers gave their captives Spanish Christian names to make it look as though they had been born in Cuba. Sengbe became José, or Joseph, Cinque. Cinque and forty-eight other adult males were secretly sold to a Cuban planter named Ruiz. Sailing from the Cuban capital of Havana, Ruiz and his partner Pedro Montes planned to take the adults, along with three little girls and a boy, to a plantation a short distance away. The name of their ship was *Amistad,* which means "friendship" in Spanish.

Mutiny

Conditions on the *Amistad* were no better physically than on the *Técora,* and psychologically they were even worse. A cook used sign language to tell the slaves that when they got to their destination, the Spaniards would slaughter them and eat them. The Africans, who had no way of knowing otherwise, believed him, and the cook's cruel joke ultimately triggered the famous *Amistad* mutiny.

Cinque seems to have emerged quickly as the leader of the slaves. He reportedly told the others, "We may as well die in trying to be free as be killed and eaten." Using a nail, he loosened the chains binding him to the wall of the vessel's cargo hold, and soon he and a fellow slave named Grabeau freed the others from their chains. Fortunately for them, their captors had foolishly stowed a large number of knives for harvesting sugar cane. Had the slavers made it to their destination, these knives would have probably served as the tools with which their slaves labored in the fields. Now they became weapons.

Leaving the four children below in the cargo hold, the armed men sneaked onto the ship's deck. The weather was on their side: it was a stormy night, and they took advantage of the rain to surprise their captors. The first one they killed was the cook, who Cinque himself handled with a single blow. They also killed the captain and all but two members of the crew, who managed to escape in a lifeboat. The only ones left were Ruiz and Montes, who themselves became captives when the mutineers placed them in chains.

But once again, the slavers took advantage of the Africans' lack of knowledge. No one but the two Spaniards knew how to sail the ship. If they wanted to get back to Africa, Cinque and the others needed to keep their former captors alive. Knowing that in sailing west to the New World,

Harper's Weekly *illustration depicting the mutiny aboard the* Amistad.

they had sailed away from the rising sun, Cinque ordered Montes to sail toward the sun. But in the next few days, Montes managed to trick the Africans. He sailed east by day, but northwest by night. If he could not get back to Cuba, Montes reasoned, he could at least steer the ship toward the southern United States. There, slavery was legal; he figured he could return his and Ruiz's "property" in the United States. As it turned out, both the Spaniards and the Africans were wrong: when the ship finally pulled into a harbor six weeks later, it was on Long Island in New York—where slavery was against the law.

Debating the fate of human lives

The U.S. Coast Guard captured the *Amistad*. At first Cinque tried to escape by jumping overboard, but he finally allowed himself to be captured. By that point, there were only forty-three African men alive on the ship, along with the four children. They were placed in jail.

The slaves might have been returned to Cuba had it not been for a group of abolitionists. These were white people, mostly in New York and New England, who wanted to see slavery abolished. Among the abolitionists who supported the cause of the *Amistad* prisoners were lawyer Joshua Leavitt and Lewis Tappan, a New York businessman. Like many Abolitionists, they were evangelical Christians opposed to slavery on moral grounds. Furthermore, Tappan believed slavery went against the principles on which America was founded. Indeed, he said that slavery was "the worm at the root of the tree of Liberty. Unless [it is] killed, the tree will die."

But President Martin Van Buren (1782–1862) was no abolitionist. Ruiz and Montes had initiated a court case to secure the return of the slaves to them, arguing that the Africans were their property, and that by revolting, Cinque and the others had in effect "stolen" themselves from their rightful owners. Van Buren was inclined to agree, especially because he wanted to maintain good relations with the Spanish authorities. To fight for Cinque and the others, the abolitionists hired attorney Roger S. Baldwin (1793–1863), who set out to prove in court that the slaves were not "property" at all, but kidnapped human beings, and that therefore Montes and Ruiz were the true criminals.

"All we want is make us free"

The trial began in Hartford, Connecticut, on September 19, 1839. By then Cinque had become something of a celebrity, and many progressive (forward thinking) Americans, including poet William Cullen Bryant (1794–1878), had spoken out in favor of the Africans. When Cinque testified in court, aided by a Mende language interpreter the abolitionists had found, he gave a stirring account of his capture and his inhumane treatment. In a powerful display, he graphically illustrated the way he and the other slaves had been crammed into the ship's hold by sitting on the floor with his hands and feet pulled tightly together.

Meanwhile, the White House was involved in sinister private dealings. In a meeting with the Spanish ambassador, Pedro Alcantara de Argaiz, President Van Buren agreed that once the trial was over, and the slaves were found guilty of mutiny, the Spanish slavers could quickly leave the country with the aid of a U.S. Navy vessel. That way, they would be out of U.S. waters before the slaves had a chance to exercise their right of appeal. This was an obvious violation of constitutional law, which guarantees that a person on trial has a right to appeal his or her case (take it to a higher court for another trial). Van Buren would later pay for this injustice.

In a move that surprised the White House, Judge Andrew T. Judson (1784–1853) of the Connecticut district court ruled on January 13, 1840, that the slaves had indeed been kidnapped, and should be returned to their homes in Africa. Van Buren filed an appeal, which meant that the case would go before the highest court in the land, the U.S. Supreme Court in Washington, D.C.

Prospects did not look good for the Africans. A majority of the Supreme Court, five of its nine justices—including Chief Justice Roger Taney (1777–1864)—were slaveholders

Is slavery a black and white issue?

Slavery has persisted in one form or another since ancient times. It has not always been a matter of white people enslaving black people. In Greece and Rome, for instance, the white upper classes of those societies "owned" other whites, as well as brown-skinned and black people captured from other countries. The system had just about died out, however, by the fifteenth century, but then several events helped to revive it.

Beginning with the voyages of Portuguese explorer Vasco da Gama (c. 1460–1524) in the 1490s, Europeans embarked on an "Age of Discovery," in which explorers such as da Gama, Christopher Columbus (1451–1506), and Ferdinand Magellan (1480–1521) mapped the continents of the world. Many positive things came from this exploration, but many negative ones as well. Whereas Europe was crowded with warring groups of people, the New World (North and South America) held vast agricultural lands, and was sparsely populated by Indians. The Europeans claimed this land for their own; looking for cheap labor to grow crops, they turned to Africa. The slave trade began in the 1400s, and continued for the next four centuries.

The system of buying and selling human lives had two components. There were the white slave traders from Europe. They sailed to the coast of Africa to buy human beings and transport them to America and other parts of the New World. These slaves then worked in fields planting tobacco, rice, and other crops. But the Europeans operated mainly on the coast, and many of the Africans lived inland. So the slave traders could not conduct their business without the help of Africans who would willingly sell them their neighbors, usually members of rival tribes. Cinque himself was initially captured, not by whites, but by an enemy tribe.

By 1839, when Cinque was captured, parts of Europe were beginning to awaken to the evils of slavery. British philosophers such as John Locke (1632–1704) held that all human beings deserved certain natural rights, which he identified as "life, liberty, and the

---

from the South. By now the Africans' supporters had formed the "Amistad Committee," which consisted of both whites and free African Americans. The Committee decided it was time to bring out the heavy firepower: U.S. representative and former president John Quincy Adams.

Though in his seventies and almost deaf, Adams was still a powerful orator, and the case of the Africans had

pursuit of property." Slowly, society was catching up: Britain abolished the slave trade in 1807, and ended slavery in England in 1833. Ironically, Cinque's homeland of Sierra Leone became a British colony in 1808 as part of British efforts to provide a place in Africa where freed slaves could settle; hence the name of Sierra Leone's capital, Freetown.

In America, people of British descent liked Locke's ideas and applied them in the Declaration of Independence (1776). (Locke's memorable phrase, of course, was altered to "life, liberty, and the pursuit of *happiness*.") But for many years, these principles applied only to white Americans. Only with the end of the Civil War (1861–65) and the subsequent adoption of the Thirteenth Amendment (1865) was slavery outlawed in the United States. Even then, it took the Civil Rights movement of the 1960s to secure full equal rights under the law for blacks living in the southern United States.

Another ironic fact about slavery is that in the late twentieth century, just about the only place on Earth where slavery still existed was in Africa. This topic made headlines briefly in 1996 when Minister **Louis Farrakhan** (1933– ; see entry in volume 2, and update on p. 71) visited the northeastern African country of Sudan and was criticized for doing so because of that nation's continuing slave trade. Farrakhan claimed that there was no slavery, but some journalists proved him wrong by travelling to Sudan and purchasing a slave, whom they set free.

What the Sudan situation proves is that slavery is not necessarily a black and white issue; it is a human issue. Considered in these terms, it is not so hard to understand that Africans would have sold other Africans into captivity. Often the most bitter rivalries are between neighbors, who fail to see that they share a common danger. The real answer to issues such as slavery is to see people as individual human beings, not as members of groups. When that happens, it is impossible for a person not to treat somebody else with the same kindness with which they would expect to be treated.

moved him deeply. Like many other Americans, he had observed the efforts of the captives, under the instruction of students from Yale College in New Haven, Connecticut, to study English and Christianity. He was particularly impressed by one of the children, a girl named Kale, who wrote him a letter that contained a stirring message: "All we want is make us free."

A victory for freedom

Adams argued before the Supreme Court for eight hours over the space of two days. Like Baldwin, who appeared with him on the slaves' behalf, he appealed to the natural laws embodied in the Constitution: "I know of no other law that reaches the case of my clients," he told the Court, "but the law of Nature and of Nature's God on which our fathers placed our own national existence." On March 9, 1841, the Supreme Court ruled that the Africans had been kidnapped, and that their mutiny had been an act of self-defense which did not violate the "eternal principles of justice."

By this time, Van Buren was no longer president. His stand on the *Amistad* issue, which infuriated northern members of his party, the Democrats, helped lead to his defeat to William Henry Harrison (1773–1841) in the 1840 election. Even with Van Buren out of office, the Amistad Committee had to raise money for the former captives' return trip to Africa. President John Tyler (1790–1862) refused to fund the voyage. (Tyler became president when Harrison died after only one month in office.)

Some of the Amistad Committee's members were from the Union Missionary Society, a group of free African Americans in Connecticut who wanted to send missionaries to Africa. Having learned English, Cinque had become an eloquent speaker, and he became a powerful spokesman for the Society's cause.

Return to Africa

On November 25, 1841, Cinque and the other former captives set sail for Africa aboard a British vessel, the *Gentleman*. It was a fitting name, because now they were travelling as free human beings, not slaves. When they arrived in Sierra Leone nearly two months later, a British government official welcomed them.

Little is known about Cinque's latter years. He returned to his home, but unfortunately many members of his family had been killed in tribal fighting. In subsequent years, African

American missionaries set up a mission in Sierra Leone. One day in 1879, an old man who said he was Cinque arrived at the missionaries' compound. He said he was dying, and he asked to be buried on the grounds of the mission. He died soon afterward, and was buried alongside the missionaries, both black and white, which were set up in Sierra Leone in the wake of the *Amistad* incident.

Subject of 1997 movie

Cinque would remain a legendary figure, a hero to all people who treasure freedom. In 1978, almost exactly a century after his death, actress Debbie Allen (1950–) became inspired by his story. Then a student at Howard University in Washington, D.C., Allen would later receive acclaim as a dancer and the star of the hit TV series *Fame*. In 1984, she purchased the film rights to a 1953 book about Cinque called *Black Mutiny,* but it would be many years before she could achieve her dream of bringing the story to film.

In 1994, however, Allen "found my John Quincy Adams in Steven Spielberg." Allen and Spielberg (1947–), one of the most successful directors of all time, teamed up to make the movie *Amistad*. The film starred Djimon Hounsou (1964–), an actor from the West African country of Benin, as Cinque; Academy Award winner Anthony Hopkins (1937–) as Adams; and many others, including Morgan Freeman (1937–). A descendant of Cinque in Sierra Leone, Samuel H. Pieh, served as a consultant in the making of the movie.

Sources for further reading

Amistad: An Extraordinary Tale of Courage, Justice, and Humanity. [Online] http://www.penguinputnam.com/amistad/ (accessed on October 8, 1998).

Amistad Trial Home Page. [Online] http://www.law.umkc.edu/faculty/projects/ftrials/amistad/amistd.htm (accessed on October 8, 1998).

Brailsford, Karen. "Don't Give Up the Ship." *People,* December 22, 1997, p. 22.

Cable, Mary. *Black Odyssey: The Case of the Slave Ship Amistad.* New York: Penguin USA, 1998.

Hudson, Wade, and Valerie Wilson Wesley. *Afro-Bets Book of Black Heroes From A to Z: An Introduction to Important Black Achievers for Young Readers.* East Orange, NJ: Just Us Books, 1997.

Jones, Howard. "All We Want Is Make Us Free!" *American History,* February 1998, pp. 22–29.

Jones, Howard. *Mutiny on the Amistad.* New York: Oxford University Press, 1997.

Jurmain, Suzanne. *Freedom's Sons: The True Story of the Amistad Mutiny.* New York: Lothrop Lee & Shepard, 1998.

Owens, William A. *Black Mutiny: The Revolt of the Schooner Amistad.* New York: Plume, 1997.

"Samuel Pieh Applauds 'Amistad' Movie About His Ancestor, Slave Revolt Leader Joseph Cinque." *Jet,* February 23, 1998, p. 39.

Zeinert, Karen. *The Amistad Slave Revolt and American Abolition.* North Haven, CT: Linnet Books, 1997.

Bill Cosby

Born July 12, 1937
Philadelphia, Pennsylvania
Comedian, actor, philanthropist

UPDATE

Bill Cosby remains one of America's most popular entertainment figures—indeed, one of the nation's most popular public figures of any kind. But in January 1997, he and his wife, Camille, faced two painful events: the murder of their son, Ennis, and a lawsuit by a woman who claimed to be Cosby's daughter from a 1973 affair. **(See original entry on Cosby in volume 1.)**

Growing up in a black neighborhood in Philadelphia during the 1940s, Cosby showed a talent for comedy, and he was equally gifted as an athlete. His grades were not good, though, and he dropped out of high school to join the Navy. During his four years in the service, he earned his diploma through correspondence courses, and enrolled at Philadelphia's Temple University following his discharge. Then in 1962, at the age of twenty-five, he left school to pursue a career in show business.

After playing the nightclub circuit for several years, Cosby had his big break with the TV series *I Spy* in 1965. Not

"Hello, friend."

—Trademark greeting of Cosby's late son, Ennis

only was the show clever, witty, and suspenseful, it was the first prime-time TV program with an African American star. In the same year that **Dorothy Dandridge** (1992–65; see entry on p. 47) committed suicide after a lifetime of frustration, young black stars such as Cosby were breaking ground. After the cancellation of *I Spy* in 1968, he launched *The Bill Cosby Show,* and in 1972 the Saturday morning cartoon series *Fat Albert and the Cosby Kids.* Cosby, who provided the voices, created the characters based on kids he had known growing up in Philadelphia.

Cosby's reputation grew during the 1970s, as he appeared in movies such as *Uptown Saturday Night* (1974), and became a spokesman for Coca-Cola, Jell-O pudding, and Kodak film. He also earned his doctoral degree from Amherst University in Massachusetts in 1977. Then in 1984 came his biggest hit of all—one of the most successful TV programs in history—*The Cosby Show.* Over the next few years, both black and white viewers would follow the story of the Huxtables. Cosby, who played Dr. Cliff Huxtable, modelled the TV family on his own, which included four daughters and a son, Ennis, the model for Theo Huxtable. *The Cosby Show* helped make its creator a very wealthy man, and Cosby has gone to great lengths to share that wealth. In 1988, for instance, he and his wife gave $20 million to Spelman College, a school for African American women in Atlanta, Georgia.

Son murdered; Cosby faces extortion by alleged daughter

The Cosby Show finished up in 1992, and in the coming years, Cosby had several other television programs. *You Bet Your Life* (1992) was an unsuccessful attempt to revive the popular 1950s game show; *The Cosby Mysteries* (1994) featured Cosby as a detective; and in *Cosby* (1996), he was reunited with his former television wife, Phylicia Rashad (1948–), from *The Cosby Show.* Cosby also hosts *Kids Say the Darndest Things,* an update of the 1950s *Art Linkletter's House Party.*

Cosby's real wife, Camille, holds a doctorate just like her husband, and in 1995 she published *Television's Imageable*

Influences, a book about stereotypes of African Americans on TV. In addition to the doctorate he had earned nearly twenty years earlier, Cosby received an honorary doctorate from Fisk University in Nashville, Tennessee, in May 1995. Honors and recognition continued through the mid-1990s: a November 1994 survey revealed that Cosby was one of the top ten celebrity endorsers on television, and a *USA Today*/MCI poll in 1996 found that Cliff Huxtable was the most memorable "TV dad" of all time. Cosby won his fifteenth People's Choice Award in January 1997.

Just a few weeks into 1997, however, Cosby entered perhaps the hardest period of his life. On January 16, his son Ennis was shot to death while changing a flat tire just off of a freeway near San Diego, California. Not only was Ennis the Cosbys' only son, he had been much-loved both within the family and outside. Diagnosed as a child with dyslexia, a reading disorder, he had devoted his life to helping those with similar disabilities. He was working on his Ph.D. in special education at Columbia University in New York City. He tutored children with reading problems, and was known for his trademark greeting: "Hello, friend." Actor Malcolm-Jamal Warner (1970–), who had played Ennis's alter ego, Theo, on *The Cosby Show,* spoke for many when he said simply, "I loved him."

In the middle of their grief over Ennis, while police searched for clues that would lead to the killer, the Cosbys were hit with another blow. Twenty-two-year-old Autumn Jackson approached Cosby with a claim that she was his daughter. Ironically, she first made contact with Cosby's lawyer on the day Ennis was shot. She threatened to go public with the story if Cosby didn't pay her $40 million. When somebody tries to obtain something through force or intimidation in this way, it is called extortion and considered illegal.

Cosby admitted publicly—and to his wife—that he had had a short affair with another woman in 1973. But he denied being Jackson's father. He even offered to undergo DNA testing, but Jackson refused. DNA (deoxyribonucleic acid) is a sort of identifying "fingerprint" that everyone carries in their blood. It is often used in cases where comparing blood types is

important. Jackson was tried and convicted of extortion and sent to prison.

By far the more painful of the two experiences was the death of Ennis. Police continued to search for the killer in the early months of 1997. State and local governments offered a reward for information leading to identification of the murderer. But the Cosbys issued a statement saying that while they appreciated the gesture, they did not want to use taxpayers' money or create the impression that they were receiving special treatment as celebrities.

Cosby did, however, challenge several tabloid newspapers such as the *National Enquirer* and *The Globe* to offer a reward, since they were profiting from the story of Ennis's murder. An offer of $100,000 from the *Enquirer* helped lead to the capture of eighteen-year-old Mikail Markhasev, an immigrant from the country of the Ukraine. He was found guilty of first-degree murder in July 1998 and was sentenced to life in prison without the possibility of parole.

Though the Cosbys were no doubt glad that justice had been done, the conviction did not bring back their son. Just a month after Ennis's death, Cosby made his first performance for a standing-room-only crowd in West Palm Beach, Florida. He came out on stage in a tee shirt emblazoned with the words "Hello Friend," and received a standing ovation before he even opened his mouth.

Since then, Cosby has thrown himself into his work. In 1998, he introduced *Kids Say the Darndest Things,* a revival of a 1960s television show hosted by humorist Art Linkletter (1912–). Cosby formed a common bond with Linkletter, who lost his own daughter to a drug overdose in 1969, and the two spent time together talking about their tragedies.

Sources for further reading

"Camille Cosby Stands by Husband, Bill, Who Admitted He Had a 'Rendezvous' Years Ago." *Jet,* February 17, 1997, p. 18.

Castro, Peter, et al. "Goodbye, Friend: Slain Son Ennis Inspired His Colleagues, His Students, But Most of All His Family." *People,* February 3, 1997, p. 68.

Conord, Bruce W. *Bill Cosby.* New York: Chelsea Juniors, 1993.

"Cosby Asks California State Officials to Take Back Reward Money Offered to Catch Son's Killer." *Jet,* February 17, 1997, p. 17.

"Cosby Makes First Return to Concert Stage Since Son's Death." *Jet,* February 17, 1997, p. 17.

Haskins, Jim. *Bill Cosby: America's Most Famous Father.* New York: Walker, 1988.

"Reward Tip Leads to Arrest of 18-Year-Old Russian Immigrant in Murder of Ennis Cosby. . . ." *Jet,* March 31, 1997, p. 12.

Schuman, N. J. *Bill Cosby: Actor and Comedian.* Springfield, NJ: Enslow Publishers, 1995.

"Son's Life Was Basis for Theo Huxtable." *USA Today,* January 17, 1997, p. 3-A.

Stambler, Lyndon, and Julia Campbell. "In Search of Justice: Ennis's Accused Killer Goes on Trial in L.A., as the Cosbys Struggle to Rebuild Their Shattered Lives." *People,* July 6, 1998, p. 80.

"The 25 Most Intriguing People '97: Bill Cosby: Struck by Loss and Scandal, He Gallantly Soldiers On." *People,* December 29, 1997–January 5, 1998, p. 54.

"Ukrainian Immigrant Mikail Markhasev Found Guilty of Murdering Ennis Cosby." *Jet,* July 27, 1998, p. 24.

Dorothy Dandridge

*Born November 9, 1922
Cleveland, Ohio
Died September 8, 1965
Los Angeles, California
Actress, singer*

Dorothy Dandridge has often been called "the black Marilyn Monroe"; in fact, Dandridge and Monroe (1926–62) were friends. Like Monroe, Dandridge was a goddess of the silver screen who would ultimately be frustrated in her desire to be taken seriously for her acting rather than her looks. Both women's lives began and ended tragically: abandoned by their fathers and abused by their mothers, they sold their beauty in a vain attempt to find love. And then, at a young age, both committed suicide.

Yet the fact that Dandridge was black, in an era when Hollywood offered black actresses few challenging roles, adds a painful aspect that is lacking in Monroe's story. Whereas Monroe became a mainstream superstar, Dandridge found herself on the sidelines. Hollywood basically had one part for her to play, that of the "tragic mulatto," a woman doomed because she can't fit in with either blacks or whites. (A mulatto is someone who has one white parent and one black parent.) The

"The [movie] industry didn't know what to do with her. Because what did black women do then? And she was searching not only to find a place in the industry, but to find love.... And I think that's what ultimately killed her, the search."

—Halle Berry

role was a stereotype (an oversimplified and prejudiced view of a class of people). When Dandridge grew tired of it, there was no place for her career to go.

Performs with sister

Born in Cleveland, Ohio, Dandridge and her sister Vivian inherited light coloring and Caucasian features from both their mother and their father. Their father left them when they were small children, and their mother, Ruby, was a lesbian. She had a minor career in comedy and pushed her children to sing, dance, and act. When Dorothy was five years old, she and her sister began touring churches in the southern United States as The Wonder Kids.

After moving to Los Angeles, Dorothy, Vivian, and a third girl, Etta Jones, formed a singing group called The Dandridge Sisters. A talent scout saw them perform and helped them get bit parts in movies such as the 1937 Marx Brothers classic *A Day at the Races*. The girls proved to be such talented singers that they became regular performers at the Cotton Club in New York City's Harlem District.

Launches her career

Dandridge was fourteen years old when she entered the world of the Cotton Club in its heyday, and she was already gorgeous. At the age of sixteen, she began dating dancer Harold Nicholas. The two were married in 1942, when Dandridge was twenty. But soon things began to fall apart. The couple's baby, Lynn, was born severely retarded and needed to be institutionalized for the rest of her life. After that, Nicholas began seeing other women.

Dandridge divorced Nicholas and continued what had become a lucrative singing career. She also began to develop her acting talent. She studied at the Actor's Laboratory in Los Angeles for two years, and in 1951 made her first major motion picture appearance as an African princess in *Tarzan's Peril*. In 1953 she had a significant role as a teacher opposite Harry Belafonte (1927– ; see entry in volume 1) in *Bright*

Road. It was one of the more notable pictures of Dandridge's career, one of the few times she did not play the "exotic seductress" role that would become common in her later work.

Nominated for an Oscar

The high point of Dandridge's career was in 1954. She starred in *Carmen Jones,* an all-black version of the famous opera *Carmen* by French composer Georges Bizet (1838–75). Dandridge's performance as the tough and sexy Carmen resulted in an Academy Award nomination for best actress. She was the first black to receive this honor. While she did not win, she had unquestionably made a big step forward. *Time* magazine hailed her as "one of the outstanding actresses of the screen." And she now had the support of the influential Otto Preminger (1906–86), who had directed *Carmen Jones* and with whom Dandridge now had a relationship. Sadly, though, it would turn out that her career had peaked just when she thought it was beginning. Dandridge would not make another film for three years.

Typecast as "tragic mulatto"

Though Dandridge appeared on the cover of *Life* magazine and was acclaimed as one of the world's most beautiful women, she was never permitted to emerge as a romantic lead (the starring actress who is romantically pursued by the starring actor). There was simply no one with whom to pair her: she might be placed opposite Belafonte or Sidney Poitier (1927– ; see entry in volume 3), who were the era's most notable black actors, but then the movie would have no chance of mainstream success. In *Island in the Sun* (1957), Dandridge and John Justin became the first black woman–white man romantic pairing ever seen in Hollywood, but that still did not make her a romantic lead. Instead, in this movie and many others, she inevitably played the beautiful, exotic creature who dazzled her white admirer but could never find romantic fulfillment.

The reason for this was simple: it was acceptable for a white man to desire a black woman, but to actually depict

Dorothy Dandridge and Sammy Davis, Jr., in a scene from Porgy and Bess.

a loving relationship between the two would go against the values of the times. So Dandridge was left to play the role of "tragic mulatto" in such forgettable movies as *The Decks Ran Red* (1958) and *Tamarango* (1959), or star in such all-black productions as *Porgy and Bess* (1959), for which she won a Golden Globe Award for best actress in a musical.

The suicide of Dorothy Dandridge

After Dandridge's romance with Preminger ended, she had a series of relationships, including one with actor Peter Lawford (1923–84). In 1959, she married a white nightclub owner, Jack Denison, but this marriage proved no better than her first.

Partly because of bad investments in Arizona oil wells, Dandridge had to declare bankruptcy in 1963. (When people declare bankruptcy, they give up rights to their possessions, which are divided among the people to whom they owe money.) Dandridge lost her home in Hollywood and could no longer pay for the care of her daughter, Lynn. She was suddenly left in the home of a mother who didn't know how to tend to her. (Ultimately Lynn wound up in a state mental institution, where she was reported to be still living in the late 1990s.)

> ### Selected films of Dorothy Dandridge
> 1941: *Sundown*
> 1941: *Sun Valley Serenade*
> 1942: *Lady from Louisiana*
> 1944: *Since You Went Away*
> 1951: *Tarzan's Peril*
> 1953: *Bright Road*
> 1954: *Carmen Jones*
> 1957: *Island in the Sun*
> 1958: *The Decks Ran Red*
> 1959: *Tamango*
> 1959: *Porgy and Bess*

On September 8, 1965, Dandridge was found in her Los Angeles apartment, dead from a drug overdose. She did not leave a suicide note, but it is generally believed that she killed herself. Yet in the months prior to her death, she seemed to be on the comeback trail: she had signed a contract to make two films, and was booked for a $10,000 two-week engagement at a New York City nightclub. But she had been abusing drugs and alcohol in the preceding years, and some say she had simply given up the will to live.

Dorothy Dandridge lives on

A generation after her death, Dandridge has become the star she never was in life. A September 1997 *Time* magazine headline said it all: "Dorothy Dandridge, Hollywood's first black film goddess, was dead at 42. Now she's back in style." The 1990s movies *To Wong Foo, Thanks for Everything! Julie Newmar* (1995) and *Girl 6* (1996) contain several references to Dandridge. In 1997, film critic and historian Donald Bogle published a popular study of her life, to which singer and actress Whitney Houston (1963– ; see entry in volume 2) has purchased the movie rights. In addition, singer Janet Jackson (1966– ; see entry in volume 2) bought the rights to Dandridge's autobiography, *Everything and Nothing,* and **Halle Berry** (1966– ; see entry in volume 1, and update on p. 13) began work in 1998 on an HBO film about Dandridge.

In today's Hollywood, opportunities are growing for black actresses, and they owe much to the one who paved the way. Dorothy Dandridge is a tough act to follow, as a 1997 *Essence* article suggested in a description of *Carmen Jones:* "Clad in a knee-length, tight, bright-red dress, Carmen saunters across the crowded army cafeteria. Immediately you're mesmerized—she's sensual, willful, mischievous and strikingly beautiful. You watch her flirt and manipulate a throng of men with the sultry confidence of a smooth hustler. She's the original home girl, bad to the bone!"

Sources for further reading

Bogle, Donald. *Dorothy Dandridge.* New York: Boulevard, 1997.

Corliss, Richard. "Lady Screens the Blues." *Time,* September 1, 1997, p. 73.

Dauphin, Gary. "Dorothy's Day." *Village Voice,* June 24, 1997, p. 84.

Russell, Yvette. "Jonesin' for Dandridge." *Essence,* May 1997, p. 114.

Scruby, Jennifer. "Halle's Comet." *Elle,* February 1998, pp. 78–80.

Dominique Dawes

*Born November 20, 1976
Silver Spring, Maryland
Olympic gymnast*

Even before she helped the U.S. women's gymnastics team win its first gold medal at the 1996 Olympic Games in Atlanta, Georgia, Dominique Dawes was famous for a number of reasons. She was only the second black woman to make the U.S. gymnastics team, which she first did in Barcelona, Spain, in 1992. Two years later, she became the second woman in history to win the all-around competition and four event titles at a national gymnastics championship.

In Atlanta, Dawes became the first African American to win a medal in the gymnastics individual event. This was particularly remarkable because, at almost twenty years old, she was at an age when most gymnasts have retired. But Dawes lived up to her motto, "D-3": dedication, determination, dynamics.

Parents didn't push her

In the case of many young people who achieve great things as entertainers and athletes, their parents pushed them

"Don't set your goals to be a star; set your goals to be the best you can be and go from there."

to succeed. This situation, in which parents of both sexes are often characterized by the nickname "stage mommy," is usually considered a bad one. But Dawes had no stage mommy—or a stage daddy, for that matter. "We did not push her at all," Dawes's mother Loretta told *U.S. News & World Report*. "We said, 'If you don't like your sport, quit. Don't do it because you'll make Mom or Dad happy.'"

But Dawes liked her sport. Born in Silver Spring, Maryland, in 1976, she was already showing herself to be a budding gymnast at the age of six. That was when she began jumping up and down on the family furniture, and tumbling down the stairs. Her mother, afraid the little girl would hurt herself, enrolled her in gymnastics classes in nearby Wheaton, Maryland. There Dawes soon attracted the attention of a young gymnastics instructor named Kelli Hill.

Up every morning at 5:00

"At first I thought [gymnastics] was a play activity," Dawes once said. "I didn't start taking it all seriously until I was 11." That was about the time Hill set up a training center in Gaithersburg, Maryland, a forty-minute drive from Silver Spring. If she wanted to be a member of "Hill's Angels," as the instructor's students were called, Dawes would have to get up every morning at 5:00 to ride to Gaithersburg for a two-hour workout before school.

And that was just in the morning. After school, another five hours of practice lay ahead of her. "I've had several children who were as God-given talented," Hill told *U.S. News*, "but the burning desire Dom had wasn't there." In spite of all her hard work, though, Dawes found time to enjoy life, and in 1994, the year she graduated high school, she was voted queen of the prom. But she had a few things to her credit that most prom queens don't: she had already participated in one Olympics, and was looking forward to the next.

From the Olympics to the Championships

In 1992, when she was a sophomore in high school, Dawes lived up to her nickname of "Awesome Dawesome" by scoring a perfect 10 in floor exercise at a U.S.-Japan meet. At the national championships that year, she placed fourth all-around, which meant that she was going to the Olympics in Barcelona. Unfortunately, she did not make a strong showing at the Olympics, finishing in 26th place overall.

Dawes's solution to this problem was simple: she worked even harder. After moving in with her coach, Dawes—still just a junior in high school—spent more hours a day training, and her work paid off with a second-place finish at the 1993 national championships. At the 1994 nationals, which she attended in the summer after she graduated high school, Dawes won the all-around title, and placed first in all four events. Only one woman, Joyce Tanac Schroeder, had ever achieved such a record, and that was twenty-five years earlier, in 1969.

Dawes became an overnight celebrity and topic of much speculation as gymnastics fans looked toward the 1996 Olympics. But she remained humble, knowing that she faced

Dominique Dawes looks more like an acrobat as she performs on the high bar.

stiff competition from fellow gymnasts Shannon Miller (1977–) and Dominique Moceanu (1981–). When Miller made a mistake in the 1995 championships, Dawes only had to do a simple maneuver to win; instead, however, she chose a difficult tumbling pattern involving eleven aerial tricks. Even with this gamble, she won the event.

Helps win first U.S. team medal

By 1996, Dawes weighed 106 pounds and stood five-foot-one, which made her a very small nineteen-year-old by ordinary standards. But she was being judged by the standards of gymnastics, and for that sport she was considered large. Also, her age, which again would be young in most careers—indeed, most sports—made her old in gymnastics. Nineteen, one commentator wrote in the *Washington Post,* "is about 100 in gymnastic years." Yet she and her teammates, including Miller and Moceanu, won the United States' first team medal—a gold—in gymnastics. The next week, she won a bronze medal in the floor exercise, becoming the first African American to do so.

Dawes's gymnastics career did not end in Atlanta. She competed in a number of events, including the 1998 Goodwill Games in New York City and the 1998 U.S. Championships in Indianapolis, Indiana—this in spite of breaking a toe in June 1998. She also found time to appear in the Broadway musical *Grease,* in which she played the part of cheerleader Patty Simcox, during late 1996 and early 1997. The gymnast proved a natural actress and performer, but one night she nearly had a case of stage fright when she looked out into the audience and saw her former competitor and teammate Miller. "I saw her and just froze," she told *Sports Illustrated.* "It was less than a second, but I was like, Shannon's here."

Dawes also remained in the public eye through a number of appearances on television and elsewhere. She has received numerous awards, including one from *Essence* magazine. As a spokeswoman for an organization called Girl Power!, she helped to educate young women about drug abuse and peer pressure. On top of everything else, she managed to continue her education at the University of Maryland at College Park.

Sources for further reading

Amazing Grace: Black Women in Sport (videorecording). Philadelphia: Black Women in Sport Foundation, 1993.

Brownlee, Shannon. "And Her Last Name Is Not Moceanu." *U.S. News & World Report,* June 10, 1996, pp. 67–68.

"Dominique Dawes." [Online] http://www.dominiquedawes.com (accessed on October 8, 1998).

Gottesman, Jane. "The Two Dominiques." *Women's Sports & Fitness,* February 1996, p. 29.

Kleinbaum, Nancy H. *The Magnificent Seven: The Authorized Story of American Gold.* New York: Bantam, 1996.

Super Stars of Gymnastics. Burbank, CA: Laurel Canyon Productions, 1995.

Wong, Kimberly. "Hopelessly Devoted." *Sports Illustrated,* December 30, 1996–January 6, 1997, p. 20.

Delany Sisters

Sadie: Born September 19, 1889
Raleigh, North Carolina
Teacher, author

Bessie: Born September 3, 1891
Raleigh, North Carolina
Died September 25, 1995
Brooklyn, New York
Dentist, author

Some people, like **Tiger Woods** (1975–) or **Venus Williams** (1980–), become celebrities at a very young age. Others have to wait a little longer. By the time the Delany sisters—Sadie and Bessie—entered the limelight, with the 1993 publication of their memoirs, Sadie was 104 years old and Bessie was 102.

One of the first questions people want to ask a centenarian (someone who has lived to be 100 years old or older) is, "How did you manage to live so long?" That was part of the reason why the *New York Times* sent a reporter, Amy Hill Hearth, to the Delanys' house in 1991. With Hearth's help as compiler and editor, the Delanys would publish two books, *Having Our Say* (1993) and *The Delany Sisters' Book of Everyday Wisdom* (1994). Bessie died in 1995, but Sadie was still going strong, and in 1997 she and Hearth published *On My Own at 107: Reflections on Life Without Bessie.*

"People assume Sadie and I don't have any sense at our age. But we still have all our marbles. . . . I do get tired . . . [but] God don't ever get tired of putting His sun out every morning, does He? Who am I to complain about being weary?"

—Bessie Delany

More than 200 years' experience

When the Delany sisters published *Having Our Say* in 1993, their combined ages totaled 206 years. Born in late 1889 and 1891 respectively, Sadie and Bessie lived through some of the most eventful decades in history. Here are historic events that happened during their lives.

1880s–1900s: the development of the automobile

1903: the development of the first airplane

1914–18: World War I

1929–41: the Great Depression

1939–45: World War II

1945–1980s: the Cold War between the United States and the Soviet Union, which lasted until the fall of Communism

1954–75: the Vietnam War

1960s: the Civil Rights movement

1960s: the assassinations of President John F. Kennedy (1917–63), Malcolm X (1925–65), the Rev. Martin Luther King (1929–68), and Robert Kennedy (1925–68)

1969: the moon landing

1972–74: the Watergate scandal that ended the presidency of Richard M. Nixon (1913–94)

1980s and 1990s: the spread of computer technology

1989: the fall of Communism

Father born a slave

Sarah (Sadie) Delany was born in 1889; her younger sister A. Elizabeth (Bessie) was born in 1891. They grew up in North Carolina, and both went to St. Augustine School, which had been established for newly freed slaves following the end of the Civil War (1861–65). Their father, Henry, had been born in 1858, just three years before the war broke out. He remembered being a slave, and he would never forget the day that the war's end brought him his freedom (see accompanying sidebar).

By the time the two sisters came along, as part of a family that included ten brothers and sisters, a new form of racial oppression had appeared in the South. After the bitterness of the Civil War and the racial turmoil of the Reconstruction (1865–77), relations between the races had become relatively peaceful in the former slaveholding states. There was still segregation (separation of whites and blacks), but it was inconsistent, and in many parts of the South, whites and blacks seemed to live in harmony. Then came the Jim Crow laws.

The origin of the name "Jim Crow" is unclear, but the meaning is not. Jim Crow meant, for instance, separate drinking fountains and bathrooms for black and white people. It was a system that would prevail until the 1960s, when Dr. Martin Luther King, Jr. (1929–68; see entry in volume 3) and other leaders of the civil rights movement brought about its downfall. But Bessie was already doing her part long before King was even born: the first time they saw a segregated drinking fountain as children, she deliberately drank out of the white side. She later remembered that it didn't taste any better than the water from the "colored" side.

Sisters start careers

Both girls chose never to marry. By the end of the 1910s, they had moved together to New York City's Harlem district, where Sadie got a job teaching while Bessie trained to become a dentist. In 1925, Bessie became the second black female dentist in New York City. She also became involved in the early civil rights movement.

Along with the rest of the nation, the Delanys endured the financial hardships of the Great Depression, which followed the stock market crash of 1929. In 1950, they asked their aging mother, Nanny, to come live with them in New York, where most of their brothers and sisters had already moved. The Delanys decided that since Bessie could not expect a pension (retirement income) as a dentist, whereas

The Delany Sisters speak

Here is a selection of quotes from the Delany sisters, as adapted from *Having Our Say* and published in "The American Century of Bessie and Sadie Delany," by Amy Hill Hearth, from the October 1993 issue of *American Heritage*.

Sadie and Bessie, on slavery: "We used to ask Papa, 'What do you remember about being a slave?' Well, like a lot of former slaves, he didn't say much about it. Finally Papa told us of the day his people were freed. He remembered being in the kitchen and wearing a little apron, which little slave boys wore in those days. It had one button at the top, at the back of the neck, and the ends were loose. And when the news of the Surrender came [in 1865], he said he ran about the house with that apron fluttering behind him, yelling, 'Freedom! Freedom! I am free! I am free!'"

Sadie, on her father's interest in astronomy: "On a clear night [Papa] would take us all outside and teach us the names of the planets and star constellations. Papa was so excited when Halley's comet came by [in 1910]. He had us all outside that night, and it was a sight to see, flickering light across the landscape. Papa said, 'I don't think any of us will be here to see Halley's comet the next time it comes around [in 1986].' Well, he was wrong about that, 'cause Bessie and I saw it again, and it wasn't as good the second time."

Sadie, on being a teacher: "[In the early 1920s] I had wanted to teach at a high school because it was considered a promotion, and it paid better. But I had to be a little clever to find ways to get around these brick walls they set up for colored folks. So I skipped [an appointment] and sent them a letter, acting like there was a mix-up. Then I just showed up on the first day of classes. Child, when I showed up that day—at Theodore Roosevelt High School, a white high school—they just about died when they saw me. But my name was on the list to teach there, and it was too late to send me someplace else. So I became the first colored teacher in the New York City system to teach domestic science [home economics] on the high school level."

Sadie—as a teacher—could, Bessie should quit work to care for their mother. Their mother died in 1955.

In the 1960s, the Delanys saw the rise of a new civil rights movement. By then they were too old to go to marches, but in 1957 they and their brother Hap helped integrate the previously all-white town of Mount Vernon, New York. After

Sadie and Bessie, on the civil rights movement of the 1960s: "The civil rights movement was a time when we thought: Maybe now it will finally happen. Maybe now our country will finally grow up, come to terms with this race mess. But it seemed like the momentum was lost when the Vietnam War happened. It was like all the energy of the young people, and the focus of the country, got shifted away from civil rights."

Sadie, on getting up and going to bed: "I wake up at six-thirty. And the first thing I do when I open my eyes is smile, and then I say, 'Thank you, Lord, for another day!' After [dinner] we say our prayers. It takes a long time to pray for everyone, because it's a very big family: We have fifteen nieces and nephews still living, plus all their children and grandchildren. We pray for each one, living and dead. The ones that Bessie doesn't approve of get extra prayers."

Sadie, on staying active: I started doing yoga exercises with Mama about forty years ago. Mama was starting to shrink up and get bent down, and I started exercising with her to straighten her up again. Only I didn't know at the time that what we were actually doing was yoga. We just thought we were exercising. I kept doing my yoga exercises even after Mama died. Well, when Bessie turned eighty, she decided that I looked better than her. So she decided she would start doing yoga too."

Bessie, on remembering her father: "Sadie and I get a kick out of things that happened a long, long time ago. We talk about folks who turned to dust so long ago that we're the only people left on this earth with any memory of them. Why, we still have a birthday party for Papa, even though he's been gone since 1928. We cook his favorite birthday meal, just the way he liked it: chicken and gravy, rice and sweet potatoes, ham, macaroni and cheese, cabbage, cauliflower, broccoli, turnips, and carrots. For dessert we'll have a birthday cake—a pound cake—and ambrosia, made with oranges and fresh coconut."

that adventure, their lives were relatively quiet for three decades. That all changed in 1991.

Centenarian celebrities

New York Times reporter Amy Hill Hearth was assigned the task of interviewing the centenarian Delany Sisters. Hearth later recalled her first meeting with the Delanys in an article for *American Heritage.* "When I met Sadie Delany and her sister, Bessie, in September 1991, I was . . . hoping to write a story on two elderly and reclusive sisters who had just celebrated their one hundred and second and one hundredth birthdays. In my hand I carried a letter written by their neighbor in Mount Vernon, New York, who had extended an invitation to come by and meet them. The Delany sisters had no phone, so I wasn't entirely sure they knew exactly when I was coming. I was prepared to be turned away.

"I knocked on the door. I waited and had raised my hand to knock again when suddenly the door swung open. The woman who answered, with her head held high, her eyes intense and penetrating, extended her hand in formal greeting. 'I am Dr. Delany,' she said elegantly. She ushered me into the house, and from across the room another elderly woman said sweetly, 'Please come in, child. Won't you sit down?' That was the older sister, Sadie. I must have hesitated for a moment. 'Go on, sit down,' Bessie urged. 'Sit down as long as you like. We won't charge you rent!' Then they both laughed uproariously at this little joke."

And so began the relationship that would make the Delany sisters some of America's most unlikely superstars. The popularity of *Having Our Say* led to a follow-up, *The Delany Sisters' Book of Everyday Wisdom,* and to the adaptation of *Having Our Say* for the stage. The Delanys became some of the most celebrated writers in the country. Their literary agent, Dan Strone, who managed comedians Jerry Seinfeld (1954–) and Paul Reiser (1957–), told *People* in 1995 that the Delany sisters received more fan mail than Seinfeld and Reiser combined. Comedian **Bill Cosby** (1937– ; see entry in volume 1, and update om p. 41) and his wife, Camille Cosby (1945–), co-produced the adaptation of *Having Our Say*). The sisters even met first lady Hillary Rodham Clinton (1947–). In spite of their newfound fame, the Delanys remained quiet homebodies who got up every morning at 5:30 A.M., never watched any TV besides the *MacNeil/Lehrer NewsHour,* and always said their prayers at night.

Sadie goes it alone at 106

Soon after seeing the play's premiere, Bessie died in her sleep on September 25, 1995, just two weeks after her 104th birthday. Sadie had often said, "I give myself two weeks without Bessie," but in 1997 she published *On My Own at 107*. As of the summer of 1998, she was still alive and looking ahead to her 109th birthday. "I'm not going to give up," she told Hearth soon after Bessie's death. "I'll just do the best I can without her."

Sources for further reading

"America's Oldest Best-Selling Author, Sadie Delany, Is on Her Own at 107." *Tennessee Tribune,* January 29, 1997.

"Bessie Delany, Candid Witness to a Tumultuous Century, Dies at 104." *People,* October 9, 1995, pp. 48–49.

Delany, Sarah, and A. Elizabeth Delany, with Amy Hill Hearth. *Delany Sisters' Book of Everyday Wisdom.* New York: Kodansha International, 1994.

Delany, Sarah, and A. Elizabeth Delany, with Amy Hill Hearth. *Having Our Say: The Delany Sisters' First 100 Years.* New York: Kodansha International, 1993.

Delany, Sarah, with Amy Hill Hearth. *On My Own at 107: Reflections on Life Without Bessie.* New York: HarperSanFrancisco, 1997.

Having Our Say. [Online] http://havingoursay-theplay.com/ (accessed on October 8, 1998).

Hearth, Amy Hill. "The American Century of Bessie and Sadie Delany." *American Heritage,* October 1993, pp. 68–79.

Kanfer, Stefan. "*Having Our Say* (play review)." *New Leader,* May 8–22, 1995, pp. 22–23.

Ralph Ellison

*Born March 1, 1914
Oklahoma City, Oklahoma
Died April 16, 1994
New York, New York
Novelist*

Novelist Ralph Ellison, who won national acclaim in 1952 with his book *Invisible Man,* died of pancreatic cancer on April 16, 1994, in New York City. Ellison's novel, a portrait of a young black man in a hostile society, has many layers of meaning, and critics view it as one of the greatest American novels of the twentieth century. **(See original entry on Ellison in volume 2.)**

Ellison grew up in Oklahoma, where he had both white and black friends. His mother, Ida, a domestic worker, often brought home books and records her employers had given her. Ellison excelled both in reading and in music, learning to play the trumpet and enrolling in Alabama's Tuskegee Institute as a music student in 1933.

In college, Ellison gained exposure to the works of a number of great writers, including British novelists Emily Brontë (1818–48) and Thomas Hardy (1840–1928), and British-American poet T. S. Eliot (1888–1965). Enchanted by

"I was taken very early with a passion to link together all I loved within the Negro community and all those things I felt in the world which lay beyond."

Eliot's long poem "The Waste Land" (1922), which had an enormous influence on twentieth-century literature, Ellison wondered why he had "never read anything of equal intensity and sensibility by an American Negro writer." Taking a course in sociology, he was disappointed to find that social science reduced the lives of African Americans to a collection of statistics. He wanted to see someone portray American black life in all of its richness, with the music and culture that made it vital.

Ultimately Ellison would realize that if anyone was going to write such a book, it would have to be him. Leaving college in 1936, he moved to New York City, where he met poet Langston Hughes (1902–67; see entry in volume 2) and novelist Richard Wright (1908–60; see entry in volume 4). Ellison began working as a writer, and served in the U.S. Merchant Marines during World War II (1939–45). After seven years of work, he finished *Invisible Man,* which won him instant acclaim.

During the next four decades, Ellison produced two collections of essays, and lectured widely in the United States and Europe. But a long-promised second novel never appeared, due, in part, to a fire at his home in the 1960s that destroyed much of the manuscript. Over many years, Ellison tried hard to reconstruct the story, a tale set in the South during the period from the 1920s to the 1960s.

A long-awaited book

On March 1, 1994, Ellison attended a dinner party in New York celebrating his eightieth birthday. Writer and longtime friend Albert Murray (1917–) reported that Ellison seemed to be in good health and was almost finished with his second novel. But just six weeks later, on April 16, 1994, Ellison died from pancreatic cancer.

In July 1995, newspapers reported some exciting news: the long-awaited second novel would soon be published. John F. Callahan, a professor of English at Lewis and Clark College in Oregon, said that he had taken on the challenging task of putting together Ellison's drafts and notes to form a finished

> ## Works of Ralph Ellison
> *The Collected Essays of Ralph Ellison.* New York: Modern Library, 1995.
> *Flying Home and Other Stories.* New York: Random House, 1996.
> *Invisible Man.* New York: Random House, 1952.

book. He hoped to be able to give the completed work to Ellison's widow, Fanny, by the spring of 1996.

As of 1998, however, the novel had not appeared. Instead, in 1996 Random House published *Flying Home and Other Stories*. Edited by Callahan, *Flying Home* contained thirteen short stories, six of which had never been published before. Callahan had discovered them while searching for parts of the manuscript to the unfinished novel. Looking through Ellison's papers, he had found a box containing a weather-beaten folder labeled "early stories."

Flying Home contains stories of not just black people, and not just conflicts between blacks and whites, but stories of white people and conflicts *within* races as well. Four of the stories concern the adventures of two young black boys, Buster and Riley. The characters in "Hymie's Bull"—a hobo (homeless man) and a "bull," a thug hired by a railroad company to chase hoboes away—are both white. "The clash here is not one of race," Alan Pusey of the *Dallas Morning News* wrote, "but of class." In "I Did Not Learn Their Names," a young black man who is "having a hard time trying not to hate" whites finds himself befriended by an elderly white couple. Pusey called *Flying Home* "a marvelous collection."

In 1997, Modern Library published a volume of Ellison's essays, also edited by Callahan. In 1998, Ellison's *Invisible Man* was the novel chosen for the annual Marathon Reading at the University of California at Los Angeles (UCLA). At the event, people take turns reading aloud for five minutes from a novel, continuing throughout the night to raise money for the

UCLA Department of English. In honor of the event, the State of California declared May 14, 1998, Ralph Ellison Day.

Sources for further reading

Bellow, Saul. "Ralph Ellison in Tivoli." *Los Angeles Times Book Review,* May 10, 1998, p. 5.

Brown, John L. "The Collected Essays (Book Reviews)." *World Literature Today,* September 22, 1997, p. 786.

Corliss, Richard. "Obituary: Invincible Man Ralph Ellison 1914–1994." *Times,* April 25, 1994, p. 90.

Graham, Maryemma, and Amritjit Singh, editors. *Conversations with Ralph Ellison.* Jackson, MS: University of Mississippi, 1995.

Kempton, Murray. "Coda for Ralph Ellison." *Newsday,* May 27, 1994, p. A13.

Polner, Rob. "Tangible Glimpse of 'Invisible Man.'" *Newsday,* April 18, 1994, p. A13.

Pusey, Allen. "Darkness Visible: Tales Prefigure 'Invisible Man.'" *Dallas Morning News,* January 5, 1997, p. 8J.

"Ralph Ellison (1914-1994)." [Online] http://www.levity.com/corduroy/ellison.htm (accessed on October 8, 1998).

"Ralph Ellison's Second Novel to Be Published." *Star Tribune,* July 14, 1995, p. 7A.

Louis Farrakhan

*Born May 11, 1933
New York, New York
Muslim minister, political leader*

UPDATE

On October 16, 1995, vast numbers of African American men gathered in Washington, D.C., for what organizer Minister Louis Farrakhan called the Million Man March. It was to be a day on which black men would take time to think about themselves and their actions in relation to their families and community in order to become better men and leaders. It would also be a time to consider the long road down which African Americans had come, and the continuing fight that they faced against white supremacy. **(See original entry on Farrakhan in volume 2.)**

The men heard speeches by such leaders as the Rev. Jesse Jackson (1941– ; see entry in volume 2) and civil rights pioneer Rosa Parks (1913– ; see entry in volume 3). Yet as celebrated as these figures were, none of them was the star of this event. That position belonged to Farrakhan. It now appeared that Farrakhan, dismissed by many as a hatemonger

"I am a servant of God and a man of peace, and I call on President Clinton and his advisors to hearken unto the voice of one born among you that can bring peace to America and peace to the world."

Louis Farrakhan | 71

and an anti-Semite (someone who dislikes Jews), had become the most powerful black man in America.

Farrakhan was born and raised in New York City, went to college in North Carolina, and later worked as a calypso singer under the name Louis X. During this time he became involved with the Nation of Islam, or "Black Muslims," under the leadership of Elijah Muhammad (1897–1975; see entry in volume 3). The Nation of Islam adopted a version of the Islamic, or Muslim, religion, which is centered in the country of Saudi Arabia and claims more than one billion followers worldwide. Among Islam's core beliefs are the doctrine that Allah is the one true God; that the founder of Islam, Mohammed, or Muhammad (A.D. 570–632), is his prophet; and that the Muslim scriptures, called the *Koran,* are the source of all wisdom. The Nation of Islam added a racial element by suggesting that whites are "blue-eyed devils" and that blacks are superior to them.

Elijah Muhammad's most famous follower, Malcolm X (1925–65; see entry in volume 3), ultimately embraced mainstream Islam and rejected the racist doctrines of the Black Muslims, a fact that some believe led to his assassination on February 21, 1965. Farrakhan, meanwhile, rose within the organization, and after Elijah Muhammad died in 1975, he became the Nation of Islam's leader. (Warith Deen Muhammad, Elijah Muhammad's son, formed a mainstream, nonracist, Muslim organization that has a much larger membership than Farrakhan's group, and he remains one of Farrakhan's most outspoken critics.)

Farrakhan burst onto the national scene in 1984 when he helped Jesse Jackson, then a presidential candidate, secure the release of an African American pilot who had been captured by the government of Syria. Farrakhan used his newfound fame to speak out against Jews. While many of his fellow Muslims condemned him, many Christian preachers embraced Farrakhan.

Farrakhan was, and remains, a magnetic figure, with a powerful speaking style that rivals Jackson's. And few could help but be impressed by Farrakhan's followers, the Fruit of Islam. Many of them former convicts, they had cleaned up their lives, and were cleaning up some of the worst neighborhoods in the country. To many it seemed that, whereas Jackson and other civil rights leaders offered only more federal programs and more talk, Farrakhan offered solutions.

Leads Million Man March

For years, a rumor circulated that Farrakhan had been behind Malcolm X's assassination. Whatever the basis for the allegations, Malcolm X's daughter Qubilah Shabazz appears to have believed them. In 1995, she was convicted of plotting to have Farrakhan killed. Then, Farrakhan appeared at a fundraiser for Shabazz's defense in May 1995, and shook hands with her mother, **Betty Shabazz** (1936–97; see entry on p. 189). In 1994, she had said she believed Farrakhan was responsible for her husband's death. But now, Farrakhan embraced Shabazz, saying that they were both "victims of a wider conspiracy." This ended a thirty-year disagreement between the two of them.

For many months, Farrakhan had planned the Million Man March with the assistance of former National Association for the Advancement of Colored People (NAACP) leader Benjamin Chavis (1948–). Chavis had been ousted from the NAACP leadership in August 1994 because of a financial and sex scandal—and because of his association with Farrakhan. They modelled the event after the 1963 March on Washington, at which Dr. Martin Luther King, Jr. (1929–68; see entry in volume 3) made his famous "I Have a Dream" speech. But whereas King envisioned a color-blind society—"I have a dream that my four little children will one day live in a nation where they will not be judged by the color of their skin, but by the content of their character"—Farrakhan had a rather different message in mind. He offered a vision of black supremacy to take the place of white supremacy.

Because of Farrakhan's anti-Semitism and racism, a few black leaders stayed away from the event, but they were in the minority. Farrakhan was the man of the moment, and the aftermath of the Million Man March saw an increase in voter registration and a rise in the membership roles of civil rights and community organizations. A writer for *Jet* marveled at "the

Louis Farrakhan speaks at the Million Man March.

power emitting from [the March's] ranks in time for a new political thrust . . . for [the 1996] presidential election." Even among many whites, Farrakhan's reputation soared, strengthened by his message of black self-reliance.

But Farrakhan failed to develop any momentum. No consistent program of political action arose from the Million Man March. His next big appearance in the news was perceived negatively by many: in March 1996, Farrakhan toured twenty-three countries, most of them enemies of the United States, such as Libya, Iraq, and Iran. Particularly controversial was Farrakhan's acceptance of financial aid from Libya leader Muammar al-Qaddafi (1942–) for a company Farrakhan was starting. Many people believe Qaddafi has been responsible for many terrorist acts around the world, such as the 1988 explosion of a civilian airliner over Lockerbie, Scotland, an incident that killed 270 people. Farrakhan also was criticized for visiting the African nation of Sudan, one of the few countries in which black people are still bought and sold as slaves. Farrakhan denied the existence of slavery in Sudan, so two reporters for the *Baltimore Sun* went to that country, where they successfully purchased—then freed—two slaves in August 1996.

The following month, Farrakhan harshly addressed the National Association of Black Journalists, calling them slaves of white newspaper owners, and telling them they were afraid to write the truth. The National Newspaper Publishers Association/Black Press of America had meanwhile voted Farrakhan their "Newsmaker of the Year." Apparently opinions about Farrakhan were as divided as estimates of the number of men actually present at the Million Man March. The National Park Service estimated 400,000; *Jet* magazine claimed "more than one million." As early as March 1996, the *Economist* reported that some black leaders were backing away from Farrakhan's movement.

In April 1997, Farrakhan acted as a racial mediator (someone who tries to help people get along with each other). Following a racial incident in Philadelphia, Pennsylvania, that city's mayor, Edward Rendell (who is Jewish) invited Farrakhan to lead a "racial unity" rally. Farrakhan wound up preaching at a Christian church for eighty-five minutes, while 500 marchers at the site of the racial incident shouted "white trash." Later that month, Farrakhan appeared on the NBC-TV news show *Meet the Press*. Host Tim Russert questioned him about his beliefs that a mad black scientist named Yakub had created white people. He was also confronted with statements he had made to the effect that Jews controlled the NAACP and other civil rights organizations, and that rich Jews had been partly responsible for the Holocaust.

The October 1997 "Day of Atonement," celebrating the two-year anniversary of the Million Man March, saw a sparse turnout at cities around the country. In March 1998, Farrakhan's name was back in the news, this time because he had placed Muhammad Abdul Aziz, one of the men convicted for killing Malcolm X, in charge of the mosque (a Muslim church) which Malcolm himself had led before his assassination.

Sources for further reading

"Dr. Betty Shabazz, Minister Farrakhan Mend 30-Year Rift During Fund-Raiser." *Jet,* May 22, 1995, p. 12.

"Fired NAACP Chief Still Backs Farrakhan." *Chicago Tribune,* August 29, 1994, p. 4.

Haskins, Jim. *Louis Farrakhan and the Nation of Islam.* New York: Walker, 1996.

Kelly, Michael. "TRB from Washington: Banality and Evil." *New Republic,* May 5, 1997, p. 6.

"Louis Farrakhan." *Time,* June 17, 1996, p. 67.

"Louis Farrakhan Tells Black Journalists They're Afraid to Write the Truth." *Jet,* September 9, 1996, pp. 8–10.

Magida, Arthur J. *Prophet of Rage: A Life of Louis Farrakhan and His Nation.* New York: Basic Books, 1996.

"Million Man March Draws More Than 1 Million Black Men to Nation's Capital." *Jet,* October 30, 1995, p. 5.

Murray, Barbra. "Interpreting the Atonement." *U.S. News & World Report,* October 27, 1997, p. 44.

The Nation of Islam Online. [Online] http://www.noi.org (accessed on October 8, 1998).

"One Man March." *Economist,* March 2, 1996, p. 30.

Ella Fitzgerald

*Born April 25, 1918
Newport News, Virginia
Died June 15, 1996
Beverly Hills, California
Singer*

UPDATE

Singer Ella Fitzgerald, often referred to as "Jazz's First Lady of Song," died on June 15, 1996, of complications resulting from diabetes. (Diabetes is a disease resulting from the inability of the pancreas to process blood sugar.) She was seventy-eight. **(See original entry on Fitzgerald in volume 2.)**

Fitzgerald had parents who were both musically inclined. Her father played the guitar, and her mother had a beautiful soprano singing voice. Fitzgerald learned to play the piano early, sang in her high school glee club, and spent many happy hours listening to records with her mother. Tragically, her parents died before Fitzgerald was an adult: her father shortly after she was born, her mother when Fitzgerald was seventeen.

Fitzgerald was adopted by bandleader Chick Webb (1909–39), who hired her to sing for his group. As she rose to fame, she developed a style of singing called "scat," making use of nonsensical syllables instead of words. Her most

"[Ella was] the greatest singer on the planet."

—Singer Mel Torme

famous song from this phase was "A-Tisket, A-Tasket," which she wrote with Webb. The two eventually married, but they soon realized that Webb was more of a father figure to Fitzgerald than a husband, so they annulled (legally cancelled) their marriage.

In the late 1940s and early 1950s, Fitzgerald recorded songs by legendary writers such as Cole Porter (1891–1964) and Irving Berlin (1888–1989). By the early 1990s, she had released some 200 recordings. She became known to a younger generation through her many talks at schools, and her appearances in commercials for Memorex recording tape (with the catch phrase "Is It Live Or Is It Memorex?") in the 1970s. She also won a number of awards, including twelve Grammys, the American Music Award (1978), a Kennedy Center award (1979), the National Medal of the Arts (1987), and a lifetime achievement award—named "The Ella" in her honor—from the Society of Singers in 1989.

The "greatest singer on the planet"

In her later years, Fitzgerald suffered from poor health, and had a series of operations. Suffering from diabetes as well as congestive heart failure, in 1993 she had to have both of her legs amputated below the knee. "I knew when that happened," said singer and longtime friend Mel Torme (1925–), "that she would probably never sing again. And that in itself is an enormous loss to all of us."

Fitzgerald had been reluctant to give up touring, because she loved her audiences. She also involved herself in charity work, helping children with learning disabilities. Meanwhile, the awards kept coming: in 1995, for instance, *The Complete Ella Fitzgerald Song Books* and *The Ella Fitzgerald Song Book on Verve* won her two more Grammys.

When Fitzgerald died on June 15, 1996, the loss was mourned by many notables in the music world and elsewhere. Torme called her "the greatest singer on the planet." Singer Tony Bennett (1926–) said, "Her recordings will live forever. She'll sound as modern 200 years from now, no matter what technique they come up with." President Bill Clinton (1946–) paid tribute, too: "Ella's phenomenal voice and wonderful phrasing will remain close to the hearts of Americans for generations to come."

Soon after her death, Ira J. Hadnot of the *Dallas Morning News* told a story that illustrated Fitzgerald's love for her audience, especially her youngest fans. Fifteen years earlier, Hadnot was backstage at a Fitzgerald concert and watched as a young boy tried to deliver a bouquet of flowers to Fitzgerald. A crowd of adults, however, forced him back. As Fitzgerald's limousine pulled away from the concert hall, she told her driver to stop, and called to the boy, "Come here, honey." Still sitting in the limousine, she reached out, lifted him off his feet, and kissed him. "When she let go," Hadnot concluded, "he slipped slowly to the ground and moved to let the car pass. As the vehicle cruised through the crowd, the little boy yelled: 'I love you, Miss Ella!' From the edge of the park, came a silence-shattering, squeaky refrain: 'I love you too, baby.'"

Sources for further reading

The Ella Fitzgerald Homepage. [Online] http://www.seas.columbia.edu/~tts6/ella.html (accessed on October 8, 1998).

Fidelman, Geoffrey Mark. *First Lady of Song: Ella Fitzgerald for the Record.* New York: Citadel Press, 1996.

Gourse, Leslie. *The Ella Fitzgerald Companion: Seven Decades of Commentary.* New York: Schirmer Books, 1998.

Hadnot, Ira J. "Jazz's Queen Treated All Like Royalty: Busy Miss Ella Always Found Time for Her Many Admirers." *Dallas Morning News,* June 18, 1996, p. 21A.

Herman, Don. "Jazz: The 'Complete Singer' Remembered." *Los Angeles Times,* June 26, 1997, p. F20.

Kliment, Bud. *Ella Fitzgerald (Black Americans of Achievement.)* Broomall, PA: Chelsea House, 1988.

Nicholson, Stuart. *Ella Fitzgerald: A Biography of the First Lady of Jazz.* New York: Scribner, 1994.

Stearns, Daniel Patrick. "Honoring the Art and Soul of Ella Fitzgerald." *USA Today,* July 11, 1996, p. 9D.

Weinstein, Henry. "Ella Fitzgerald, Jazz's First Lady of Song, Dies." *Los Angeles Times,* June 16, 1996, p. A1.

Whitcomb, Dan. "Music World Mourns Loss of Jazz Legend Fitzgerald." Reuters, June 16, 1996.

Wyman, Carolyn. *Ella Fitzgerald: Jazz Singer Supreme.* Danbury, CT: Franklin Watts, 1993.

George Foreman

*Born January 10, 1949
Marshall, Texas
Professional boxer*

Boxer George Foreman has the distinction of earning the world heavyweight title twice. The first time was in 1973, when at twenty-five he defeated the reigning champion, Joe Frazier (1944–). A year later, Foreman lost to Muhammad Ali (1942– ; see entry in volume 1) in Kinshasa, Zaire. Nicknamed "The Rumble in the Jungle," the Foreman-Ali fight was one of the most celebrated matches of all time, and later was documented in the 1996 film *When We Were Kings*. As for Foreman, by 1977 the defeated former champion had hit rock-bottom. In despair, he underwent a religious conversion and became a Christian minister. And it seemed that his years in the ring were a part of the past.

Then in the mid-1980s, Foreman made an historic comeback. Famous as a hearty eater, he shed more than forty pounds and underwent a grueling regimen of training. Critics were skeptical at first, but Foreman defied them all. In 1991, he put up a good fight against then-champion Evander Holy-

"I want [to train] kids with murder on their faces. I'll trick 'em with boxing and sports and get them straightened out and going to school."

field (1962–); then, on November 5, 1994, he defeated Michael Moorer (1967–) to regain the heavyweight title. At almost forty-five years of age, Foreman had become the oldest heavyweight champion in boxing history.

"A reputation for savage butt kickings"

Growing up in the depressed Fifth Ward district of Houston, Texas, Foreman learned early that he had to be tough to survive. He was the fifth of seven children, raised by a single mother, and he was soon drawn to the gang lifestyle as a way to survive. According to pro football player Lester Hayes, who grew up in the same neighborhood, Foreman "was a very, very big kid and had a reputation for savage butt kickings."

Foreman's idea of a hero at that time was a man who had killed someone, or at least one with a scar on his face as proof of his masculinity. Foreman didn't kill anyone, but he would wear a bandage on his face to make it look like he had scars, and he and his friends conducted regular muggings and robberies. It all seemed normal to them: "We didn't even know we were criminals," he later said.

A commercial changes his life

By the age of fifteen, Foreman had quit school, and it appeared likely that he would live out his days as a gangster on Houston's mean streets. But around this time, he saw a commercial that changed his life. The ad was for Job Corps, a government program designed to teach job skills to kids from poor neighborhoods. The program was endorsed by one of the few men Foreman respected—football legend Jim Brown (1936–).

Foreman wound up in a Job Corps camp in Pleasanton, California. There he got into a fistfight with another trainee, which caught the attention of a Job Corps supervisor named Doc Broadus. Broadus later recalled that the young Foreman seemed to be crying out for help, and for a positive role model. Broadus had the solution: he took Foreman to a gym and began teaching him how to box.

Heavyweight boxer George Foreman won the gold medal at the Olympic Games in Mexico City, Mexico, in 1968.

During the next two years, Foreman learned construction, and became interested in academic subjects ranging from Latin to anthropology (the study of different cultures). He earned his high-school equivalency diploma in 1967, when he was eighteen. Meanwhile, his boxing progressed, and Broadus helped him get work as a Job Corps boxing instructor. In 1968 Foreman, who had only been boxing for two years, qualified for the Olympics in Mexico City. He went on to win the gold medal in the heavyweight division.

Foreman defeats Frazier; Ali defeats Foreman

In 1969, Foreman turned pro. He won his first forty fights, more than half the time defeating his opponents in fewer than two rounds. Then on January 22, 1973, he was set to fight the world heavyweight champion, Joe Frazier, who had taken the title from Ali. Although Foreman was undefeated, he was not considered a serious contender for the title because few of his past opponents had been particularly talented boxers. Frazier was not concerned about Foreman; he had his eyes on his next match with Ali. But it was Frazier, not Foreman, who hit the canvas—six times in two rounds, before Foreman was declared the winner.

Now Foreman had beaten the man who had defeated the boxer considered by many to be the greatest fighter in the world, Muhammad Ali. After two more victories, Foreman was ready for his October 30, 1974, match against Ali. Ali had become the unquestioned superstar of boxing in the 1970s—a "golden age" for the sport. And the crowd of 60,000 in Zaire was pulling for him. In the fight, Ali employed his brilliant "rope-a-dope" strategy, staying against the ropes and letting Foreman tire himself out. In the end, Ali proved too much for Foreman, knocking him out in the eighth round.

Death and salvation

The next three years were a kind of living death for Foreman. He had never known defeat before. He began indulging in a lavish, wasteful lifestyle that included fancy cars, jewelry, a pet lion and tiger, lots of women, and plenty of false friends. On January 24, 1976, he fought a brutal match against Ron Lyle (1942–) in which Foreman emerged the victor, but on March 17, 1977, he suffered a humiliating twelfth-round defeat to Jimmy Young.

After that, Foreman became obsessed with death, and suffered a breakdown which he compared to death. He had the sensation of falling "into a deep, dark nothing, like out in a sea," he later told *Sports Illustrated,* "with nothing over your head or under your feet. Nothing but nothing. A big dark lump of it. And a horrible smell came with it. A smell I haven't forgotten. A smell of sorrow. . . . And then I looked around and I was dead." Confronted with the emptiness of his lifestyle, he reached out to the only person or thing that seemed to offer an answer: Jesus Christ.

Foreman became an ardent Christian, and soon began preaching. He eventually established the Church of the Lord Jesus Christ in a mobile home outside Houston, and tried to avoid the media spotlight. But he hadn't solved all of his problems: between 1981 and 1983, he was married and divorced three times, and was involved in a bitter child-custody battle. But by 1983, he was in a stable marriage (his fifth), and was teaching boxing to local kids in a gym next to his church. In his late thirties, it seemed that Foreman had finally found peace. There was only one problem: he needed money.

The great comeback

Not only did Foreman's church and gym cost more than they brought in, but several of his children—Foreman has eight in all—were nearing college age. He tried raising money for his ministry by speaking at churches, but that seemed humiliating to him. He later said that at this point he thought, "I know how to get money. I'm going to be heavyweight champion of the world. Again."

When Foreman announced his return to the ring in 1987, few observers took him seriously: he was thirty-eight years old and weighed 315 pounds. But he underwent a period of exhausting training that included strapping a punching bag on the back of his pickup truck and running for ten miles behind it, punching the bag the whole way. By 1990, he had won twenty-four matches, and in January 1990 he defeated another aging boxer, Gerry Cooney (1956–).

But Foreman knew he could only re-establish himself if he took on a younger, tougher fighter. On April 19, 1991, he took on the new champion, Evander Holyfield. Holyfield had been a boy when Foreman fought his last title bout, and though the younger man won in the twelfth round, Foreman made an impressive showing. "He was strong all the way to the end," said Holyfield.

Regains heavyweight title

After defeating twenty-four-year-old Tommy Morrison (1969–) in 1993, the now forty-four-year-old Foreman retired. But the following year, on November 5, 1994, he was back again. This time he faced Moorer, who had defeated Holyfield for the title. Foreman made boxing history when he defeated Moorer in the tenth found. Few men ever earn the world heavyweight title, and fewer still ever regain it, as Ali had done at Foreman's expense in 1974; but no one had ever done so at nearly forty-five years of age.

In the meantime, outside the ring, Foreman enjoyed a brief run on television in 1993 as the star of *George,* a situation comedy about an aging boxer. Foreman also published an autobiography, *By George,* in 1995. Royalties from the book, his winnings from boxing, and lucrative endorsement deals ensured that he was financially sound. According to *Forbes* magazine, Foreman's $8 million in product endorsements in 1995 meant that advertisers had paid him more to promote their products than all but a handful of athletes.

"All this marks a distinct personality change from the Foreman of the 1970s," wrote *Forbes*'s Randall Lane, who quoted Foreman as saying that back then "I never did a commercial, never did anything like that. Didn't want to be bothered with it. [But] this time around, whether I became champ or not, I was going to really go out there and show these guys how to sell."

"Still cookin'"

In 1995, Foreman lost his title, not due to defeat but because he failed to schedule matches to defend his crown in accordance with boxing federation rules. He fought again in 1996 and 1997 in lesser bouts, but in November 1997, just a month before his forty-eighth birthday, Foreman retired from boxing. "It's time for the young guys to chase the young guys," he said. "The way to beat George Foreman now is to outsmile and outsell him." By now, Foreman had clearly created for himself a role as a hero of aging baby-boomers, a man loved by millions as much for his good humor and good nature as for his comeback in the boxing ring.

Foreman has come a long way from the tough streets of Houston. He continues to pursue a number of activities involving his church, his commercial enterprises, and, especially, his gym. In his gym, he helps train kids who, like he was, are troubled, aggressive, violent—and desperately in need of someone to believe in them. "Kids will do the right things if people sincerely pay attention to them," he told *Southern Living.* "I was rescued from the gutter. . . . I was mean and bad until somebody cared. I'm thankful to . . . the Job Corps for helping turn my life around."

The ex-boxer has even published a cookbook. Says Foreman, "When people ask one day, 'Where is George? He's got to be retired by now,' they'll hear, 'No, no, no. He's in the kitchen—still cookin!'"

Sources for further reading

"Black Celebrities Who Are Also Ministers." *Jet,* December 18, 1995, pp. 54–57.

Dieffenbach, Dan. "Sport Lifestyle: Sparring with George Foreman." *Sport,* June 1995, pp. 80–81.

Foreman, George, and Cherie Calbom. *George Foreman's Knock-Out-the-Fat Barbeque and Grilling Cookbook.* New York: Villard, 1996.

Foreman, George, and Joel Engel. *By George, The Autobiography of George Foreman.* New York: Villard, 1995.

Gee, Denise. "The Gospel According to George." *Southern Living,* February 1997, pp. 94–95.

Kram, Mark. "The Burger King." *Esquire,* February 1995, pp. 98–102.

Lane, Randall. "Mickey Mouse, Meet George Foreman." *Forbes,* December 18, 1995, p. 210.

"A Literary Knockout–*By George, the Autobiography of George Foreman* by George Foreman and Joel Engel." *Sport,* September 1995, p. 6.

McCallum, Jack, and Hank Hersch. "A Gentle Warrior Says Goodbye." *Sports Illustrated,* December 1, 1997, pp. 22–24.

When We Were Kings (motion picture). PolyGram Filmed Entertainment/Gramercy Pictures, 1996.

Arthur Gaston

Born July 4, 1892
Demopolis, Alabama
Died January 19, 1996
Birmingham, Alabama
Entrepreneur

UPDATE

Arthur G. Gaston, one of the richest black men in America, died on January 19, 1996, at the age of 103. Among Gaston's many businesses was the Booker T. Washington (BTW) insurance company, which he founded in 1932, and which was valued at almost $40 million in 1992. Gaston was also known for his behind-the-scenes efforts on behalf of the civil rights movement in the 1960s. **(See original entry on Gaston in volume 2.)**

Gaston was born in a log cabin in 1892, and grew up in segregated Alabama. But he let neither racial prejudice nor his family's poverty stand in his way. As a young salesman for a black newspaper, the *Birmingham Reporter,* he gained such a good reputation that the paper's owner got him a job with the post office in Mobile. When he arrived in Mobile, however, Gaston learned that there was no job; and by the time it actually became available, he was making so much money as a hotel bellhop that he decided against taking the

> "Dr. Gaston was not an entertainer or star athlete. He did not make his money instantly, which seems to be the norm these days, but he saved and invested in his community, which is abnormal for a lot of wealthy people now."
>
> —Washington Afro-American *columnist James Wright*

post office job. Gaston later remembered that a British salesman offered him a job while Gaston was still working as a bellhop. Had he taken the position, he recalled, he might well have died with his employer, who lost his life when the ocean liner *Titanic* sank in 1912.

Gaston fought in World War I (1914–18) during 1917 and 1918, and afterward went to work for a coal company. Yet he wanted to be an entrepreneur (independent businessman). He soon developed a number of businesses of his own. The most promising was a burial insurance business, for which members of the local African American community paid premiums (scheduled, predetermined amounts) to offset the cost of burying their loved ones. By 1932, this business had become the Booker T. Washington (BTW) Burial Insurance Company. In 1939, Gaston established BTW Business College to train black students for secretarial jobs.

During the 1950s and 1960s, Gaston's business interests increased. For instance, he owned the Gaston Motel in downtown Birmingham, Alabama; at the time, it was the only motel in the city where black travellers could stay. Dr. Martin Luther King, Jr. (1929–68; see entry in volume 3) and other civil rights leaders often stayed there when they were in town. Gaston also bailed King and others out of jail when they were arrested for marching.

In 1968, Gaston published *Green Power, the Successful Way of A. G. Gaston,* in which he discussed the "secrets" of acquiring wealth. Due in part to that wealth, Gaston and his wife Minnie became targets of a kidnapping attempt in 1976. The kidnapper was caught and, miraculously, neither Minnie nor Gaston—by then eighty-four years old—was harmed. In 1987, Gaston in effect gave BTW Insurance to his employees when he sold it to them for a fraction of its $34 million value. Over the years, Gaston acquired a number of honors, including an honorary doctorate in 1975 from Pepperdine University. This was quite an achievement for someone who had never gone past tenth grade in school.

Dies at 103

In the mid-1980s, one of Gaston's legs had to be amputated. In 1992 the 100-year-old businessman suffered a stroke. Yet despite his health problems, he continued to go to the office every day. Two of the many enterprises he developed were among the largest black-owned businesses in the United States: BTW was the sixth largest black-owned insurance company, and Citizens Federal was the seventeenth largest black-owned financial company. In 1992, *Black Enterprise* magazine named him "entrepreneur of the century" and established an A. G. Gaston Lifetime Achievement Award. Gaston also was the first recipient of Birmingham's A. G. Gaston Distinguished Citizen Award.

Gaston lived to be not only one of the richest, but one of the oldest, black people in America. When he died in Birmingham on January 19, 1996, he was 103 years old. "He was loved by many people," wrote Betsy Butgereit of the *Birmingham News,* "and he loved people." His was a life that had spanned more than a century, during the greatest period of change in history.

In a tribute to Gaston, *Washington Afro-American* columnist James Wright observed that Gaston was a strong believer in the self-help philosophy of educator Booker T. Washington (1856–1915; see entry in volume 4). Gaston, Wright wrote, "counseled Black men to 'work hard, save your money, watch for opportunity and invest wisely,' and 'not to live beyond your means.' Dr. Gaston was not an entertainer or star athlete. He did not make his money instantly, which seems to be the norm these days, but he saved and invested in his community, which is abnormal for a lot of wealthy people now. I never had the chance to meet Dr. Gaston personally, which I deeply regret, but I am glad that he lived to help make our lives easier."

Sources for further reading

Butgereit, Betsy. "A. G. Gaston Dies: 103-Year-Old Businessman Broke Barriers." *Birmingham News,* January 19, 1996.

Gaston, A. G. *Green Power, the Successful Way of A. G. Gaston.* Birmingham: Southern University Press, 1968.

Smith, Eric L. "Blazing a Path for 100 Years: A. G. Gaston, [*Black Enterprise*'s] 'Entrepreneur of the Century,' Set the Tone for a Generation to Follow." *Black Enterprise,* March 31, 1996.

Wright, James. "A. G. Gaston Worked Hard for His Millions; Was an Inspiration." *Washington Afro-American,* January 27, 1996.

Zelma Watson George

Born December 8, 1903
Hearne, Texas
Died July 3, 1994
Cleveland, Ohio
Sociologist, musicologist, singer, social worker, humanitarian

UPDATE

Zelma Watson George, the first black woman appointed to the United States' United Nations (UN) delegation, and the first black woman to sing the leading role in an opera on Broadway, died on July 3, 1994, at the age of ninety. Clearly a woman of many talents, she was remembered by the people of her adopted hometown of Cleveland, Ohio, for her contributions to the community. **(See original entry on George in volume 2.)**

George was born Zelma Watson in Heanre, Texas, in 1903. Her father was a Baptist minister, and her mother taught George at home, along with her siblings and others. The family moved to Topeka, Kansas, when George was in high school, and later she attended college at the University of Chicago. There she had several experiences of racial harassment, but she later maintained positive memories of her college years.

After college, George worked in a variety of community-service jobs, and honed her abilities as a singer. In 1932 she

"She leaves behind a legacy of 'salt-of-the-Earth' goodness that is rarely found these days."

—Journalist Armetta Landrum

became dean of women at Tennessee Agricultural and Industrial State College in Nashville. Toward the end of the 1930s, during a brief marriage to a young minister she had known in Topeka, George began work on her Ph.D. degree. In the early 1940s, she married her second husband, attorney Clayborne George, and moved to Cleveland. There she became involved in a wide variety of humanitarian and community organizations. Meanwhile she continued her education, receiving a Ph.D. in sociology and intercultural relations from New York University in 1954. In her doctoral dissertation, George catalogued some 12,000 songs written or inspired by African Americans.

George also continued to develop her musical talent. In 1949, she played the title role in Gian-Carlo Menotti's opera *The Medium*. When the show went to New York City the following year, she became the first African American woman to sing the lead in a Broadway opera.

Even greater recognition followed, when she served in a variety of national offices under President Dwight D. Eisenhower (1890–1969). In 1959, she conducted a six-month lecture tour of Asia, Africa, and Europe, and in 1960 became the first black female member of a U.S. delegation to the UN, where she served on the Economics and Finance Committee. Over the next thirty years, George served as executive director of the new Cleveland Job Corps Center for Women, taught at Cuyahoga Community College, and was a popular speaker, college lecturer, and civic leader.

Remembered for her many contributions

George died of heart failure at University Hospitals of Cleveland on July 3, 1994. She was best remembered, not only for her achievements in the world of music and international politics, but for her contributions to the community. Cleveland's Job Corps Center was the oldest of its kind in the nation, and it had remained open due to her efforts. In the late 1960s, when President Richard M. Nixon (1913–94) wanted to close down the local Job Corps in a budget-cutting move,

George called Nixon, who she knew from her days in the Eisenhower administration when Nixon was vice president. She persuaded Nixon not to close down the center.

The community remembered her with high praise. "Though she leaves behind a legacy of 'salt-of-the-Earth' goodness that is rarely found these days," wrote Armetta Landrum in the *Call and Post,* "she also leaves a shelter for women and children named in her honor, that needs our community's continued support." Margaret Ford-Taylor, executive director of the city's Karamu House, said, "The world is so much richer because she lived, and so much poorer because she is gone."

Sources for further reading

Forte, Roland. "Cleveland's Grand Dame, Zelma George, Dies at Age 90." *Call and Post,* July 7, 1994.

Landrum, Armetta. "Dr. Zelma Watson George." *Call and Post,* July 14, 1994.

[Obituary.] *St. Louis Post-Dispatch,* July 5, 1994, p. 4B.

Smith, Jessie Carney, ed. *Notable Black American Women.* Detroit: Gale, 1992.

Charles Gordone

Born October 12, 1925
Cleveland, Ohio
Died November 16, 1995
College Station, Texas
Playwright, actor, director, educator

UPDATE

Charles Gordone, the first black playwright to win the Pulitzer Prize, died of cancer in College Station, Texas, on November 16, 1995. He was seventy years old. Gordone won the acclaimed literary award in 1970 for his play *No Place to Be Somebody.* **(See original entry on Gordone in volume 2.)**

Growing up in Indiana, Gordone, a light-skinned African American youth, experienced discrimination from both whites and blacks. He went to college at the University of California at Los Angeles (UCLA), then spent a tour of duty in the U.S. Air Force. He returned to school, earned his B.A. degree in 1952, and went to New York to find work as an actor.

During the next few years, Gordone built a reputation for himself in the theatre, appearing in plays that included Moss Hart's (1904–61) *Climate of Eden,* an all-black production of *Of Mice and Men* by John Steinbeck (1902–68), and *Tobacco Road,* an adaptation of a novel by Erskine Caldwell

> "[Gordone] believed in a multiracial American theater. It had become black theater, Chicano theater, lesbian theater—he wanted a truly American theater."
>
> —Poet Buck Ramsey

(1903–87). In 1964, he was associate producer of the pioneering film *Nothing But a Man*. Throughout the 1960s, Gordone worked on writing the play *No Place to Be Somebody,* which finally opened in 1969 to rave reviews. Drawn from Gordone's own experiences as a waiter, the play takes place mostly in a New York City bar filled with out-of-work customers, some of them bitter, some merely sad that they have "no place to be somebody."

Gordone followed up with several more works, and in the late 1970s turned his attention to helping others. From 1977 to 1978, he served as an instructor in two drama programs for prison inmates, and from 1978 to 1979 he taught at the New School for Social Research in New York City. After completing a coveted D. H. Lawrence fellowship in Taos, New Mexico, he joined the faculty of Texas A&M University in College Station, Texas. Gordone had a few film appearances, most notably in 1987's *Angelheart*.

Contrasting memories of Gordone

Gordone died on November 16, 1995, following a six-month illness. Critic Richard H. Costa remembered Gordone in an online article called "The Short Happy Afterlife of Charles Gordone," using a phrase borrowed from the title of a short story by Ernest Hemingway (1899–1961), about a man who dies on a safari in Africa after having faced death in the form of a lion. Costa quoted "Amarillo [Texas] cowboy poet" Buck Ramsey (1938–98) as saying that Gordone "believed in a multiracial American theater. It had become black theater, Chicano theater, lesbian theater—he wanted a truly American theater." Playing on the title of Gordone's most famous play, Ramsey added, "That essentially left him no place to be."

Emerging playwright OyamO (1943–) certainly remembered Gordone. OyamO, who jokes that his name means "black man with typewriter" in an unidentified African language, adopted it because his real name is Charles Gordon, and he did not want to be confused with the more well-known playwright. Actress Shezwae Powell, in an interview with the *Independent,* remembered her first substantial role, in *No*

Place to Be Somebody in 1969. After the male lead had quit, Gordone "went drinking in a Manhattan bar and decided that the best person to give the part to was the bartender, who claimed to be an actor." The event proved a disaster, as Powell remembered in a humorous story. Many students also paid tribute to Gordone in a memorial service. Emerging filmmaker Greg Carter recalled falling "under the spell of visiting professor Charles Gordone" while at Texas A&M.

Gordone's long-time companion, Susan Kouyomjian, described him as having a vision that went beyond race: he was looking for "a truly American America," she told Costa. In the end, Costa suggested, Gordone's failure to produce a follow-up to *No Place to Be Somebody* could be compared to a similar situation with novelist **Ralph Ellison** (1914–94; see entry in volume 2, and update on p. 67), who never followed up his *Invisible Man* (1952). By seeing the larger perspective, Costa indicated, and by having a view of things that saw people as people, rather than as members of races, Gordone and Ellison were not fashionable. Perhaps that was why Gordone said, after accepting his Pulitzer in 1970, "I'm still as mean, arrogant, silly, paranoid, and scared as ever."

Sources for further reading

Cavendish, Dominic. "Theatre: Debut." *Independent,* July 1, 1998, p. 11.

Contemporary Black Biography, Volume 15. Detroit: Gale, 1997, pp. 106–8.

Costa, Richard. "The Short Happy Afterlife of Charles Gordone." *The Touchstone,* February/March 1996. [Online] http://www.rtis.com/reg/bcs/pol/touchstone/February96/costa.htm (accessed on October 8, 1998).

Vognar, Chris. "Different Road to the 'Hood: First-Time Filmmaker Is a Talkative, Ambitious Auteur." *Dallas Morning News,* April 2, 1998, p. 1C.

Florence Griffith Joyner

Born December 21, 1959
Los Angeles, California
Died September 21, 1998
Mission Viejo, California
Track and field athlete

At the 1988 Olympic Games in Seoul, South Korea, Florence Griffith Joyner, or Flo-Jo as she was better known, was a blur on the racetrack, winning gold medals in the 100– and 200–meter dashes and with the U.S. 4 x 100–meter relay team. By doing so, Griffith Joyner became known as "The World's Fastest Woman." She also made news with her unusual track outfits, her long fingernails, her flowing hair, and her bright smile. After she retired from racing, she started new careers in acting, clothes designing, modeling, and writing. In 1993, she accepted President Bill Clinton's invitation to be co-chairperson for the President's Council on Physical Fitness and Sports. Her life was cut short on September 21, 1998, however, when she suffered an epileptic seizure and suffocated in her sleep at her home in Mission Viejo, California. She was 38 years old.

Delorez Florence Griffith was born December 21, 1959, in Los Angeles, California. One of 11 children, she was raised

"We were dazzled by her speed, humbled by her talent, and captivated by her style."

—President Bill Clinton

in the Jordan housing project in the tough Watts section of Los Angeles by her mother, Florence, a seamstress. (Her parents were divorced when she was four.) Her mother had a hard time earning enough money to support her family, but her daughter didn't mind. "We learned something from how we grew up," Griffith Joyner told the *Sporting News*. "It has never been easy, and we knew it wouldn't be handed to us, unless we went after it." To avoid being confused with her mother, she was given the nickname "Dee Dee," a name her friends and family always called her.

Her own person

Griffith Joyner showed early signs of becoming her own person. In kindergarten, she braided her hair with one braid sticking straight up. In high school she wore her pet boa constrictor (a very large snake) like a necklace. She read a lot, wrote poetry, and kept a diary. "I always wanted a gun set for Christmas, which no other girls wanted," she told the *Chicago Tribune*, "or something in a color no one had." Her mother tried to discipline the young rebel, attention she didn't like at the time but later appreciated. "Everybody in the family survived," she told *Newsweek*. "Nobody does drugs, nobody got shot at. I used to say it was because we were afraid of Mama's voice. We didn't know how poor we were. We were rich as a family."

At the age of seven Griffith Joyner began to compete in 50– and 70–meter dashes at the Sugar Ray Robinson Youth Foundation (named after the famous boxer), a program for poor children. "I would always win," she told the *Chicago Tribune*. In 1973 she won the annual Jesse Owens National Youth Games (named after the legendary track star) and the next year she won again. In 1978 she graduated from Jordan High School in Los Angeles after setting school records in sprint races and the long jump.

Wins Olympic medal

After high school Griffith Joyner attended California State University at Northridge, but ran out of money, quit school, and worked as a bank teller. In college, she met a young track coach named Bobby Kersee, who helped her apply for financial aid. When Kersee changed jobs in 1980 and went to the University of California at Los Angeles (UCLA), Griffith Joyner followed him. In 1980 she barely missed qualifying for the Olympic team in the 200–meters and in 1982 she ran the 200–meters in 22.39 seconds for the National Collegiate Athletic Association (NCAA) championship. She was also a threat in the 400–meters, winning the NCAA championship in 1983. She qualified for the Olympic team in 1984, finishing second in the 200–meter race.

Takes time off

After the Olympics Griffith Joyner cut back on her training and competing, gaining weight and falling out of shape in the process. She worked as a customer service representative for a bank and as a hair-dresser and nail stylist. At her beauty shop she developed elaborate styles of braiding hair and painting long nails. Griffith Joyner was engaged to be married to Olympic hurdle runner Greg Foster, but broke off the engagement. She then became close to Al Joyner (1960–), who had won a gold medal in the triple jump at the 1984 Olympic Summer Games. The two met at the 1980 Olympic trials, began dating in 1986, and married on October 10, 1987, in Las Vegas, Nevada. They later appeared on *The Newlywed Game* TV show.

Trendsetter

Griffith Joyner brought her sense of style onto the race track. Her outfits were different, to say the least—she wore white bikini bottoms over most unusual tights. The right leg was completely covered in fabric; the left leg completely bare, except for the shoe on her foot. Her long nails also showed a distinctive style, and the designs she painted on them showed her individualism. "Looking good is almost as important as running well," she once said. "It's part of feeling good about myself."

Record breaker

In 1987 Griffith Joyner returned to serious competition and began training under Coach Kersee's very strict program. She finished second in the 200–meters at the World Championships in the summer of 1987, and became even more determined to improve. "When you've been second-best for so long, you can either accept it, or try to become the best," she told *Ms.* magazine. "I made the decision to try to be the best." During the U.S. Olympic trials in July of 1988, she shattered the world 100–meter record with a time of 10.49 seconds—.27 seconds better than the previous record held by American sprinter Evelyn Ashford (1957–).

Olympic champ

Heading to the Olympics in Seoul, South Korea, Griffith Joyner was favored in the 100– and 200–meter races, and was a member of the U.S. 400– and 1600–meter relay teams. In the 100–meter dash she won with a time of 10.54 seconds. She followed that up by breaking the world record in the 200–meter competition twice—once in the semifinals and again in the finals. In the 400–meter relay, she shared a gold medal with three U.S. teammates in a time of 41.98. Finally, she shared a silver medal with three other teammates in the 1600–meter relay, won by the Soviet Union in a world and Olympic record time of 3:15.18. In both the 100– and 200–meter dashes, Griffith Joyner would have had better times, but she couldn't resist throwing her arms up and flashing a brilliant smile for the cameras.

Drug-free

Following the Olympics, some of Griffith Joyner's competitors claimed she used illegal drugs called steroids to build up her strength. She denied the charges, pointing to her training program as the reason she ran so fast, and passed every drug test she was asked to take. The charges "hurt me, but [they] didn't bother me," she told *New York Newsday.* "I know that I'm a champion. I am anti-drugs.... Chasing all those

Florence Griffith Joyner competes at the U.S. Olympic Track and Field trials in July 1988.

records and giving the young kids coming up something to chase, that's what the sport is all about."

With her performance in the Olympics, Griffith Joyner earned the title "The World's Fastest Woman." She was honored with the 1988 Jesse Owens Award as the year's outstanding track and field athlete and the 1988 Sullivan Award as the top American amateur athlete. In February of 1989, she announced that she was retiring from competition to start commercial and entertainment careers. "With all I want to do—[fashion] designing, writing, acting, modeling—I realized there was no time to train," she told the *Chicago Tribune*. Griffith Joyner became the spokesperson for several products, designed her own line of sportswear for Starter, appeared as an actress in several television shows, and made a fitness video. She also continued her childhood hobby of writing, and was the author of more than 30 books for children.

The president calls

In 1993 President Clinton announced that Griffith Joyner and former NBA basketball star and U.S. congressman Tom McMillen would be co-chairpersons for the President's Council on Physical Fitness and Sports, a group that advises the president on ways to promote fitness and sports programs for all Americans. Griffith Joyner hoped to use her new position to help children. "I love working with kids, talking with them and listening to them," she told the *New York Times Magazine*. "I always encourage kids to reach beyond their dreams. Don't try to be like me. Be better than me." As co-chairperson she strove to encourage all Americans, but especially children, to exercise and eat right. But, she admitted, nobody is perfect. "I don't always have the best eating habits," she told the *New York Times Magazine*. "I like butter and ice cream. There are days I should work out and I don't. But it's never too late to change old habits."

Off the track

Griffith Joyner was part of a very successful track and field family. Her sister-in-law is Jackie Joyner-Kersee, who has won three Olympic gold medals, one silver, and one bronze in three Olympic Games. Her coach was Bob Kersee, who is married to, and coaches, Jackie Joyner-Kersee. Griffith Joyner fired Kersee before the 1988 Olympics, but the two couples remained friendly. At the time of her death, Griffith Joyner lived with her husband and daughter, Mary Ruth, in Mission Viejo, California.

In November 1995 Griffith Joyner was one of six inducted into the National Track and Field Hall of Fame. She founded the Florence Griffith Joyner Youth Foundation, through which she worked with inner-city youth. Remembering her childhood, running at the Sugar Ray Robinson Foundation, Griffith Joyner's ultimate goal, as she told the *New York Times Magazine* was to "make sports and athletics available to every youth in America, not just one day a week like it was for me, but every day."

Sudden death

On September 21, 1998, Griffith Joyner died in her sleep. Early reports suggested she had died as a result of a heart condition. But on October 22, Orange County officials released the findings of her autopsy, which reported that she died of an epileptic seizure, resulting from a brain abnormality that caused blood to build up near normal blood vessels. The seizure caused her to suffocate while she was sleeping.

Many people paid tribute to Griffith Joyner. President Clinton said: "We were dazzled by her speed, humbled by her talent, and captivated by her style. Though she rose to the pinnacle of the world of sports, she never forgot where she came from, devoting time and resources to helping children—especially those growing up in our most devasted neighborhoods—make the most of their own talents." U.S. Olympic Committee president Bill Hybl stated, "The Olympic family is saddened and stunned by her passing. She was a role model for girls and young women in sports and her legacy will be one that included kindness and an interest in children. She will be missed."

Sources for further reading

Aaseng, Nathan. *Florence Griffith Joyner: Dazzling Olympian.* Minneapolis: Lerner Publications Co., 1989.

Chicago Tribune, July 22, 1988.

Detroit Free Press, November 30, 1995, p. D2.

Detroit News, October 23, 1998.

Koral, April. *Florence Griffith Joyner: Track and Field Star.* Danbury, CT: Franklin Watts, 1992.

Los Angeles Times, July 22, 1997.

New York Times, September 22, 1998, p. C26.

New York Times Magazine, July 21, 1993.

Newsday, July 24, 1988; September 7, 1988; September 30, 1988.

Newsweek, August 1, 1988.

The Olympics Factbook: A Spectator's Guide to the Winter and Summer Games. Detroit: Visible Ink Press, 1992.

Sporting News, October 10, 1988; October 17, 1988; February 23, 1989.

Stewart, Mark. *Florence Griffith Joyner.* Danbury, CT: Children's Press, 1996.

Women's Sports + Fitness, September 1995, pp. 44–45.

Greg Gumbel

Born May 3, 1946
New Orleans, Louisiana
Sports commentator

Sports commentator Greg Gumbel has come a long way since he was growing up in Chicago, Illinois, with his younger brother Bryant Gumbel (1948– ; see entry in volume 2), the well-known former host of NBC-TV's *Today* show. As kids in Chicago, the two stood in front of the mirror and pretended to be baseball play-by-play announcers. By 1994, Greg was "calling the plays" in front of an estimated 200 million viewers at the Winter Olympics in Lillehammer, Norway, where he served as the prime-time anchor. Two years later, during the 1996 Summer Olympics in Atlanta, Georgia, he hosted NBC's daytime coverage of the Games.

In spite of his success, Gumbel is known as "the humble Gumbel," to quote the title of a 1994 article about him. Whereas Bryant has a reputation as a hard-hitting television journalist who sometimes makes enemies with his aggressive style, Greg is more cool, calm, and friendly. "Watching him," said *People* magazine, "is like dropping in on a neighbor who is savvy and fanatical about sports."

"Probably the biggest difference between Bryant and me is our admitted self-confidence. Bryant . . . is extremely self-confident . . . and doesn't fail to let that be known. I'm confident . . . but I certainly admit to having occasional butterflies."

Sportscaster with an audience of one

Though he was born in New Orleans, Louisiana, Gumbel grew up in Chicago, the oldest of Richard and Rhea Gumbel's four children. Even then, he and Bryant didn't always agree: Greg's favorite hometown baseball team was the Chicago White Cox, whereas Bryant's was the Cubs. The two boys, Greg later told *People,* would "grab our gloves, stand in front of a full-length mirror, wind up, pitch, and announce entire imaginary games, taking turns every half inning." Greg became involved in sports, and played on several varsity teams in high school.

"Bryant didn't hire me"

After he graduated from high school, Gumbel went to Loras College in Dubuque, Iowa, where he played baseball. In his senior year, he batted .378, and won the team's most valuable player award. In 1967 he earned his bachelor's degree in English, and got a job selling hospital supplies. His work took him to Detroit, Michigan, where he met his future wife, Marcy. They married in 1976, and Gumbel adopted Marcy's daughter, Michelle.

Though he did well in his work, Gumbel was not finding fulfillment. "I was good at the job," he told a reporter for the *Chicago Tribune,* "but I hated it." Meanwhile Bryant was succeeding as a newscaster in Los Angeles, California. When Bryant told his brother about a sports anchor opening at WMAQ-TV in Chicago, Greg applied for the job. To his surprise, he got it. In later years, people often asked him how much of a role Bryant played in his later success. "I'm sure it didn't hurt me that Bryant was just making inroads into network sports," he told *People.* But "Bryant didn't hire me, and he never renewed my contract. The station did."

One of ESPN's first anchors

Even though he got the job at WMAQ, Gumbel's career did not immediately take off. He was so nervous in front of the cameras that he sweat heavily, earning him the nickname

"Waterfall." He was moved to the position of sports reporter, but he triumphed, winning two local Emmy awards.

After seven years at WMAQ, from 1973 to 1981, Gumbel was ready for a change. He moved to the brand-new Entertainment and Sports Programming Network (ESPN). Although the network would grow to become a giant in cable television, in the early days it was a little rough around the edges. "The announcers doing the show were pretty much responsible for the content," Gumbel recalled, and this meant that he had to sometimes make things up as he went along.

In 1986, Gumbel moved to New York City to work for the Madison Square Garden Network. During this time he also hosted a drive-time radio sports talk show on WFAN. One of his listeners was Ted Shaker, executive producer of CBS Sports. In 1988 Shaker asked Gumbel to become a play-by-play announcer on the network's broadcast of National Football League (NFL) games. Gumbel also began covering basketball and baseball, and soon was offered a much bigger role with CBS Sports.

From *The NFL Today* to the Olympics

In 1990, CBS placed Gumbel alongside former Pittsburgh Steelers quarterback Terry Bradshaw (1948–) as cohost of the game-day *NFL Today*. The two men were opposites, with Gumbel smooth and cool, and Bradshaw loud and enthusiastic. After a slow start, their show became a hit.

During the early 1990s, Gumbel also served as sports commentator for *CBS This Morning,* which competed with his brother's *Today* show. In this capacity, he hosted morning broadcasts of the 1992 Winter Olympics from Albertville, France. Though it gave him lots of exposure, Gumbel was not initially excited about his Olympic job, because he didn't like cold weather. Nonetheless, he received good reviews from critics, and in 1994 was back as sole anchor for the Winter Games in Lillehammer. Never a big fan of winter sports, Gumbel even became an expert on such events as the luge and bobsledding.

CBS sports commentator Greg Gumbel, center, with basketball analysts Dean Smith, left, and Clark Kellogg, right.

Hosts the biggest games of all

"Greg Gumbel is the kind of guy you'd talk to at a cocktail party," wrote Kate Meyers in *Entertainment Weekly* in 1994. She quoted a CBS executive who said Gumbel was "a nice guy to hang out with. What Greg is in real life, he is on the air." Television critics liked his smooth, conversational style, and they gave him good reviews for his performance as 1994 Olympics host.

Back at CBS, though, the future did not look good. The network had lost pro football broadcast rights, meaning the end of *The NFL Today*. Gumbel soon began negotiations with NBC Sports, and became host of *The NFL on NBC*. He also served as pregame host for the coverage of Superbowl XXX in 1996.

But the biggest coup for Gumbel was getting the daytime anchor spot for the Summer Olympic Games in Atlanta. The 1996 Olympics had an estimated audience of as many as 200 million U.S. viewers. And since many countries purchase Olympic coverage from the U.S. network, Gumbel's worldwide audience was well into the hundreds of millions. It was the most widely watched Games of all time. As usual, Gumbel remained humble about his role. Commenting on his larger exposure compared to two years earlier, he told *USA Today,* "The philosophy's the same wherever you are. The Games themselves are the story. But, as with CBS, we couldn't do this thing without the help of producers and researchers."

Few in 1996 could have predicted that by 1998, NFL football would return to CBS—and so would Gumbel. In January 1998, he hosted the pregame show for the Superbowl, NBC's last NFL program after thirty-three years of pro football coverage. "I felt really terrible for all the people at CBS when we lost [football rights] to Fox," he said. "I can only feel happy for them now. But now I feel the same way for the NBC people and what they're going through." Gumbel signed a five-year contract for an average of $1.75 million a year. Returning to his old network and his old friends, Gumbel said, "I can't stop giving out hugs."

Sources for further reading

Contemporary Black Biography, Volume 8. Detroit: Gale, 1995, pp. 89–91.

Dixon, Oscar. "Greg Gumbel Agrees to Deal with CBS." *USA Today,* January 22, 1998, p. 3C.

Gumbel, Greg (host). *Stride to Glory: The History of African American Achievement in the Olympic Games* (videorecording). Santa Monica, CA: Trans World International/ Xenon Entertainment Group, 1997.

Martzke, Rudy. "Gumbel Primed 'To Put the Lights Out' for NBC." *USA Today,* January 23, 1998, p. 18E.

Martzke, Rudy. "Return of NFL Lights a Fire at CBS." *USA Today,* May 21, 1998, p. 2C.

Martzke, Rudy. "Same Opportunity, Different Network for Greg Gumbel." *USA Today,* July 20, 1996, p. 2C.

Meyers, Kate. "The Humble Gumbel." *Entertainment Weekly,* February 18–25, 1994, p. 102.

Alexis Herman

*Born July 16, 1947
Mobile, Alabama
U.S. secretary of labor*

In May 1997, President Bill Clinton (1946–) swore in Alexis Herman as U.S. secretary of labor. Herman was the first African American to hold this position, and was one of the first black Cabinet members. The Cabinet is a group of top presidential advisors who oversee key departments of the government. As secretary of labor, Herman is one of the most powerful black women in America. She is responsible for making sure that businesses comply with labor laws regarding such matters as overtime pay and worker's compensation. She also works to ensure good relations between employers and workers. In this capacity, she helped resolve a dispute between the United Parcel Service (UPS) and a large union (an organized group of workers) in August 1997.

"It's important that we set high goals for ourselves. It never occurred to me that I couldn't be anything I wanted to be."

Father beaten by Klansmen

Herman grew up in Mobile, Alabama, during the troubled years leading up to the 1960s, when the Rev. Martin

Luther King, Jr. (1929–68; see entry in volume 3) and others helped secure equal rights for African Americans. One night when she was a little girl, she and her father were riding in a car when they were stopped by members of the Ku Klux Klan (white supremacists). The Klansmen beat her father, but it did not break his spirit. This had a powerful effect on Herman.

Herman's parents, Alex and Gloria, sent her to Catholic schools. After graduating from high school in 1965, she attended several colleges, ultimately obtaining her B.S. degree from Xavier University in New Orleans, Louisiana. She became involved in community work throughout the South, and in 1972 earned her graduate degree from the University of South Alabama in Mobile. In 1972, she became director of a program for the Southern Regional Council in Atlanta, Georgia, helping African American women obtain higher-paying positions as executives. This project, the Minority Women Employment Program, became a national organization under Herman's leadership in 1974.

A national position

During the administration of President Jimmy Carter (1924–), Herman served as director of the Women's Bureau under Secretary of Labor Ray Marshall. She was the Bureau's youngest director ever. In this role, she encouraged women to start businesses and addressed economic and social concerns of women in the marketplace.

At the end of the Carter administration in 1981, Herman entered the private sector as co-director (and, later, sole director) of a consulting firm. She advised businesses on how to comply with government regulations regarding minority hiring. During this time, she worked closely with a number of African American political leaders, most notably the Rev. Jesse Jackson (1941– ; see entry in volume 2). She also became acquainted with the late commerce secretary **Ron Brown** (1941–96; see entry in volume 1, and update on p. 17), leading to even larger roles for Herman.

Labor secretary Alexis Herman reads to children at the annual Easter Egg Roll on April 13, 1998.

A job at the White House

When Brown became chairman of the Democratic National Committee (DNC) in 1989, he invited Herman to become his chief of staff. Later he promoted her to chairwoman, and in 1992 she served as chief executive officer for the Democratic National Convention in New York City, where Clinton became the party's presidential nominee. After Clinton was elected, he appointed Herman deputy director of the Presidential Transition Office. This office is designed to help smooth the transition between the outgoing and incoming presidential administrations.

Herman then served as director of the White House Public Liaison Office from 1993 to 1997. Herman's job was to encourage public support when Clinton would introduce new government plans. It was an important position, and Herman's role—as well as that of Maggie Williams (1954–), who became the first black chief of staff for a first lady under Hillary Rodham Clinton (1947–)—underscored the gains made by African American women. Half a century before, the only White House job available to a black woman was as a maid. But an even bigger role awaited Herman in Clinton's second term.

Helps resolve UPS strike

One month after Clinton was reelected in November 1996, he nominated Herman to take the place of outgoing secretary of labor Robert B. Reich. Cabinet secretaries must be approved by the U.S. Senate (to make sure there isn't anything in the nominee's past that would make him or her unsuitable for the position). Herman was confirmed by a wide majority, 85 to 13, on April 29, 1997.

Herman's first great challenge as labor secretary came in 1997, during a strike of some 185,000 UPS workers. Because thousands of American businesses depend on UPS, by far the largest private package service, the strike had wide-ranging effects. It was crucial that it be resolved as quickly as possible. Among the demands of the UPS workers were higher wages and full-time status for part-time employees, many of whom worked as many hours as full-time employees without enjoying the benefits of full-time employment. Herman could not force an end to the strike—that was a matter for UPS and the union to resolve between themselves—but she did encourage both sides to come to a deal as quickly as possible. The strike ended after fifteen days, and many observers gave Herman credit for helping to end it.

Good and bad news

In late 1997 and early 1998, however, Herman's name was in the news for less positive reasons. Attorney General Janet Reno (1938–) appointed an independent counsel to investigate whether Herman accepted a bribe. There were allegations that Herman had taken $25,000 in return for help in obtaining a license for a satellite telephone company.

On a happier note, in November 1997, Herman was honored in her hometown of Mobile with a weekend of festivities to celebrate her successes. As for the challenges ahead, Herman, who remains a strongly religious Catholic, refers to a special passage in the Bible, James 1:1-8. During the Senate confirmation hearings, two friends mentioned the verses to her, and when she went to open her mother's Bible, she found that her mother had written "In times of trouble, read James 1:1–8." As Herman told *Essence* magazine, "That passage said consider yourself lucky when your faith is tested, because if you survive, your faith will carry you all the way. I stopped trying to rely on me and my understanding."

Sources for further reading

Cohen, Gary. "Labor Secretary on the Griddle." *U.S. News & World Report,* January 26, 1998, p. 41.

Contemporary Black Biography, Volume 15. Detroit: Gale, 1997, pp. 109–11.

Edwards, Tamala M. "Labor of Love." *Essence,* March 1998, pp. 86–90+.

Elvin, John. "Yet Another Independent Counsel." *Insight on the News,* June 22, 1998, p. 33.

Fix, Janet. "When Social Security Might Not Be Enough." *Detroit Free Press,* June 22, 1998, p. 4F.

Randolph, Laura B. "A Black-and-White Alabama Homecoming." *Ebony,* November 1997, pp. 124–32.

Smith, Jessie Carney, ed. *Notable Black American Women, Book II*. Detroit: Gale, 1996, pp. 287–88.

Jesse Jackson, Jr.

*Born March 11, 1965
Greenville, South Carolina
Congressman*

Jesse Jackson, Jr. is more than just the oldest son of the Rev. Jesse Jackson (1941– ; see entry in volume 2). In 1995, at the age of thirty, he became one of the youngest members of the U.S. Congress when he was elected to fill the seat for the second congressional district in Chicago, Illinois.

Because he is the son of a famous civil rights leader, Jackson has enjoyed plenty of exposure in the national media. But he intends to make a name for himself in his own right: "I'm having a study done," he told *Chicago* magazine. "I want to know what the most successful freshmen [first-term members of Congress] have accomplished in their first term. So when the media says that Jesse Jackson, Jr. hasn't done anything, I can hold up this study and say, 'I bested the best.'"

Almost named "Selma"

When Jackson was born, his father was hard at work in the civil rights movement alongside the Rev. Martin Luther

"It's a name that's synonymous with public service, with helping people, and I've striven to live up to that commitment. But it's also a double-edged sword. You inherit your father's friends, your parents' friends, and you inherit their detractors."

King, Jr. (1929–68; see entry in volume 3). Jackson, Sr., was in Selma, Alabama, at a voting rights march on March 11, 1965, while back home in Greenville, South Carolina, Jacqueline Jackson was giving birth to their first child, a son. Jackson, Sr., wanted to name his son "Selma," in honor of the historic event taking place at the time; but as Jackson, Jr., later said, "Thank God I have a mama." Instead he was named after his father, and even as an adult, he is often referred to simply as "Junior."

Growing up on the south side of Chicago, Jackson and his four siblings had a very strict upbringing. They were not allowed to go to friends' houses after school, to watch television at night, or to play loud music. Some of his father's friends, such as musician Quincy Jones (1933– ; see entry in volume 2) remembered Jackson as a high-spirited boy who got into a lot of trouble, but was very smart.

In order to teach him more discipline, Jackson's parents sent him and his brother Jonathan away to a military school. His father later told *Chicago* magazine that he wanted his sons to grow up in "an environment free of me being on the radio and TV every day, but one that was close enough for them to be home for the holidays and give them some space for independent development."

Four degrees in ten years

Jackson excelled at Le Mans Military Academy in Rolling Prairie, Indiana, and later attended St. Albans, an Episcopal preparatory school in Washington, D.C. There he distinguished himself both as a student and as a football player, becoming leader of the debate team and gaining 1,000 yards and scoring thirteen touchdowns during his senior year.

After his graduation in 1983, Jackson received a number of scholarship offers from prestigious universities. He decided to attend his father's alma mater (college), North Carolina Agricultural and Technical State University, where the student body is mostly black. He majored in business and played football, but quit the team during his sophomore year in order to concentrate on his studies.

Jackson earned his bachelor's degree in just three years, then went on to Chicago Theological Seminary, another school that his father had attended. In 1990, he earned his master's degree, then earned his law degree from the University of Illinois in 1993. In just ten years, Jackson had earned four degrees: his high school diploma and bachelor's, master's, and law degrees.

Introduces father at Democratic convention

Long before he finished his schooling, Jackson had gone to work in two civil rights organizations led by his father—Operation PUSH (People United to Save Humanity), then the Rainbow Coalition. "Dad wasn't someone I should just be casually comfortable with," he told the *Christian Science Monitor,* "but one I should also respect as a champion of social justice." In spite of his father's reputation, however, his parents had always encouraged him to make his own decisions about his career; on his own, he chose to work in "the family business."

At the 1988 Democratic national convention in Atlanta, Georgia, Jackson and his siblings introduced their father, then a candidate for president. The senior Jackson sibling's introduction, said one friend, "brought the house down," and helped earn him a national reputation. Soon the young law school student was commanding fees as high as $7,500 per speech. Around the time of the convention, he met his future wife, Sandra, who was working for the eventual Democratic candidate, Governor Michael Dukakis of Massachusetts (1933–). The two married in 1991.

Wins congressional race

In 1993, Jackson became national field director for the Rainbow Coalition. Under his leadership, the organization modernized many of its operations, and he personally oversaw the establishment of a website and a weekly faxed newsletter called "JaxFax."

By 1995, Jackson had his eye on a much more prominent position. He and Sandra had moved to the second congres-

U.S. representative Jesse Jackson, Jr., left, shares a laugh with his father, the Rev. Jesse Jackson.

sional district of Chicago, where U.S. congressman Mel Reynolds (1952–) was forced to leave office following a scandal. In September 1995, Jackson became a candidate for the vacant seat.

Despite his famous name, Jackson's election was not automatic. At just thirty years old, he was by far the youngest among the four Democratic candidates, and most observers favored state senate leader Emil Jones to win. But Jackson's campaign appealed to younger voters with its theme of "A New Generation." He won the support of a broad base of voters in a district whose neighborhoods included extremely poor blacks, upper-middle class whites, and racially mixed groups. Among candidate Jackson's plans was to build a third Chicago airport (in addition to O'Hare and Midway) in an economically depressed area of the district.

Jackson surprised many observers by winning the Democratic nomination and, then, the general election. On December 14, 1995, Jackson was sworn in to Congress. The new congressman's father found it difficult to express his pride: "I wish I had a bigger word. Like I feel elephant joy, or dinosaur excitement."

Active congressman and "sexiest politician"

Although members of Congress are all equal in theory, each member does not hold equal power. To a large extent, power depends on the Congressional committees to which a congressperson belongs. Among the most significant is the Ways and Means Committee, which drafts most tax laws and thus governs the amount of money the federal government receives from its citizens. Jackson wanted an appointment to that committee, but settled for the relatively obscure Banking and Financial Services Committee.

Nonetheless, Jackson made the most of the situation, attending every meeting he could, and involving himself heavily in committee business. He also championed the third Chicago airport, a cause also supported by his Republican colleague, Henry Hyde (1924–). The airport issue, popular among Chicagoans because of the economic boost it would give their city, gained Jackson further support from his white and middle-class constituents (group of voters). In 1996, Jackson had to run for reelection, since his first term only completed his predecessor's term. This time he ran unopposed in both the Democratic primary and the general election.

In November 1997, *People* magazine gave Jackson a different sort of vote when it chose him as "sexiest politician" on its list of "Ten Sexy Men." His wife Sandra told *People,* "He is by far the most intellectually stimulating person I've ever met. That's probably the sexiest thing about him." Jackson himself said that "nothing is more unattractive than someone who doesn't have anything on his mind." That same month *Jet* magazine listed Jackson's election to Congress as one of the highlights of the past twenty-five years of African American events. At his website, Jackson tells visitors: "Visit this site often. You'll learn about important events as soon as they happen. Stay informed. Get involved. With your help we can make a difference."

Sources for further reading

Congressman Jesse Jackson, Jr. Web Site. [Online] http://www.jessejacksonjr.org/about.cgi (accessed on October 8, 1998).

Contemporary Black Biography, Volume 14. Detroit: Gale, 1997, pp. 129–33.

"Generation Next." *People,* November 18, 1996, pp. 50–53.

"Growing Up with a Famous Father." *Ebony,* June 1996, pp. 122–125.

"Jet Milestones: 1951-1997." *Jet,* November 3, 1997, pp. 10–19.

"Like Father, Like Son." *Jet,* January 27, 1997, p. 32.

"Relieving O'Hare." *Economist,* January 10, 1998, pp. 22–23.

Richardson, Kevin R. "Jesse Jackson, Jr." *Elle,* September 1996, p. 318.

"Ten Sexy Men." *People,* November 17, 1997, p. 97.

Earvin "Magic" Johnson

Born August 19, 1959
Lansing, Michigan
Basketball player, businessman, activist

UPDATE

Magic Johnson may have retired from basketball—more than once, as a matter of fact—but he was far from inactive during the mid- to late 1990s. He left his team, the Los Angeles Lakers of the National Basketball Association (NBA), after the 1991 announcement that he had HIV, the virus that causes the fatal disease AIDS. But Johnson returned to the game twice, and retired twice more. He remained a committed AIDS activist, and in 1997 he and his wife Cookie discovered that the traces of HIV in his bloodstream had all but disappeared, something Cookie called a miracle. Johnson also started a highly successful chain of movie theatres, but proved less successful as host of a late-night talk show. **(See original entry on Johnson in volume 2.)**

Born Earvin Johnson in Lansing, Michigan in 1959, the future basketball star grew up in a working-class family. His father, for whom he was named, watched games on TV with him, and gave him tips on how to play. Every day and every

> "I honestly feel that the Lord is going to heal [Magic] and that we are going to live together forever and have more children and be happy.
>
> —Cookie Johnson

night, Johnson was on the court. He didn't love the game because he was good; he became good at it because he loved the game. "In the schoolyard," he later said, "the only way you can stay on the court when there are lots of people around is keep winning.... And I wanted to keep playing. All day and all night long." As a high-school player, he was given the nickname "Magic" by a local sportswriter.

Johnson's final game as a college player for Michigan State University (MSU) saw him square off against another future legend, Indiana State University's (ISU) white forward, Larry Bird (1956–). After MSU defeated ISU in the 1979 National Collegiate Athletic Association (NCAA) championships, Johnson was drafted by the Lakers, while the Boston Celtics picked Bird. Johnson became a superstar for the Lakers, twice winning the most valuable player (MVP) award, and helping his team win the championship five times. (Johnson and Bird met three times in the NBA finals.)

In September 1991, Johnson married his longtime girlfriend, Earletha "Cookie" Kelly, and a few weeks later he discovered that he had HIV. On November 7, he let his teammates know, and soon afterward retired from basketball. He became involved with the National AIDS Commission, but quit over differences with U.S. president George Bush (1924–). In 1992, Johnson played with the U.S. team at the Olympic Games in Barcelona, Spain, and the following year he attempted a comeback with the Lakers. But many other players feared they might contract AIDS by coming into close contact with Johnson on the court, so he again retired. In 1994, he coached the Lakers' final 15 games of the season.

HIV disappears; invests in the black community

In February 1995, Johnson and Cookie adopted a baby girl, Elisa, Johnson's third child. (He had a son, Andre, from an earlier relationship, as well as his and Cookie's son, Earvin III.) Cookie, who gave a long interview with the *New York Times* concerning her role as Magic's partner and supporter, became heavily involved in the Magic Johnson Foundation, an organization Johnson established in December 1991 to promote AIDS awareness. The Johnsons are also involved in numerous other AIDS-related causes, and are faithful members of, and financial contributors to, the West Angeles Church of God in Christ in Los Angeles, California. Johnson is so committed to charities that he even turned his star-studded thirty-seventh birthday party in 1996 into a benefit to raise money for AIDS awareness.

Raising money for AIDS led Johnson onto the basketball court again in October 1995, when he and the American All Stars faced an Italian team in a benefit game. In an unsurprising result, Johnson's team won, 135–81. Then in February 1996, he made his second comeback with the Lakers. Thanks in part to Johnson's own AIDS education programs, though, players now realized that they weren't likely to catch the virus on the court. Referring to a sweepstakes represented by a well-known TV personality, the New Jersey Nets' Jayson Williams (1968–) said, "You've got a better chance of Ed McMahon knocking on your door with $1 million than you have of catching AIDS in a basketball game."

But in June 1996, Johnson retired once more. But this time, it was on his own terms. Unlike before, when he was all but forced out of the game because of other players' fears, Johnson had been given an opportunity to come out onto the court and prove that he could still play. Now he was ready to turn his attention to other things.

In April 1997 came some stunning news: tests had shown no sign of HIV in Johnson's body. Five years earlier, Cookie had told the media, "I honestly feel that the Lord is going to heal him and that we are going to live together forever and have more children and be happy"; now, she said, although "doctors think it's the medicine" that caused the HIV to disappear, "we claim it [as a miracle] in the name of Jesus."

Meanwhile, Johnson began taking the millions of dollars he earned from basketball, endorsements, and business ventures, and invested it in some struggling communities. Johnson opened the Magic Johnson Movie Theatres, a twelve-screen complex in the heart of L.A.'s South Central area.

White businesspeople had been afraid to invest in the area, not simply because it is black and poor, but because of its reputation for heavy crime and violence, as exhibited during the 1992 riots. Johnson said, "Most people go on what they read and see on TV, and if that's all you know, no one would come in here. But Sony [the company that invested jointly with him] had the good business sense to come for themselves." What they saw in the neighborhoods were cut lawns, trimmed hedges, and nice cars.

Blacks were at least as skeptical, and as surprised, as whites over the success of Johnson's black-run enterprise. Johnson said a black woman came up to him once and said, "You know, I told myself I would never go to your theatre because I knew they would disrespect me, I wouldn't get the proper service, there would be a lot of craziness. So my girlfriend talked me into going one night, and I must apologize to you. I've never been treated like that anywhere else—'Welcome to the theatre, may we help you, thank you for coming'—the whole thing."

Buoyed by the success of the L.A. theatres, Johnson began expanding his thriving business. In May 1998, Johnson, singer Janet Jackson (1966– ; see entry in volume 2), and former Motown Records president Jheryl Busby bought controlling shares in Founders National Bank, also in South Central Los Angeles. It is now the only black-owned and -operated bank in California. Johnson told the *Wall Street Journal,* "This is not a charity case. We made a smart business deal. Hopefully, we can knock down some doors and take the bank to the next level." In addition to his theatres and his part ownership in the bank, Johnson is involved in restaurants, coffee shops, and shopping centers.

Less successful was Johnson's venture into show business. His late-night TV talk show, *The Magic Hour,* debuted in June 1998. He had always wanted to host a show; but within two months, it was cancelled due to a lack of ratings. As a writer for *Jet* observed, the world of late-night TV, dominated by Jay Leno (1950–) and David Letterman (1947–), is "an even more competitive arena" than professional basketball.

Magic Johnson laughs it up with guest Arnold Schwarzenegger on The Magic Hour. *Johnson's talk show lasted only two months.*

But just because he had failed to win in the tough late-night arena did not mean that Johnson was not still a winner. In April 1998, Kofi Annan, secretary-general of the United Nations (UN), appointed Johnson a "United Nations Messenger for Peace." In an interview, Johnson said, "I always thought I was more than a basketball player." He planned to promote the UN and the cause of world peace in speeches at high schools and elsewhere, adding that he could reach an audience that most political leaders could never reach.

Sources for further reading

Braxton, Greg. "Time's Up for 'Magic Hour'." *Los Angeles Times,* August 7, 1998, business section, p. 2.

"Cookie Johnson Says 'The Lord Has Healed Earvin' in April's *Ebony.*" *Jet,* April 7, 1997, p. 50.

Frank, Steven. *Magic Johnson.* New York: Chelsea House Publishers, 1995.

Haskins, James. *Sports Great Magic Johnson*. Hillside, NJ: Enslow Publishers, 1992.

"Janet, Magic, and Jheryl Busby Buy Majority Stake in Los Angeles Bank." *Jet,* May 18, 1998, p. 14.

Johnson, Earvin "Magic," with Richard Levin. *Magic*. New York: Viking Press, 1983.

Johnson, Earvin "Magic," with Roy S. Johnson. *Magic's Touch*. Reading, MA: Addison-Wesley, 1989.

Johnson, Earvin "Magic," with William Novak. *My Life*. New York: Random House, 1992.

Johnson, Earvin "Magic." *What You Can Do to Avoid AIDS*. New York: Times Books, 1992.

Katz, Lee Michael. "U.N. Honors Magic Johnson." *USA Today,* April 17, 1998, p. 3-C.

"Magic Johnson and Wife Cookie Adopt Baby Girl." *Jet,* February 6, 1995, p. 53.

"Magic Johnson Enters the Talk Show Arena with 'The Magic Hour.'" *Jet,* June 22, 1998, p. 58.

Magic Johnson Foundation. [Online] http://www.magicjohnson.org (accessed on October 8, 1998).

"Magic Johnson Retires Again, Saying It's on His Own Terms This Time." *Jet,* June 3, 1996, p. 46.

"Magic Makes Comeback with L.A. Lakers." *Jet,* February 19, 1996, p. 52.

Noble, Kenneth B. "Magic Johnson Finds Success in a New Forum." *New York Times,* January 8, 1996, p. 8.

Pascarelli, Peter F. *The Courage of Magic Johnson: from Boyhood Dreams to Superstar to His Toughest Challenge*. New York: Bantam Books, 1992.

Rothaus, James R. *Magic Johnson*. Mankato, MN: Child's World, 1991.

Schwabacher, Martin. *Magic Johnson*. New York: Chelsea Juniors, 1994.

Strauss, Larry. *Magic Man*. Los Angeles: Lowell House Juvenile, 1992.

Weinraub, Bernard. "At Work with Cookie Johnson: Moving Forward, with Hope." *New York Times,* May 2, 1996, p. C-1.

Barbara Jordan

*Born February 21, 1936
Houston, Texas*
*Died January 17, 1996
Austin, Texas*
Legislator, lawyer, educator

UPDATE

Barbara Jordan attained national attention for her role on the House Judiciary Committee during the 1974 impeachment hearings of President Richard M. Nixon (1913–94). Though she had only been in Congress for two years, her abilities gained her a place as keynote speaker at the 1976 Democratic National Convention, and many predicted that she would become the nation's first black female vice president; instead, she retired from politics in 1979. On January 17, 1996, Jordan died of pneumonia that arose as a complication of leukemia. **(See original entry on Jordan in volume 2.)**

Jordan grew up poor in the fifth ward of Houston, Texas, an area that was later depicted in the 1994 film *Jason's Lyric*. Jordan's father, Benjamin, a Baptist minister, maintained strict standards that included no movies, dances, or parties. From her mother, Arlyne, Jordan picked up skills as an orator, which she put to use on her high school debate team. Inspired by

"I believe in brain power, not black power."

black lawyer Edith Sampson (1901–79; see entry in volume 4), who spoke at her school on Career Day, Jordan decided to become a lawyer herself. She attended college at Texas Southern University, and law school at Boston University.

In 1959, Jordan, who had too little money to open an office, started her law practice at the dining room table of her parents' home. She also became involved in Harris County's Democratic party, and after two unsuccessful bids for the state house of representatives in 1962 and 1964, in 1966 she became the first black woman ever elected to the Texas state senate.

In 1972, Jordan ran for Congress and won. As a member of the House Judiciary Committee, the inexperienced congresswoman found herself in the limelight during the 1974 Watergate hearings, and she gained respect with a nationwide audience who tuned in to the proceedings on television. This led to her selection as keynote speaker at the 1976 Democratic National Convention, and to rumors that she might become the nation's first black female vice president (see accompanying sidebar).

This did not happen, however, and in 1979, after just three terms as an enormously popular congresswoman, Jordan retired from politics to become a professor at the Lyndon B. Johnson School of Public Affairs at the University of Texas in Austin. Johnson had lost fifty pounds during her time in Washington, the result of a tough diet; and her weight loss, coupled with her retirement, led to rumors that she was ill. She was not ill, she indicated, but she *was* ready to step out of the spotlight. She returned to Texas, lived quietly in Austin with longtime companion Nancy Earl, and only emerged on the national scene occasionally, as when she again addressed the Democratic National Convention as its keynote speaker in 1992.

Awarded Presidential Medal of Freedom

In 1994, President Bill Clinton (1946–) awarded Jordan the distinguished Presidential Medal of Freedom in recognition of her many achievements. Also that year, Jordan was back in

The first black female vice president?

The *Washington Post* called Barbara Jordan "the first black woman everything." In 1972, she ran for Congress and won, becoming the first black female from the South ever elected to the nation's highest legislative body. Yet she did not present herself as a black woman, but rather as a human being, a fact that upset some African Americans. Jordan, however, responded that she was in favor of "brain power, not black power."

Appointed to the House Judiciary Committee, she soon found herself at the center of one of the major political dramas of the twentieth century. The committee had to decide whether or not President Richard Nixon should be impeached for his role in a break-in at the Democratic National Committee headquarters in Washington's Watergate Hotel prior to the 1972 national elections. In the hearings, Jordan won recognition nationwide as an articulate speaker and a thoughtful legislator. She indicated that she did not like the idea of impeaching a president but, she said, "It is reason and not passion which must guide our decision."

As a result of her fame from the impeachment hearings, the Democratic Party in 1976 made her the first black woman ever to make the keynote address at a national convention. Many speculated that the Democratic presidential candidate, Governor Jimmy Carter of Georgia (1924–), might choose her as his vice presidential candidate. Jordan had plenty of supporters, but she and Carter did not warm up to one another personally. More important, though, was the fact that she did not want the job. A black vice presidential candidate, she said, "would not be a viable political possibility" in 1976; and even if it were, "I really do not have much interest in being a symbol." When Carter finally did offer her a job—that of U.S. ambassador to the United Nations—she turned it down. Carter opted for Minnesota senator Walter Mondale (1928–) as his running mate; eight years later, as the Democratic presidential nominee, Mondale ran—unsuccessfully—with New York congresswoman Geraldine Ferraro (1935–), making her the first woman to be on a major party's presidential ticket.

the public eye, leading efforts to reform immigration policy as chairman of the Commission on Immigration Reform (CIR). Immigration was a sensitive topic. On the one hand, many Americans believed that aliens (people living in one country who are citizens of another country) from Mexico were taking

U.S. jobs, welfare money, and other benefits of citizenship such as free schooling. On the other hand, others believed that such opposition was a form of racial bias. According to CIR executive director Susan Martin, "The chair had to be someone whose intelligence and moral authority is so strong that if she says [a strategy] makes sense, it will be considered seriously."

Many people hoped that Jordan would reemerge nationally, even fifteen years after her retirement from politics. But it was not to be. Jordan had long suffered from multiple sclerosis (a disease that weakens the muscles and leads to paralysis), which had kept her confined to a wheelchair for several years. In the 1990s she was diagnosed with leukemia, a type of cancer. She died on January 17, 1996, of pneumonia, which her doctor said was a complication of the leukemia.

Jordan's funeral service was at the Good Hope Missionary Baptist Church in Houston, where Jordan's father had preached for years. President Clinton recalled how, in the 1974 Watergate hearings, Jordan had referred to the words "We the people," which introduce the U.S. Constitution. "When the document was completed on the 17th of September in 1787," she had said, "I was not included in the 'we'," because most black Americans were then still slaves. In a comment that brought loud applause, Clinton said, "If Barbara wasn't in the Constitution when it was first written, she made sure that once she got in, she stayed in it all the way." Jordan was laid to rest in the State Cemetery in Austin, where other Texas heroes before her had been buried.

Sources for further reading

Barbara Jordan. [Online] http://www.rice.edu/armadillo/Texas/jordan.html (accessed on October 8, 1998).

Blue, Rose. *Barbara Jordan.* Broomall, PA: Chelsea House, 1992.

Bryant, Ira B. *Barbara Charline Jordan: From the Ghetto to the Capitol.* Houston: D. Armstrong Co., 1977.

Franks, Jeff. "Barbara Jordan Remembered as 'American Original'." Reuters, January 20, 1996.

Hines, Cragg. "Barbara Jordan Lived as Pioneer and Prophet." *Houston Chronicle,* January 17, 1996.

Jeffrey, Laura S. *Barbara Jordan: Congresswoman, Lawyer, Educator.* Springfield, NJ: Enslow, 1997.

Johnson, Linda Carlson. *Barbara Jordan: Congresswoman.* Woodbridge, CT: Blackbirch, 1997.

Jordan, Barbara, and Shelby Hearon. *Barbara Jordan, A Self-Portrait.* Garden City, NY: Doubleday, 1979.

Patrick-Wexler, Diane. *Barbara Jordan.* Austin, TX: 1995.

Puente, Maria. "Familiar Voice Leads Way in Reform Effort." *USA Today,* July 14, 1994, p. 5.

Rhodes, Lisa Renee. *Barbara Jordan: Voice of Democracy.* Danbury, CT: Franklin Watts, 1998.

Roberts, Maurice. *Barbara Jordan, The Great Lady from Texas.* Chicago: Childrens Press, 1984.

Rogers, Mary Beth. *Barbara Jordan: American Hero.* New York: Bantam Doubleday Dell, 1998.

Michael Jordan

February 17, 1963
Brooklyn, New York
Basketball player

UPDATE

The most important event for Michael Jordan in the mid-1990s was the murder of his father, James Jordan, on August 3, 1993. This began a period of soul-searching during which Jordan, one of the most successful basketball stars in history, left the Chicago Bulls to play a sport in which he was not a star, baseball. Jordan ultimately returned to his first love, basketball, where he continued to excel. He gained honors both on and off the court, and emerged as a marketing phenomenon. **(See original entry on Jordan in volume 2.)**

Jordan was born in Brooklyn, New York, but grew up in Wilmington, North Carolina. He loved basketball from an early age but—amazing as it may sound now—was too short to make his school's team in ninth grade. Only in his junior year was he tall enough, and he soon emerged as one of the best high school players in the country. This led to a basketball scholarship from the University of North Carolina at Chapel

"My ultimate dream is to get a pot belly. . . . I know it sounds bad and everything, but I've had to stay focused and stay in shape. . . . I just want to . . . sit around and relax, and [not] focus on what I have to do the next day."

Michael Jordan pulls up for a jumper.

Hill (UNC), where he began to attract national attention even during his freshman year.

Jordan played on the U.S. basketball team at the Pan American Games in 1983 and at the 1984 Summer Olympics. Recruited by the Chicago Bulls of the National Basketball Association (NBA), he quit college after his junior year, though he finished his degree in the off-season. Under Jordan's leadership, the Bulls went from being one of the worst teams in the league to being regular NBA champions. He acquired the nickname "Air Jordan" for his ability to seemingly fly toward the hoop, dunking balls effortlessly. Shoemaker Nike began marketing its "Air Jordan" line in 1985, the first of many Jordan product endorsements.

Jordan led the Bulls to their best season ever in 1988, and he won the Most Valuable Player award (MVP) for several years running. Besides his popularity as a celebrity endorser for Nike, he was also seen in ads for Coca-Cola, McDonald's, and other products. Jordan began actively supporting a number of charities through his Michael Jordan Foundation. Not only was he popular for his ability on the court, but even non-sports fans admired him for his lectures on drug abuse, his visits to sick children in hospitals, and his generosity to kids from poor neighborhoods. Then, tragedy struck.

On August 3, 1993, Jordan's father, James, was brutally murdered at a rest stop in North Carolina. The two eighteen-year-olds accused of the murder, Larry Demery and Daniel Green, claimed they had no idea who he was. They were just interested in stealing his car. Green was later sentenced to life in prison, though Demery, who testified against his partner, managed to get a lighter sentence.

Sports kudos

Having retired from basketball in the fall of 1993, Jordan in January 1994 signed on with the Birmingham Barons, a minor league baseball team affiliated with the Chicago White Sox. From a world in which he had been a superstar, Jordan was suddenly in one where, with a .202 batting average, he was far from the best. Many fans criticized him for the move, but many more admired his courage in stepping out to do something new, different, and a little scary.

In part because of his disgust over the baseball strike of 1994, Jordan returned to basketball in April 1995; but he did not stop trying new things. In 1996, he co-starred with—of all "people"—Bugs Bunny in the animated/live-action movie

Comedian Bill Murray, cartoon legend Bugs Bunny, and basketball star Michael Jordan in a scene from Space Jam.

Space Jam, and in 1998 made a cameo appearance in *He Got Game,* directed by Spike Lee (1957– ; see entry in volume 3). Jordan could also be found on the golf course, and though he couldn't give his friend **Tiger Woods** (1975– ; see entry on p. 239) any advice on that particular game, he did find himself giving the younger man advice about how to handle fame. In June 1998, he told *Jet* that he had found a new way to work off tension: playing the piano. Teammate Scottie Pippen complained, "He's up there banging; he's not playing." But Jordan was philosophical: "I can get a note every now and then and feel gifted."

One place where his gifts continue to be without question is on the basketball court. In February 1997, Jordan made basketball history when he received more than 2.45 million all-star votes from fans, well over a half-million votes ahead of the second highest vote-getter. In January 1998, Jordan was voted the most powerful person in sports in a *Sporting News* poll. It was the first time an athlete, as opposed to a coach or a team owner, had led the list. In April of that year, he became only the third player in NBA history, after Kareem Abdul-Jabbar (1947–) and Wilt Chamberlain (1936– , see entry in volume 1) to score 29,000 career points.

Has $10 billion impact on U.S. economy

Jordan's honors extended outside basketball: a 1997 *Wall Street Journal*/NBC poll found that he was the third-most popular person in America. (This poll represented a milestone, in that the top three were all African American men: **Colin Powell** [1937– ; see entry in volume 3, and update on p. 171] and Woods were second and third, respectively.) Back home in North Carolina, part of Interstate-40 was renamed for Jordan, as was the gymnasium at Laney High School—where Jordan had once been unable to make the team.

Jordan continued to support a number of charities through his Michael Jordan Foundation, and he was heavily involved in business as well. It seemed that everything Jordan touched turned to gold. Perhaps for that reason, Oakley, a sunglasses manufacturer, asked him to join its board of directors in September 1995. In 1996, Jordan became the highest-paid player in the NBA when he signed a one-year contract for $30 million with the Bulls. But this was less than the $38 million he would earn that year in endorsements for Nike, Wheaties, Gatorade, and other products. Together with Nike, in 1997, he launched his own line of athletic shoes and clothing, which was expected to generate $250 million in sales during its first year.

Fortune magazine reported in June 1998 that Jordan had a $10 billion impact on the U.S. economy. He generated an estimated $5.2 billion in sales for Nike alone—not to mention $3.1 billion in increased sales of NBA-licensed products, such as caps.

After winning his sixth NBA championship with the Bulls in 1998, Jordan hinted that he may retire. As for the future, Jordan sees himself as a role-model and has suggested that he might become more involved in social issues after he retires. "I want to go to Southeast Asia to see the Nike plants for myself," he told *ESPN* magazine in 1998. (There have been claims that Nike factories in Asia underpay and mistreat their workers. For more about the Nike controversy, see the entry on Andrew Young, p. 249.) "I really think that when I'm done," he continued, "I will take a bigger stand in social and political things."

But what is the ultimate dream of the man who seemingly has everything, including a wife and three children? "This is going to sound wild," he told Keenan Ivory Wayans (1958–) in March 1998, "but my ultimate dream is to get a pot belly.... I know it sounds bad and everything, but I've had to stay focused and stay in shape, and I've never really gotten out of shape. I just want to get a pot belly, sit around and relax, and [not] focus on what I have to do the next day."

Sources for further reading

Burton, Elizabeth, with Lynn Offerdahl. *Cinderfella & the Slam Dunk Contest* (fiction; illustrated). Boston: Branden Pub. Co., 1994.

Dolan, Sean. *Michael Jordan* (introductory essay by Coretta Scott King). New York: Chelsea House, 1994.

Ellis, David, Linda Kramer, and Brant Clifton. "Justice Delayed: The Alleged Killers of James Jordan Still Await Arraignment." *People,* August 22, 1994, p. 77.

"Friends, Fans Salute Michael Jordan During Chicago Tribute at New Stadium." *Jet,* November 21, 1994, p. 54.

"Green Sentenced to Life in Prison for Murder of James Jordan." *Jet,* April 1, 1996, p. 36.

Hoover, Ala. "Jordan Will Take Another Swing: Mr. Basketball Finds Fulfillment as Baseball's Mr. Average." *Washington Post,* August 31, 1994, p. B-1.

Jordan, Michael. *I Can't Accept Not Trying: Michael Jordan on the Pursuit of Excellence.* San Francisco: HarperSanFrancisco, 1994.

Jordan, Michael. *Rare Air: Michael on Michael.* San Francisco: HarperSanFrancisco, 1993.

"Jordan Takes Piano Over Golf for Relaxation." *Jet,* June 22, 1998, p. 50.

Knapp, Ron. *Michael Jordan: Star Guard.* Hillside, NJ: Enslow Publishers, 1994.

Kornbluth, Jesse. *Airborne Again!: The Triumph and Struggle of Michael Jordan.* New York: Aladdin Paperbacks, 1996.

Krulik, Nancy E. *Space Jam.* New York: Scholastic Inc., 1996.

Lazenby, Roland. *Yo, Baby, It's Attitude!: The New Bad Boyz of the NBA Take the Jordan Test.* Lenexa, KS: Addax Pub. Group, 1997.

"Michael Jordan Has $10 Billion Impact on U.S. Economy." *Jet,* June 22, 1998, p. 48.

"Michael Jordan Reveals He Gives Advice to Golf Sensation Tiger Woods." *Jet,* May 5, 1997, p. 50.

The Michael Jordan Ring. [Online] http://www.bomis.com/rings/bulls_jordan/ring_home.html (accessed on October 8, 1998).

"Michael Jordan Says His Ultimate Dream Is to Spend More Time 'Watching My Kids Grow Up.'" *Jet,* March 9, 1998, p. 34.

"Michael Jordan Says 'I'm Back for the Love of the Game!'" *Jet,* April 10, 1995, p. 51.

"Michael Jordan Talks About Playing Reggie Miller, Family, and the End of His NBA Career." *Jet,* April 20, 1998, p. 51.

The Official Michael Jordan Web Site–CBS SportsLine. [Online] http://jordan.sportsline.com (accessed on October 8, 1998).

Owens, Thomas S. *Michael Jordan: Legendary Guard.* New York: PowerKids Press, 1997.

"Powell, Woods, Jordan Most Popular Americans." *Jet,* May 19, 1997, p. 5.

"Ties to Michael Jordan Still Remain in His Hometown of Wilmington, NC." *Jet,* June 23, 1997, p. 50.

Alan Keyes

*Born August 7, 1950
New York, New York*

Politician, lecturer, author

Alan Keyes first attracted widespread national attention in 1996, when he ran for president of the United States as a Republican, becoming that party's first African American presidential candidate in the twentieth century.

Being a black Republican is unusual enough (see accompanying sidebar), but even within a party known as a stronghold of American conservatism, Keyes's staunch "family values" campaign was too conservative for many. Central to Keyes's political position was a belief that abortion should be outlawed, and that American morality should be influenced through politics. To some, Keyes is a dangerous enemy of free speech who wants to impose his own values on the rest of the country; to others, his voice is a breath of fresh air in the confused climate of American politics.

Growing up as an "army brat"

Keyes was born in New York City, the youngest of five children. Keyes's father was in the U.S. Army, so the Keyes fam-

"If folks become more involved at the community level, in our families, in our churches, in our community organizations, we can restore this nation as an environment conducive to a good family life."

ily moved around a great deal when he was a child. At various times they lived in Italy and in a number of stateside locations, including San Antonio, Texas, where Keyes attended high school in the mid-1960s. A good student, he became president of the student council, and at the age of sixteen, was elected the first African American president of the American Legion Boys Nation. This organization was founded in 1946 by the American Legion, a military veterans' group, to promote citizenship and patriotism among American youth. Among the other well-known members of Boys Nation, ironically, was President Bill Clinton (1946–), who, as a teenager, traveled with the group to Washington, D.C., where he met then-President John F. Kennedy (1917–63). Already a political conservative, Keyes won a Boys Nation contest for a speech in which he defended American participation in the Vietnam War (1954–75), which by then had become highly unpopular among many young people.

Keyes attended Cornell University in New York, where he studied under humanities professor Allan Bloom, who later wrote the 1987 bestseller *The Closing of the American Mind*. In 1969, when Keyes was a freshman, black students at Cornell took over the university's student center. In his book, Bloom condemned this and similar acts, which were common in the late 1960s. The gun-wielding students, Bloom wrote, used brute force in a place where people were supposed to resolve their differences with reason, not violence. Keyes, too, was horrified by these actions, and quit the school's African American Society. This earned him so much harassment from fellow black students that he left Cornell.

Rises in the U.S. State Department

Keyes spent a year in Paris, then returned to the United States to enroll at Harvard University, where he earned his Ph.D. degree in political science in 1979. In 1978 he went to work for the U.S. State Department, which manages relations between the United States and other countries. As a desk officer for southern African affairs, he angered a number of American civil rights leaders because he opposed economic sanctions against South Africa. At that time, South Africa was

Alan Keyes has become well-known for his powerful public speaking style.

dominated by a system of white racism called apartheid (pronounced "uh-PAR-tide"). African American leaders such as Jesse Jackson (1941– ; see entry in volume 2) urged President Ronald Reagan (1911–) to punish the South African government by imposing economic sanctions—that is, by refusing to sell American goods to the South Africans. Reagan and Keyes, however, argued that if the United States cut off economic

Left, right—Which way is up?

Nobody who follows politics for very long can avoid hearing the terms "Right" and "Left," along with a similar pairing, "conservative" and "liberal." These words may seem hard to understand in their political context, and indeed they confuse many people. Even the dictionary does not offer much help, because in practice the words sometimes mean different things.

Many people use the first set of terms interchangeably with the second pair, equating liberals with the Left and conservatives with the Right. This is often correct, but not always. "Right" and "Left" are easier to define, because they describe two different sets of *values.* "Liberal" and "conservative," though, identify two different practical approaches to political situations.

Generally speaking, the Right places a high value on tradition and on traditional institutions. The slogan "For God and Country" suggests a right-wing viewpoint. The Right emphasizes the family and institutions—such as the church, the police, and the military—that help to preserve order in a society. The Left, on the other hand, places a high value on *ideals,* such as justice, equality, and unity, rather than on institutions.

Liberals usually have left-wing values, and conservatives usually have right-wing values. But unlike "Right" and "Left," definitions of "liberal" and "conservative" tend to change with the times. Virtually all of America's great presidential leaders, from George Washington (1732–99) and Thomas Jefferson (1743–1826) to Abraham Lincoln (1809–65) and John F. Kennedy (1917–63) were considered liberals in their day, but would probably be viewed as conservatives if they were around in the 1990s.

Dictionary definitions of "liberal" and "conservative" are not very helpful in describing the actual behavior of liberals and conservatives in American politics. In general, in recent decades, liberals have tended to belong to the Democratic Party, while conservatives have belonged to the Republican Party. But this, too, has changed with

ties, the South African government would simply purchase its goods elsewhere. As a result, the U.S. government would miss an opportunity to influence affairs in South Africa.

From the desk officer position, Keyes next became a member of the State Department's Policy Planning Council.

time. Democrats were the chief supporters of the Civil Rights Movement in the 1960s, but Southern Democrats supported slavery in the years leading up to the Civil War (1861–65). The Republican Party, on the other hand, was the home of anti-slavery Abolitionists before the Civil War, and remained the favored party of African Americans until the 1930s. But Republican opposition to affirmative action (an effort to improve employment and educational opportunities for minority groups) in the 1980s and 1990s has not helped the party's standing with many black voters.

Though studies show that most African Americans tend to be conservative about many issues, they still vote overwhelmingly for Democratic candidates. This is in part due to the leadership of popular Democrat Jesse Jackson, who ran for president in 1984 and 1988. But in the 1990s, many African Americans began questioning blacks' seemingly total loyalty to a single political party. Some believed that Democrats had come to assume that they would receive the majority of black votes, and had quit working as hard for their African American constituents.

At the same time, some analysts saw a rise in black conservatism, symbolized in part by Keyes's presidential candidacy. But other observers questioned whether this was really happening. For instance, a 1995 article in the liberal magazine *Nation* suggested that the large number of conservative blacks did not mean that there was a growing "black conservative movement." Certainly black conservatives were few in number, and did not enjoy widespread support in the African American community. But the movement appeared to be there.

African Americans are even presented with a third option in the person of Minister **Louis Farrakhan** (1933– ; see entry in volume 2, and update on p. 71) and his Nation of Islam, a group that identifies itself with neither political party.

Then he was appointed U.S. ambassador to the United Nations Educational, Scientific, and Cultural Organization (UNESCO), from which he moved to a position as assistant secretary of state for international organizational affairs. By 1987, Keyes was the highest-ranking African American in the State Department; but that year he abruptly quit after a dispute with Deputy

African American conservatives—Who are they?

In 1997, the African American conservative magazine *Headway* published its list of the "20 Most Influential Black Conservatives." Along with Keyes, these included Supreme Court Justice Clarence Thomas; economists Walter Williams (1936–) and Thomas Sowell (1930–); Democratic congressman Floyd Flake (1945–) of New York and Republican congressman J. C. Watts (1957–) of Oklahoma; historian Shelby Steele (1946–); and pro basketball player Charles Barkley (1963–), who has suggested that he might run as a Republican for governor of his home state, Alabama.

Absent from the list, but still important public figures, were civil rights activists Roy Innis (1934– ; see entry in volume 2) and James Meredith (1933– ; see entry in volume 3); as well as radio talk-show hosts Ken Hamblin (1940–) and Armstrong Williams; television commentator Tony Brown (1933–); and scholar Glenn Loury. Then there is the most popular "black conservative" of all (though far less conservative than most people on the list): Colin Powell.

Many of these figures are routinely attacked by Jesse Jackson and other civil rights leaders, who consider them servants of the white establishment because they favor an end to affirmative action and drastic cuts to welfare. In fact, these conservatives believe welfare and affirmative action are simply more ways for black people to be dependent on whites, as opposed to making opportunities for themselves. Conservative radio talk-show host John Doggett believes the Republicans Party's principles are similar to those of Marcus Garvey (1887–1940; see entry in volume 2) and Malcolm X (1925–63; see entry in volume 3). On the other hand, without federal programs such as the Job Corps, boxer **George Foreman** (1949– ; see entry on p. 81) might never have won the heavyweight title; likewise government-funded food stamps sustained **Tina Turner** (1939– ; see entry on p. 217) following her breakup with her husband, Ike.

Secretary of State John C. Whitehead (1922–), who Keyes said had treated him badly because he was black.

Two Senate runs and a talk show

In 1988, Keyes, who had settled in Maryland, ran for the U.S. Senate against Paul Sarbanes (1933–). Sarbanes was a

Democrat in a heavily Democratic state. He was also the incumbent (a person already holding the position), which made him an especially tough candidate to defeat. Keyes won 38 percent of the vote, a strong showing considering the odds.

During the next few years, Keyes served as a member of an organization called Citizens Against Government Waste. He also earned a reputation as a powerful speaker, just like his political opposite, Jesse Jackson. In 1992, Keyes again ran for the Senate, this time against the other incumbent, Democrat Barbara Mikulski (1938–). Keyes lost, receiving only 29 percent of the vote. He also became involved in a scandal when supporters learned that he had paid himself a monthly salary of $8,500 from campaign donations, and had failed to repay a $44,500 debt to the campaign fund. A year later, Keyes became host of his own successful radio talk show in Baltimore, *America's Wake-Up Call: The Alan Keyes Show.*

Runs for president

On March 26, 1995, Keyes announced his candidacy for president. A Catholic, Keyes ran as a religious conservative, gaining the support of the so-called religious Right—that is, Christians who are on the "right" side of the political spectrum (see accompanying sidebar for more on "right" and "left").

The "religious Right" is mostly white, and as in his two Senate races, when black voters tended to support Democratic candidates, Keyes's chief support came from whites. His opposition to affirmative action and his support of controversial African American Supreme Court Justice Clarence Thomas (1948– ; see entry in volume 4) won Keyes few friends among the civil rights leadership. Even among white conservatives, he lacked the appeal of **Colin Powell** (1937– ; see entry in volume 3, and update on p. 171), who many considered a possible Republican candidate in 1996.

Linda Feldman of the *Christian Science Monitor* called Keyes "hands down, the best orator in a crowded Republican field, a Jesse Jackson of the right, only without the rhymes."

As for his earlier campaign-finance problems, he had solved those by not paying himself a salary. Yet his actions in the 1988 senate race cost him a great deal of support.

Keyes's presidential candidacy generated few votes. (Former U.S. senator Bob Dole [1923–] won the Republican nomination.) But Keyes gained a place in the national spotlight, which helped draw attention to the Black America's Political Action Committee (BAMPAC), a group he founded in 1993 to help black conservatives in their campaigns for public office. After the 1996 elections, Keyes continued to work as a radio talk-show host and lecturer. Since 1981 he has been married to Joyce Martel; they have three children.

Sources for further reading

Contemporary Black Biography, Volume 11. Detroit: Gale, 1996, pp. 145–47.

Feldman, Linda. "Alan Keyes." *Christian Science Monitor,* January 11, 1996, p. 10.

Ireland, Doug. "Alan Keyes Does the Hustle." *Nation,* October 30, 1995, pp. 500–503.

Keyes, Alan. *Masters of the Dream: The Strength and Betrayal of Black America.* New York: Morrow, 1995.

Keyes, Alan. *Our Character, Our Future: Reclaiming America's Moral Destiny.* Grand Rapids, MI: Zondervan, 1996.

"Media Focuses on Conservative GOPer Alan Keyes in 1996 Presidential Race." *Jet,* April 17, 1995, p. 6.

Newsmakers, 1996 cumulation. Detroit: Gale, 1997.

Terry McMillan

Born October 18, 1951
Port Huron, Michigan
Novelist, screenwriter

UPDATE

In the early 1990s, Terry McMillan published a number of successful novels, including *Waiting to Exhale* (1992). The mid-1990s saw the spread of her fame as that book became an enormously popular 1995 movie starring Angela Bassett (1958–), Whitney Houston (1963– ; see entry in volume 2), Loretta Devine, and Lela Rochon (1966–). In the mid-1990s, McMillan experienced some extreme ups and downs in her personal life. In 1996, she wrote another bestseller, *How Stella Got Her Groove Back* (1996), whose storyline resembled her own life. In 1998, this book, too, became a movie starring Bassett, with McMillan writing the screenplay, as she had done with *Waiting to Exhale*. **(See original entry on McMillan in volume 3.)**

McMillan was born into a working-class family in Michigan in 1951. Her mother divorced her father, a violent alcoholic, when McMillan was thirteen years old. Soon afterward, a job at a local library inspired McMillan's first interest

"I exhale every day and count my blessings."

in books. She moved to California after high school, and began writing.

At the University of California at Berkeley, McMillan studied journalism, and in 1976, the year she graduated, she published her first short story. She moved east to work on her master's degree at Columbia University in New York City, but left the school because she felt it was racist. In 1984, she and her lover, Leonard Welch, had a son they named Solomon. Meanwhile, McMillan had begun work on her first novel, *Mama,* which she completed the following year.

In part because of her promotional efforts, the book was a success, and in 1987 she accepted a position at the University of Wyoming as a visiting writer. By this time her relationship with Welch was coming to an end, but Welch would later charge that she used elements of it in the plot of her next novel, *Disappearing Acts* (1989). In 1990 he filed an unsuccessful $4.75 million defamation suit against her, claiming that she had used the story to get revenge on him in public. With *Waiting to Exhale* two years later, McMillan continued themes she had begun developing in her first two novels: of strong, independent women whose only real problem is the men in their life.

Personal tragedy, book and movie successes

By early 1996, *Waiting to Exhale* had sold more than three million copies, and was at the number one position on the paperback bestseller lists. But McMillan herself experienced personal tragedy. In September 1993, her mother, Madeline, died suddenly of an asthma attack. McMillan, who was on an author tour at the time, had spoken to her mother on the phone just a few hours before her death, and nothing had seemed to be wrong then. Later she told *People* magazine, "Do you know how hard it is to take your mother out of your address book?" Distraught over her loss, McMillan stopped work on her novel *A Day Late and a Dollar Short,* which featured a character very much like her mother. Then, in Septem-

Works of Terry McMillan

Mama. Boston: Houghton Mifflin, 1987.

Disappearing Acts. New York: Viking, 1989.

Waiting to Exhale. New York: Viking, 1992.

How Stella Got Her Groove Back. Rockland, MA: Wheeler Pub., 1996.

---

ber 1994, McMillan lost her best friend, New York City novelist Doris Jean Austin, who died of liver cancer.

Meanwhile, her professional reputation soared with the 1995 release of the movie *Waiting to Exhale,* which took in some $70 million at the box office. McMillan, still reeling from her personal losses, went to Negril, Jamaica, for an extended vacation and a chance to do some thinking. It was there that she met Jonathan Plummer.

Later, when she published *How Stella Got Her Groove Back,* fans would see parallels between Plummer and the character of Winston Shakespeare: both were Jamaican, both were young men in their twenties "whose encounter with a certain rich, 40-plus single woman," in the words of *People* magazine, "helps transport her from loneliness to joy." McMillan herself downplayed the similarities; whatever the case, she met Plummer, and soon afterward—again, much like the book—he came to live with her in California. The two were married on September 5, 1998, on a beach in Maui, Hawaii.

McMillan wrote *How Stella Got Her Groove Back* quickly after returning from Jamaica, and the book proved even more successful than McMillan's other works. Authors usually receive an advance from their publishers, a sum based on what the publisher thinks the book will earn; McMillan's advance for *Stella* was more than $1 million, as was the fee paid by 20th Century Fox to make the movie. She wrote the script, as she had done on *Waiting to Exhale,* and announced plans to complete *A Day Late and a Dollar Short*. Plans were also in the works for a movie of *Disappearing Acts,* with a screenplay also to be written by McMillan. "I exhale every day," she told *People* in February 1996, "and count my blessings. I'm grateful to God, my mom, and anyone else out in the ozone who caused all this good fortune to come my way."

Sources for further reading

Contemporary Black Biography, Volume 17. Detroit: Gale, 1998.

How Stella Got Her Groove Back (motion picture). 20th Century Fox, 1998.

Hubbard, Kim, and Penelope Rowlands. "On Top of Her Game: A New Book and a New Guy Have Terry McMillan Breathing Easy." *People,* April 29, 1996, p. 111.

"Talking with . . . Terry McMillan." *People,* February 5, 1996.

Waiting to Exhale (motion picture). 20th Century Fox, 1995.

"Whitney Houston, Angela Bassett, Lela Rochon, Loretta Devine Star in 'Waiting to Exhale.'" *Jet,* December 25, 1995–January 1, 1996, p. 22.

Ronald McNair

Born October 21, 1950
Lake City, South Carolina
Died January 28, 1986
Near Cape Canaveral, Florida
Astronaut, physicist, astronomer

Ronald McNair initially became famous as America's second black astronaut, after Guy Bluford (1942–). In February 1984, he made his first space flight on the *Challenger* shuttle. (A space shuttle is a vehicle that looks like a cross between a rocket and airplane; it orbits the Earth for a period of days or weeks before returning home.) McNair was later assigned to his second flight, again aboard the *Challenger*—on January 28, 1986.

The flight attracted great public interest, largely because its seven-member crew would include the first civilian in space, teacher Christa McAuliffe (1948–86). Up to that time, all astronauts had either been in the military, or like McNair, employees of the National Aeronautics and Space Administration (NASA), which operates space flights. When *Challenger* lifted off at 11:38 on the morning of January 28, a large national audience was watching—and a nation reacted in horror as the shuttle exploded and crashed into the Atlantic Ocean, killing everyone on board.

"The true courage of space flight . . . is not sitting aboard 6 million [pounds] of fire and thunder as one rockets away from this planet. True courage comes in enduring . . . and believing in oneself."

Dreamed of space flight as a child

Growing up in Lake City, South Carolina, McNair was fascinated with space flight from an early age. In 1957, when he was seven years old, the Soviet Union launched *Sputnik,* the first satellite to orbit the earth. It was the beginning of the "space race" between the Soviet Union and the United States, and for McNair it was the beginning of an obsession. "That's all Ronald talked about—Sputnik, Sputnik, Sputnik," a classmate later told *Ebony.* "We got tired of hearing it."

McNair, who had learned to read when he was just four years old, also read comic books and stories about outer space, and avidly followed the competition between the superpower countries. In 1958, the United States launched its first satellite, *Explorer.* The Soviets put the first living creature into space, a dog named Laika in the late 1950s; the first man, Yuri Gagarin (1934–68) in 1961; and later, even the first woman, Valentina Tereshkova (1937–) in 1963. Meanwhile Alan B. Shepard (1923–98) became the first American in space in May 1961, and the following year, John Glenn (1921–) orbited the Earth in a space capsule. (America did not put a woman into space until 1983, when Sally Ride [1951–] went up in the space shuttle.)

As a student, McNair developed his interests in science. His parents stressed the importance of education, and his father taught him car repair, which gave him a basic knowledge of engineering. Less exciting was his work picking beans and cotton in the summers, but it allowed him to earn a few dollars. Opportunities were limited for a young black man in South Carolina in 1962, when McNair entered the segregated Carver High School in Lake City. Nonetheless, he excelled in his studies, as well as in athletics.

Joins space program

In 1967, McNair started school at North Carolina Agricultural and Technical State University, a predominantly black school whose most famous graduate is the Rev. Jesse Jackson (1941– ; see entry in volume 2). In his junior year, McNair had a breakthrough opportunity when he participated

Cheryl and Ronald McNair share some quiet moments only two days before the Challenger *disaster.*

in a one-year exchange program initiated by the Massachusetts Institute of Technology (MIT), one of the world's most prestigious technically oriented universities. MIT arranged to bring promising students such as McNair from minority schools in the South, and sent instructors from MIT's Boston, Massachusetts, campus to teach at schools such as North Carolina A&T.

Following his graduation in 1971, McNair returned to MIT as a graduate student. He received his doctorate in physics in 1976, and married Cheryl Moore soon afterward. The couple moved to Malibu, California, where McNair worked for Hughes Research Laboratories, a large contractor with the U.S. Defense Department. McNair heard that NASA was looking for astronaut candidates, and he decided to apply. He knew that his chances were slim—over 10,000 people had applied, and out of that number only a few dozen would be selected to receive training. But McNair was one of those few.

In 1978, the McNairs moved to Houston, Texas, where McNair began six years of training at the Johnson Space Flight Center. During those years, he and his wife had two children. In February 1984, McNair made his first space flight, on which he was responsible for conducting a number of tests. His next flight was the January 28, 1986, *Challenger* launch.

The *Challenger* tragedy

Problems had plagued mission control at the Kennedy Space Center in Cape Canaveral, Florida, in the days leading up to January 28. The weather had been bad, and temperatures were unusually low for that part of Florida. But NASA chose to go ahead with the launch: largely because of McAuliffe, much of the nation—especially schoolchildren—were watching. The launch was a great public relations spectacle for 1986, which NASA had planned to be one of its biggest years ever. Among other events that year, NASA would be observing the return of Halley's Comet, which passes the earth once every seventy-six years. McNair was responsible for putting in place a telescopic camera to photograph special pictures of the comet.

What the *Challenger* crew did not know was that the spacecraft had a fuel leak after a rubber gasket called an O-ring had come loose. Just two minutes after liftoff, when *Challenger* was nine miles in the air, the spacecraft exploded, and the orbiter capsule carrying the astronauts careened into the ocean.

A lawsuit and a legacy

Later it was discovered that officials at NASA and Morton Thiokol, the company responsible for the O-rings, knew that the gaskets were defective at temperatures below 51 degrees Fahrenheit. But they had decided to go ahead anyway, a fact that would greatly hurt NASA's credibility for many years. (NASA had planned to send up fifteen shuttle flights in 1986, but after the *Challenger* explosion it was three years before another shuttle went up.)

As for Morton Thiokol, it became the target of lawsuits from the families of the seven victims. Cheryl McNair was the first to file a suit, and the company later settled with her and with the family of Judith Resnick (1949–86) for several million dollars. Over the following years, it would pay many millions more to the McAuliffes, and the families of the other four crew members, Gregory B. Jarvis (1944–86), Ellison Onizuka (1946–86), Dick Scobee (1939–86), and Mike Smith (1945–86)—all because of a $900 synthetic rubber gasket.

The first of many tributes to the *Challenger* crew came from President Ronald Reagan (1911–), who was scheduled to give his annual State of the Union address that night, but instead spoke about the tragedy. McNair, who had been honored in his lifetime by the renaming of Lake City's Main Street, was memorialized in several ways. His hometown renamed its high school—long since integrated—after McNair, and MIT christened its Center for Space Research the Ronald E. McNair Building. In Brooklyn, New York, a park was named in his honor, and in 1994, a nine-foot memorial to him was unveiled. There is also a Ronald McNair Elementary School in Germantown, Maryland; and McNair, like the other six *Challenger* crew members, has a crater on the moon named after him.

But no doubt McNair's greatest legacy lies with his family. Cheryl works with the Challenger Center for Space Science Exploration, a Houston-based group founded by a fellow *Challenger* widow, June Scobee, to educate kids about math and science. She is also involved with a foundation for unwed teenage mothers; but her primary responsibility is to her own two teenagers, who were so young at the time of their father's death that they barely remember him. She told *Ebony* in 1996, "Ron left a legacy for his children and the nation. The legacy of inspiration and motivation. The legacy of a person who achieved against difficult odds. He has really been an inspiration to me. I know that no matter how discouraging the situation, I have to keep trying."

Sources for further reading

Dowling, Claudia. "Ten Years Ago Seven Brave Americans Died As They Reached for the Stars." *Life,* February 1996, pp. 38–43.

Haskins, Jim. *One More River to Cross: The Stories of Twelve Black Americans.* New York: Scholastic, 1992.

Kessler, James H., et al. *Distinguished African American Scientists of the 20th Century.* Phoenix, AZ: Oryx Press, 1996, pp. 249–53.

"Monument Honoring Memory of Space Shuttle Astronaut Dr. Ronald McNair Unveiled in Refurbished Brooklyn Park." *Jet,* July 11, 1994, p. 26.

Naden, Corinne. (Introductory essay by Coretta Scott King). *Ronald McNair.* New York: Chelsea House, 1990.

Shaw, Dena. *Ronald McNair.* New York: Chelsea House, 1994.

Townsel, Lisa Jones, and Kevin Chappel. "Cheryl McNair: Transcending the *Challenger* Disaster." *Ebony,* May 1996, p. 94.

Thelma "Butterfly" McQueen

Born January 8, 1911
Tampa, Florida
Died December 22, 1995
Augusta, Georgia
Actress

UPDATE

Thelma "Butterfly" McQueen, best known for her portrayal of the maid Prissy in the 1939 movie *Gone with the Wind*, died on December 22, 1995, when a kerosene heater exploded in her three-room bungalow in Augusta, Georgia. She was eighty-four years old. **(See original entry on McQueen in volume 3.)**

McQueen was born in Tampa, Florida, in 1911. Her father, who hauled cargo on the Tampa docks, left home when she was five years old. Eventually she and her mother relocated to New York City's Harlem district, and by the time McQueen was thirteen, they had settled in Long Island.

Though she studied nursing after high school, acting was McQueen's dream. In 1935, she appeared in the "Butterfly Ballet," which gave her a nickname that stuck, and in 1937 she made her Broadway debut in the murder drama *Brown Sugar*. It was the first of several roles in which she was cast as a maid, the typical role for black women at that time. In 1939,

"[The] fluttering hands and eyelids [of McQueen's Prissy] were a wicked satirization of the very mistress whom she served, Scarlett O'Hara."

—Journalist Syl Jones

How do blacks view *Gone with the Wind*?

Butterfly McQueen became famous in the 1939 film *Gone with the Wind* as Prissy, Southern belle Scarlett O'Hara's shiftless, whiny maid who didn't "know nothin' 'bout birthin' no babies." The movie was set partly during the Civil War (1861–65), and Prissy and all the other blacks in the movie were slaves.

At that time, blacks were depicted either as foolish scatterbrains, like Prissy, or as dangerous outlaws, like the freed slaves who attempt to rape a white girl in D. W. Griffith's *Birth of a Nation* (1915). Because of its screenplay and its production, *Birth of a Nation* is often considered the first great motion picture in history; but it was also a racist epic, and its release—which some African Americans at the time protested—led to the reestablishment of the Ku Klux Klan in Stone Mountain, Georgia.

In fact, the "blacks" in *Birth of a Nation* were played by white actors in blackface (make-up that made them appear black). As for black actors themselves, they had few choices but to play servants or slaves; the only difference between the two seemed to rest on whether the movie was set before or after 1865. Had McQueen not accepted the role of Prissy in *Gone with the Wind,* it is hard to imagine how she could have attained the international fame she did.

Still, most black viewers considered the role of Prissy a demeaning one. At least Hattie McDaniel (1895–1952; see entry in volume 3), who played Mammy, the other main black female role in the movie, got to boss Miss Scarlett. Mammy seemed wise in comparison to her often immature mistress, while Prissy's foolishness and laziness fit with what many white people at the time thought about blacks. For this reason—and the obvious fact that the movie seemed to glorify the system of slavery—*Gone with the Wind* has had few African American defenders.

---

she appeared as Prissy, Scarlett O'Hara's squeaky-voiced maid in *Gone with the Wind*. The movie became one of the most popular of all time, and McQueen would long be remembered for her famous line: "Miss Scarlett, I don't know nothin' 'bout birthin' no babies."

Her fame was a mixed blessing. Though she was proud of her success, McQueen hated the stereotypes her role had

Gone with the Wind is an epic love story, the tale of a strong, selfish woman and the men she loves. It is set against the sweeping drama of a war and the aftermath of that conflict. In 1998, the movie was re-released in a technically enhanced version. Jack Garner of Gannett News Service wrote: "The skies over burning Atlanta haven't been this vibrantly red since the original release in 1939." As for the movie, "At this point, the film itself would seem to be beyond reviewing. It is a legendary movie, and needs to be seen." But there was that old demon again: "The exaggerated shiftlessness of [Prissy]," wrote Garner, ". . . doesn't age as well [as the rest of the movie]; it's one of the aspects that has made racial attitudes in 'Gone with the Wind' problematic for modern audiences."

Many blacks saw it as more than "problematic." But Syl Jones of the *Star Tribune* offered a different perspective in a tribute to McQueen shortly after her death. Referring to McQueen and McDaniel, he said, "Hatred of [the film's] message does not include condemnation of its black stars. . . . To them we owe a debt of gratitude that will never be repaid." He particularly singled out McQueen for praise, and found in her exaggerated behavior a subtle mockery of Prissy's white "owner." Her "fluttering hands and eyelids," Jones wrote, "were a wicked satirization of the very mistress whom she served, Scarlett O'Hara."

At the time of Jones's writing, the film *Waiting to Exhale* had recently been released. Based on a novel by **Terry McMillan** (see entry in volume 3, and update on p. 155), which depicted four intelligent, successful black women, the film showed how far African Americans had come. "Today," Jones concluded, "'Waiting to Exhale' marks a kind of coming-out party for black actresses as well as black women. But Whitney Houston [1963– ; see entry in volume 2], Angela Bassett [1959–] et al. might never have gotten the chance to hold their collective breath on screen if not for the pioneering performances of Butterfly McQueen."

helped to promote. Eventually she refused to play any more maid roles, which meant an end to her acting career. During the 1950s and 1960s, she acted in stage productions and on TV, and sometimes had to work jobs that ranged from running a restaurant to selling toys at Macy's.

Meanwhile, actors such as **Dorothy Dandridge** (1992–65; see entry on p. 47) and Sidney Poitier (1927– ; see entry in volume 3) opened up new opportunities for African Americans on the screen. By the 1970s, McQueen was able to return to acting. But her real comeback only happened in the 1980s, as a result of celebrations marking the fiftieth anniversaries of the novel and movie versions of *Gone with the Wind*. She became a frequent TV talk show guest, and appeared in a few movies, including *Mosquito Coast* in 1986.

Dies in a Fire

By the early 1990s, McQueen had made her winter home of Augusta her permanent home. She owned rental property as well as two homes. Having never married, she lived quietly in a small, wooden cottage, and enjoyed the warm weather year-round. On December 22, 1995, the kerosene heater in her house ignited. Neighbors said they heard two explosions, which probably came from two five-gallon containers of kerosene that she kept for her portable heaters. The blast blew the windows out, and the house was engulfed in flames. McQueen suffered third-degree burns, and died in the hospital ten hours later.

McQueen was a generous woman. Her two wills specified that her rental houses be given to the tenants living in them; that her various awards be donated to the Schomberg Center for Research at the New York Public Library; and that the contents of her bank accounts should go to the American Society for the Prevention of Cruelty to Animals and the Freedom from Religion Foundation in Madison, Wisconsin.

Controversy Surrounding Death

Her donations to the Freedom from Religion Foundation caused a controversy. McQueen had long proclaimed herself an atheist (one who doesn't believe in a god). She had even been quoted once as comparing religion with slavery. But some of McQueen's friends claimed that the actress "had returned to her roots" and her Christian upbringing in the weeks preceding her death.

This was not the only controversy surrounding McQueen's death. Friends charged that in the confusion of the fire, a number of people had looted her home, stealing personal papers and other memorabilia. "One person literally backed a truck up to the place while the fire was still going," claimed one friend.

In April 1996, a sale of McQueen's belongings was held, with the proceeds going to the creation of a bronze plaque in her honor. Confusion surrounded the sale, however, because of the looting and the fact that she had not left a detailed list of her possessions. The same year, McQueen was honored with a Hall of Fame Award from the National Association for the Advancement of Colored People (NAACP).

Sources for further reading

"Butterfly McQueen Remembered." *Freethought Today,* January/February 1996. [Online] http://www.infidels.org/org/ffrf/fttoday/jan_feb96/butterfly.html (accessed on October 8, 1998).

"Clothes Ignite, Butterfly McQueen Dies." *USA Today,* December 26, 1995.

Garner, Jack. "'Gone with the Wind' Deserves This Re-Release." Gannett News Service, June 24, 1998.

Jones, Syl. "Despite Hating Her Big Film, Blacks Owe a Debt to McQueen." *Star Tribune,* December 31, 1995, p. 19A.

Kane, Gregory P. "'Gone with the Wind': Racism Just One of Its Faults." *Star Tribune,* July 9, 1998.

McCarthy, Rebecca. "Remains of Actress's Estate a Mystery: Tracking Down GWTW Player's Belongings Futile." *Atlanta Journal and Constitution,* December 18, 1996, p. D7.

McCarthy, Rebecca. "Some Fear McQueen's Home Looted After Death." *Atlanta Journal and Constitution,* December 30, 1995, p. A1.

Morehouse, Macon. "Butterfly McQueen Dies of Burns." *Atlanta Journal and Constitution,* December 23, 1995, p. A1.

Smith, Jessie Carney, ed. *Notable Black American Women.* Detroit: Gale, 1992, pp. 710–15.

Warner, Jack. "Actress McQueen's Charred Belongings Go on Sale at Hotel." *Atlanta Journal and Constitution,* April 13, 1996, p. E4.

Colin Powell

*Born April 5, 1937
Harlem, New York*

*Army officer,
chairman of the Joint Chiefs of Staff*

UPDATE

Every election year, millions of Americans *don't* run for the office of president of the United States, and this is not considered news. But when Gen. Colin Powell did not run in 1996, Americans discussed the fact at great length. This was because many people believed Powell stood the greatest chance of any black man in history of being elected president. **(See original entry on Powell in volume 3.)**

Powell was born the son of Jamaican immigrants in New York City's Harlem district in 1937. He attended the City College of the City University of New York, where he took part in the Reserve Officers' Training Corps (ROTC). After graduating in 1958, he took a commission in the U.S. Army as a second lieutenant. He served first in Germany, and then, shortly after marrying his wife Alma, in Vietnam. By the mid-1960s, the United States was heavily involved in the Vietnam War (1954–75). Powell was wounded while rescuing two of his comrades, an act for which he earned several medals.

"When discrimination still exists, or where the scars of past discrimination contaminate the present, we must not close our eyes to it . . . and hope it will go away by itself. It did not in the past. It will not in the future."

In the early 1970s, Powell earned his master's of business administration (MBA) degree from George Washington University. He got his first taste of government life as a military advisor to Frank Carlucci (1930–), deputy director of the Office of Management and Budget in the administration of President Richard M. Nixon (1913–94). Later, after serving in a number of different Army posts, Powell returned to Washington to again work with Carlucci, who by now was secretary of defense under President Ronald Reagan (1911–).

During the 1980s, Powell became one of the most powerful black men—indeed, one of the most powerful *men*—in the nation. Working with Carlucci, he helped plan the 1983 invasion of Grenada, in which the United States restored democratic rule to a Caribbean island nation that had been taken over by a dictatorship (government rule by one person). Powell also helped plan the 1986 bombing of Libya, whose leader, Muammar al-Qaddafi (1942–), was believed to be a primary force behind international terrorism. In 1986, Reagan appointed Powell director of the National Security Council (NSC), an extremely vital position for the coordination of defense and foreign policy.

In 1989, Powell became chairman of the Joint Chiefs of Staff, which includes the commanding officers of all U.S. military forces, and which serves as the principal advisory group for the secretary of defense. Powell was the youngest man—and the first African American—to hold that position. In this capacity, he helped direct the 1989 invasion of Panama after President George Bush (1924–) charged that nation's leader, Manuel Noriega (1940–), with involvement in international drug trafficking. Then in 1990, when the Middle Eastern nation of Iraq invaded its neighbor, Kuwait, the United States again mobilized for war. The result was the Gulf War, or Operation Desert Storm, which took place during the early months of 1991 and resulted in a U.S. victory over Iraq and its dictator, Saddam Hussein (1937–).

When President Bill Clinton (1946–) took office in 1993, Powell found himself at odds with the new administration. Clinton, who had avoided military service as a young man in the 1960s, was not known as a friend of the armed forces. Powell disagreed with the new president's plan to cut defense budgets and give homosexuals equal rights in the military. He stepped down from his job, though he continued to advise Clinton on subsequent military actions.

Chooses not to run for president in 1996

In 1995, Powell published *My American Journey,* which was both an autobiography (his life story), and a statement of his political beliefs. In it he sharply criticized the Clinton administration, but he also had negative observations about members of the Reagan and Bush administrations. By then, speculation was high that Powell might run for president, but analysts were unsure of which political party he would choose. Powell declared himself "a fiscal conservative with a social conscience" (for more about conservatives and liberals, see the entry on **Alan Keyes** on p. 147). This meant that he believed in cutting government budgets, but favored affirmative action (an effort to improve employment and educational opportunities for minority groups) and abortion rights, neither of which are popular ideas with many conservatives.

On balance, however, he made it clear that he was a Republican—but that he wasn't going to run for president in 1996. This announcement, which he made in November 1995, almost exactly a year before the 1996 elections, was greeted with widespread disappointment. Powell was very popular. Conservatives liked his pro-military stance, and his desire to cut the budget; liberals liked his views on affirmative action and abortion rights; and people across the spectrum liked the idea that America might elect a black man as its president.

In July 1996, Powell announced that he would not run as a vice presidential nominee, even if the Republican presidential nominee, former U.S. senator Bob Dole (1923–), offered him the job, as some suggested he might. Yet Powell did make the keynote address (the main speech other than the one by the presidential nominee) at the July Republican Convention in San Diego, California. In a speech that drew multiple standing ovations, Powell urged Republicans to exercise a broader vision, and to bring in minorities and others who shared their values of law and order, a strong defense, and a smaller government: "It is our party," he said, "the party of Lincoln, that must always stand for equal rights and fair opportunity for all. And when discrimination still exists, or where the scars of past discrimination contaminate the present, we must not close our eyes to it . . . and hope it will go away by itself. It did not in the past. It will not in the future."

One of the reasons why Powell chose not to run in 1996 was because his wife, Alma, did not want him to. Along with letters "telling me what a wonderful man I was married to and how much the country needed him," she received hate mail concerning his candidacy. She worried about the public exposure they would endure during a presidential campaign.

Outside of his political life, Powell worked with charitable and civic organizations. Many groups wanted him to join their boards, and in early 1996 he chose the Boys and Girls Clubs of America, as well as the Childrens' Health Fund. In April 1997, he joined Clinton and former presidents Bush, Jimmy Carter (1924–), and Gerald Ford (1913–) at a Philadelphia, Pennsylvania, rally in which they called on Americans to volunteer for civic organizations to wipe out poverty and stop crime.

In September 1996, Powell helped dedicate the first memorial to the 200,000 black soldiers who served in the Civil War (1861–65). The Washington, D.C., monument, he said, would help to make up for "the terrible overlooking of Black heroism in the military." In January 1997, the first black wax museum in the nation unveiled a monument of sorts to him, a likeness of Powell that joined the other wax statues in the Baltimore, Maryland, museum. His alma mater, City College of the City University of New York, dedicated its Colin L. Powell Center for Public Policy Study in April 1997.

Meanwhile, speculation about Powell's political future remained. At one point it was suggested that Clinton might ask him to join his Cabinet (the president's group of chief advisors). In December 1997, Powell clashed with Senate Republicans over Clinton's nominee for assistant attorney general for civil rights, Bill Lann Lee, who Powell supported; and he continued to disagree with a number of Republican leaders over affirmative action. Nonetheless, Powell remained within the Republican camp. In June 1998, *Jet* reported that political observers had suggested an "unbeatable" Republican team for the 2000 elections: Texas governor George W. Bush (1946– ; son of the former president) as president, and Powell as vice president. The possibility remained that Powell might make a run for national office in the future.

Sources for further reading

Apple, R. W., Jr. "In Book, Powell Says a 3d Party May Be Needed." *New York Times,* September 10, 1995, p. 1.

Applegate, Katherine. *The Story of Two American Generals, Benjamin O. Davis, Jr., Colin L. Powell.* New York: Dell Publishing, 1992.

Banta, Melissa. *Colin Powell.* New York: Chelsea House, 1995.

"Colin Powell's Wife Reveals She Got Hate Mail During Time He Considered Bid for President." *Jet,* May 6, 1996, p. 12.

Cummings, Judith, and Stefan Rudnicki. *Colin Powell and the American Dream.* Beverly Hills, CA: Dove Books, 1995.

Finlayson, Reggie. *Colin Powell.* Minneapolis: Lerner Publications, 1997.

"Gen. Powell Praises Plans for First Memorial Honoring Black Civil War GIs." *Jet,* September 30, 1996, p. 51.

"The Greatest Love Stories of the Century: Colin Powell & Alma Johnson." *People,* February 12, 1996, p. 168.

"How Blacks Participated in the Republican Convention." *Jet,* September 2, 1996, p. 4.

Hughes, Libby. *Colin Powell: A Man of Quality.* Parsippany, NJ: Dillon Press, 1996.

Powell, Colin. *In His Own Words: Colin Powell.* New York: Berkley, 1995.

Powell, Colin L., with Joseph E. Persico. *My American Journey.* New York: Random House, 1995.

"Powell Gives Opening Keynote Speech at GOP Convention." *Jet,* September 2, 1996, p. 12.

Roth, David. *Sacred Honor: A Biography of Colin Powell.* Grand Rapids, MI: Zondervan, 1993.

Schraff, Anne. *Colin Powell: Soldier and Patriot.* Springfield, NJ: Enslow Publishers, 1997.

Strazzabosco, Jeanne. *Learning About Responsibility from the Life of Colin Powell.* New York: Rosen, 1996.

Chris Rock

*Born February 7, 1966
Brooklyn, New York
Comedian, actor, author*

The years 1997 and 1998 were busy ones for comedian Chris Rock. On the heels of his November 1996 marriage to public relations executive Malaak Compton, he had a string of successes: a popular HBO comedy show, two Emmy awards and two CableACE awards for his television performances, a comedy album, a Grammy Award, and a best-selling book. He made memorable TV appearances, such as his spot as host of the 1997 *MTV Video Music Awards,* and he appeared alongside Danny Glover (1948– ; see entry in volume 2), Mel Gibson, and Joe Pesci in *Lethal Weapon IV.* Chris Rock, as many magazine headlines announced—making a pun on his last name—was on a roll.

Yet life hasn't always been this successful for Rock, and he's philosophical about the way success comes and goes. "I've achieved all my goals; now I've got to maintain [them]," he said in a July 1998 *USA Weekend* article. "If everybody died at 35, this would be great, but fortunately or unfortunate-

"Parts of me need to get out. I've got ideas in my head, things I want to do. I've got jokes to tell."

ly, that doesn't happen. You're always fighting the monster you created at 25 or 30."

Taunted about his name

Is his name really Chris *Rock*? The answer is yes. "It was the worst name as a kid to have," he said in a 1996 Prodigy on-line chat. "They called me Piece of the Rock, Plymouth Rock. . . ." And those were not the worst names he heard as a boy growing up in the tough Bedford-Stuyvesant district of New York City's Brooklyn borough.

In the 1970s, when Rock was in elementary school, much of the United States tried a racial experiment called busing. The idea was to bring black kids into predominantly white schools, and white kids into predominantly black schools. This meant that a lot of children were forced to leave the schools where they had friends, and go to places where they weren't always wanted. That was the situation for Rock, who was bussed to an equally tough, but mostly white, neighborhood called Bensonhurst. "It was horrible," he told *Ebony* magazine years later. He said that his time in school "was like Vietnam. They spit on me, called me n—r, not once in a while, every single day."

"Discovered" by Eddie Murphy

Fortunately for Rock, he had the support of a loving family. The oldest of six children, he was especially close to his father, Julius, who drove a newspaper truck for the *New York Daily News.* Julius and Rose Rock encouraged their son's talents. Discussing his ability years later in *People* magazine, Rock said, "I never realized I'm funny. I just realized that sometimes when I'm serious, people tend to laugh."

Whatever it was, Rock had a gift, and when he was seventeen years old, he quit school to pursue comedy. (He later earned a general equivalency diploma, and encourages young people to get an education.) The next few years were not easy. By day he worked as a busboy, mental hospital orderly, and a laborer unloading trucks at the *Daily News;* by night he worked as a stand-up comedian.

He had his first show in 1984, and by 1985, when he was about twenty years old, Rock decided that he wanted to be a full-time comedian. In 1986, while appearing at the Comic Strip Club in Manhattan, superstar comedian Eddie Murphy (1961– ; see entry in volume 3) saw him. Murphy was not just a star in Rock's eyes, he was a hero, a comic whose style Rock respected. Murphy was so impressed with Rock that he gave him a small role in his upcoming film *Beverly Hills Cop II*. It was Rock's first break.

Almost quits comedy for good

Rock moved to Hollywood, and on the heels of his first movie appearance, played "the rib joint customer" in the 1988 spoof of African American movies, *I'm Gonna Git You Sucka*. Again he attracted the attention of a superstar, talk show host Arsenio Hall (1955– ; see entry in volume 2). Rock's appearance on Hall's talk show led to an audition for the popular late-night comedy program *Saturday Night Live* in 1990. *SNL* had launched the careers of many successful comedians, including Murphy, and it seemed like a good sign when Rock became a featured player.

The next year, Rock made a memorable appearance as the crack addict Pookie in the critically acclaimed drama *New Jack City*. The role of Pookie showed that Rock could perform in a serious role as well as a comic one, and his fame grew. Yet just as his career was taking off, Rock faced challenges in his personal and professional life. His father died in 1988 of complications resulting from an ulcer, and Rock called the loss "the most traumatic experience of my life." Partly because of his grief, and partly because of his inexperience, he started to get a reputation for not giving his best on *Saturday Night Live*.

In an interview, Rock said, "*SNL* was great, but I felt like the adopted [black] kid with the great white parents." So he left the show in 1993, and signed on with its chief competition, the primarily black *In Living Color* on Fox. "Then I went to the black family," he continued, "and it was like I really fit in. But then they canceled the show."

Nothing else seemed to work for him, either. The comedy film *CB4,* which he co-produced and wrote, did not do well at the box office. He made some television appearances, but had no TV series or movie offers. He decided to leave the prestigious William Morris Agency to find a different agent. Suddenly, as he later told *Entertainment Weekly,* "no one wanted me. Literally every agent in town turned me down." By then it was early 1996, and Rock was thirty years old. Rock told himself that if nothing changed by the end of the year, he would take it as a sign that he should quit comedy and do something else with his life.

Rock on a roll

Rock may have been a high-school dropout, but in 1996 he became a serious student of comedy. He carefully studied the routines of his heroes, and worked on his own act. During this time, he also taped a special for HBO. Entitled *Bring the Pain,* it got good reviews from critics and showed the results of Rock's hard work and study. As a result, Comedy Central's *Politically Incorrect* asked him to conduct its humorous coverage of the 1996 presidential elections, a take-off on the serious reporting of the big networks.

Suddenly everything looked up for Rock. Thanks to a number of commercials, especially his appearance as "Li'l Penny" on Nike ads, his voice and face seemed to be everywhere. In 1997, he saw even greater success, with the publication of his book *Rock This!,* two Emmy awards for *Bring the Pain,* and an appearance as host of the *MTV Music Video Awards.* HBO invited him to have a full-time talk show, which earned him two CableACE awards, and his album *Roll with the New* led to the hit video "Champagne." In 1998, he appeared in *Lethal Weapon IV,* and his voice was featured in a film starring his old friend Murphy—*Dr. Doolittle,* in which Rock provides the voice of a guinea pig.

Starts humor magazine

Rock's talk show has featured a wide spectrum of black personalities, ranging from emcee Sean "Puffy" Combs

The wit and wisdom of Chris Rock

Chris Rock isn't just funny: he's got a lot of wisdom. Mixed in with the humor are good observations about society, politics, and relations between people. Here are some of his collected thoughts on...

His mother's frugality: "My mother would never buy brand-name foods. You know the cheapest thing my mother ever bought? The peanut butter with the jelly in it. That's like buying a shoe with the sock sewn inside."

Soul food: "Soul food is not black food. That's some nasty [stuff] they fed to the slaves. You think a ham hock tasted good the first time the white man gave it to us? We put some seasoning on it and made it work."

Racism and the N-Word: "This country is fascinated by anything a white man can't do, like say that word. The whole [N-word] thing is all blown out of proportion. Don't people have other things to do? Clean up the crack house, find a cure for something. . . . Racism's hysterical. . . . When you laugh at it, you forget about it."

Popular images of intelligence: "Any show on television, especially with kids, the smart kid is always made out to be the kid you would least want to be like. So it's kind of like an anti-education thing that we promote. . . . To me, [that's] worse than violence and profanity."

The President: "You know what I like about Clinton? He's got real problems. He don't got President problems, he's got real problems like you and me. He's runnin' out of money. . . . All his friends are goin' to jail. I know Bill Clinton. I am Bill Clinton."

Loaning money: "You ever had someone owe you money and have the nerve to wear new clothes around you? 'Hey, look what I just picked up.' Did you see my money while you were down there?"

Learning from others (quoting his father): "Never be the smartest guy in the room. You never learn anything that way."

Success: "I want to be the best. When they have the contest for who's the best, I'd at least like to get invited."

Humility: I know I'm going to fall. All this hoopla that's going on now is going to stop. But as long as I put in the proper amount of work, the fall won't be that steep."

Chris Rock hams it up for the cameras after he won two Emmy awards in 1997 for his HBO special, Bring the Pain.

(1969–) to actress Vivica Fox (1964–) to Republican congressman J. C. Watts, Jr. (1957–). Two of his guests, comedian Whoopi Goldberg (1955– ; see entry in volume 2) and political activist Rev. Jesse Jackson (1941– ; see entry in volume 2), have gotten into heated discussions with Rock about aspects of his social commentary. He upset some African Americans for criticizing former football star and acquitted murder suspect O. J. Simpson (1947– ; see entry on p. 207), and Washington, D.C., mayor Marion Barry (1936– ; see entry in volume 1, and update on p. 9), who was reelected in spite of his record as a crack user.

Yet Rock has never forgotten his roots. In February 1998, he announced that he was offering an unusual contribution to the black community: the creation of a black college humor magazine to rival the Harvard *Lampoon*. The *Lampoon*, which led to the creation of the popular humor magazine *National Lampoon*, helped a number of comedy writers get their start.

By locating his magazine at Howard University, a predominantly African American school, Rock hopes to create opportunities for black comedy writers. Though he did not attend Howard, Rock has joked that the Washington, D.C., institution is "the closest black university to my house in Brooklyn."

Rock continues to be humble about his success. His next-door neighbor is a plumber, and he gets his hair cut at the local barber shop. Much of his comic material comes from his surroundings: "You just keep quiet and observe, try to be around normal people," he told *Jet*. "The barber shop is a great place. . . . You just draw from all the people around you. I read about four or five newspapers a day and every magazine I can get my hands on to try to get a sense of what's going on in the country." His goal is similarly modest: to make people laugh. Remembering two of his fellow *Saturday Night Live* cast members who died in the late 1990s, Phil Hartman (1948–98) and Chris Farley (1964–97), Rock said, "Phil Hartman's in a box right now saying, 'I hope they think I was funny.' Chris Farley's right now hoping his movie was funny. Hey, at the end of the day, I just want to be funny."

Sources for further reading

"Chris Rock Talks About His Comedy, New Wife and Fame." *Jet,* October 20, 1997, pp. 32–36.

Contemporary Black Biography, Volume 3. Detroit: Gale, 1993, pp. 218–20.

Fretts, Bruce. "Chris Rock." *Entertainment Weekly,* December 26, 1997–January 2, 1998, p. 20.

Grove, Lloyd. "Chris Rock: Stone Cold Funny." *Washington Post,* April 10, 1997, p. B1.

HBO: The Chris Rock Show. [Online] http://www.hbo.com/rock/ (accessed on October 29, 1998).

Mendelsohn, Jennifer. "Rock of Pages." *People,* December 1, 1997, p. 53.

Nelson, Jill. "Alternative Rock." *USA Weekend,* July 10–12, 1998, pp. 4–5.

Newsmakers 1998, issue 1. Detroit: Gale, 1998.

Rock, Chris. *Rock This!* New York: Hyperion, 1997.

"Rock to Launch Comedy Magazine at Howard." *Black Issues in Higher Education,* February 19, 1998, p. 8.

Stein, Joel. "Q & A." *Time Canada,* February 9, 1998, p. 75.

Tucker, Ken. "Rocking Late Night." *Entertainment Weekly,* November 28, 1997, p. 61.

Wilma Rudolph

*Born June 23, 1940
Bethlehem, Tennessee
Died November 12, 1994
Nashville, Tennessee
Athlete, Olympic gold medalist, teacher*

UPDATE

Wilma Rudolph, who won three gold medals in track and field at the 1960 Olympics in Rome, Italy, died on November 12, 1994, of complications resulting from throat cancer and a brain tumor. Rudolph, who was fifty-four years old, was born with polio. She could hardly move her left leg, and suffered from pneumonia and scarlet fever as a child. But hard work and determination changed her life. **(See original entry on Rudolph in volume 3.)**

Born the twentieth of twenty-two children in 1940, Rudolph was raised near Nashville, Tennessee. At the age of five, she was fitted with a steel leg brace, which she wore for the next six years. In seventh grade, she experienced a turning point in her life when she discovered sports. She excelled as a runner, and competed with great success throughout junior high and high school.

In 1956, the sixteen-year-old Rudolph became the youngest member of the U.S. women's Olympic track team.

"You'll never know what you can accomplish until you get up and try."

She competed in the Olympics in Melbourne, Australia, where she helped her relay team win a bronze medal. Enrolling in college at Tennessee State University (TSU) in Nashville, she ran track on the Tigerbelles team under the guidance of coach Edward Temple (1927–). During the 1960 Olympics in Rome, she competed in the 100-meter, 200-meter, and relay events—and won gold medals in all three.

With her success in Rome, Rudolph became an international celebrity. She competed in a number of athletic competitions, but continued her college education as well. Following her 1963 graduation, she went to work as a schoolteacher, and in 1967 Vice President Hubert Humphrey (1911–78) invited her to participate in a national program designed to train star athletes from disadvantaged backgrounds. She worked as a teacher and social worker throughout the 1970s and 1980s, and directed the Wilma Rudolph Foundation, a non-profit group she organized in 1981 to train young athletes.

A legacy of honors

In July 1993, the National Sports Council selected Rudolph as the only woman on its list of the five greatest athletes of all time. She was inducted into the National Women's Hall of Fame on September 24, 1994, and in November, the Jackie Joyner-Kersee Community Foundation—founded by fellow Olympic gold medalist Jackie Joyner-Kersee (1962– ; see entry in volume 2)—announced that it would also honor Rudolph with an award.

Rudolph was unable to attend either of the 1994 ceremonies, however, due to poor health. United States Olympic Committee (USOC) president Leroy Walker, speaking at the opening ceremonies of the Olympic Congress on November 11, said "I'm sad to report that not too far from here, Wilma is in grave health, fighting for her life." The next day, Rudolph died of complications resulting from throat cancer and a brain tumor.

Temple, her former coach, remembered her attitude: "She had a great outlook on life. She could relate to anybody.

She would say, 'You'll never know what you can accomplish until you get up and try.'" Three-time Olympian Mae Faggs-Starr, who as a fellow member of the Tigerbelles had helped to train Rudolph, recalled that "Coach Temple said [to] keep your eye on the tall, thin one. She was all arms and legs, but I knew then she was going to be great. She had the talent and that spirit; she wanted to be the best."

The USOC announced in November 1994 that it intended to set up an athletic scholarship in Rudolph's name; and a year later, TSU dedicated its Wilma G. Rudolph Residence Center, which would house some 420 female students. The Women's Sports Foundation established its Wilma Rudolph Courage Award, which it presents each year to "a female athlete who exhibits extraordinary courage in her athletic performance." In November 1995, the North Nashville Matthew Walker Comprehensive Health Center named a birthing center for Rudolph. The choice was fitting, Rudolph's sister Charlene told the *Tennessee Tribune,* because "she preferred kids over adults any time."

Sources for further reading

Baines, Gwendolyn. "The Matthew Walker New Birthing Center to Honor Wilma Rudolph." *Tennessee Tribune,* November 23, 1995.

Climer, David. "Wilma Rudolph Dead at 54." Gannett News Service, November 12, 1994.

Coffey, Wayne. *Wilma Rudolph.* Woodbridge, CT: Blackbirch Press, 1993.

Dixon, Otis. "Admirers Gather to Honor Rudolph." *USA Today,* November 18, 1994, p. 2.

Dixon, Otis. "Mentor: 'I Knew That She Was Going to Be Great." *USA Today,* November 14, 1994, p. 2.

Greenlee, Craig T., "Rekindling Wilma's Legacy: Tennessee State University Struggles to Revive Olympic Tradition." *Black Issues in Higher Education,* August 8, 1996.

Krull, Kathleen. *Wilma Unlimited: How Wilma Rudolph Became the World's Fastest Woman.* San Diego: Harcourt Brace, 1996.

Mitchell, Ralph E. "TSU Names Building in Honor of Olympic Great Wilma Rudolph." *Tennessee Tribune,* August 8, 1995.

Sherrow, Victoria. *Wilma Rudolph: Olympic Champion.* New York: Chelsea House, 1995.

Weir, Tom. "Olympic Congress Opens with Tribute to Rudolph." *USA Today,* November 11, 1994, p. 7.

Betty Shabazz

*Born May 28, 1936
Detroit, Michigan
Died June 23, 1997
New York, New York
Nurse, educator, activist*

Betty Shabazz was best known to the world as the wife of civil rights leader Malcolm X (1925–65; see entry in volume 3). For seven short years, she experienced with him the many changes that characterized his career. When that career came to an end, she was beside him. On February 21, 1965, pregnant with twins, she was sitting near the front row of the Audubon Ballroom in New York City with her four daughters when gunmen fired sixteen shots at Malcolm. She rushed to the stage in a futile effort to save him, but it was too late: at twenty-eight, she became a widow.

But Shabazz was more than simply the woman behind Malcolm X. Her attempt to save his life came from something more than a wife's concern for her husband. She was a registered nurse, and after his death, she would go on to further her education. She raised the six daughters, too, ensuring that they learned about a variety of cultures. As for carrying on her husband's work, Shabazz would be much less vocal than her

"I don't feel sad. I feel fortunate. I feel very blessed spiritually. My soul is at peace. My heart is full of concern and love, and I understand the meaning of my own life and the lives of others. So, no, no, I'm never alone. I'm never cut off."

counterpart, Coretta Scott King (1927– ; see entry in volume 3), widow of the Rev. Martin Luther King (1929–68; see entry in volume 3). She seldom made public appearances, and her most outspoken statements concerned a rival of her late husband within the religious organization Nation of Islam. When death came to her at the age of sixty-one, it would come, like her husband's passing, under ironic circumstances—and much too soon.

A regular childhood

"Pick a week out of your life," Shabazz told *Essence* magazine in 1992. "If you understood that week, you understood my life." Born Betty Sanders, Shabazz had an extremely ordinary childhood as the adoptive daughter of a middle-class couple in Detroit, Michigan. As a teenager during the late 1940s and early 1950s, her life was as regular as clockwork. From Monday to Friday, she attended school, and each Friday night went to the movies. Saturdays she worked at her parents' store, and sometimes on Saturday nights she went to parties with her sorority, the Delta Sprites, a high-school version of Delta Sigma Theta. Sunday mornings, the devout Methodist family went to church.

Growing up in a sheltered environment, Shabazz had seldom experienced racism. Therefore when she went away to college in the South—at Tuskegee Institute in Alabama, where her father had attended—she encountered a harsh reality. At first she was hurt by the treatment she received from local whites. Her parents offered little help; she recalled later that they responded as though she had somehow brought it on herself. Then she resolved to move north, to New York City.

Marriage to Malcolm X

In New York, Shabazz enrolled at the Brooklyn State Hospital School of Nursing, where she earned her bachelor's degree and registered nurse (R.N.) certification in 1958. But that was not the most important thing that happened to her in 1958. That was the year Betty Sanders married Malcolm X.

As a junior in college, she attended a lecture at a Muslim temple run by the Nation of Islam. Under the leadership of its founder Elijah Mohammed (1897–1975; see entry in volume 3), the Nation of Islam had adapted the Muslim, or Islamic, faith and combined it with political doctrines about the superiority of blacks over whites, and the need for struggle between the two races. To an innocent young girl from Detroit, this was all very new and shocking; so too was the fiery orator she went to hear. His name was Malcolm X (born Malcolm Little), and she later recalled her first impressions of him: "I looked over and saw this man on the extreme right aisle sort of galloping to the podium. He was tall, he was thin, and . . . it looked as though he was going someplace much more important than the podium. . . . I sat up straight. I was impressed with him."

Malcolm, to whom she was introduced, quickly became impressed with her as well. Shabazz recalled, "I knew he loved me for my clear brown skin—it was very smooth. He liked my clear eyes. He liked my gleaming dark hair. I was very thin then, and he liked my Black beauty, my mind. He just liked me." Within a year or so, she converted to Islam, and began teaching classes for women. Malcolm suggested topics, and she often helped him with his papers. "He would actively seek me out, ask me questions," she remembered. "He was different. He was refreshing, but I never suspected that he thought of me in any way other than as a sister who was interested in the Movement. . . . There were too many people in line for his attention."

The two never "dated" as such, because the Nation of Islam frowned on the idea of single men and women spending time alone; instead, they saw each other only in large groups. Still, the attraction was clear, and when Malcolm called her one day from Detroit and asked her to marry him, she accepted. Within a week, Betty Sanders had become Mrs. Malcolm X.

Witnessing her husband's death

The next seven years were far from restful ones. Malcolm X was the kind of man who questioned what he was told.

Thus, under the guidance of Elijah Muhammad, he had questioned the values of a society that often viewed whites as better than blacks. He eventually began to question Elijah Muhammad's teachings as well. This led to a break with the Nation of Islam in March of 1964, and Malcolm's transformation continued with a trip to the holy city of Mecca, in present-day Saudi Arabia. The trip—a *hajj,* or pilgrimage—is a tradition of Islam, and a devout Muslim tries to visit Mecca once in a lifetime. In the course of his hajj, when he saw Muslims of all races worshipping together, Malcolm turned against the racist doctrines of Elijah Muhammad.

Malcolm came back to the United States with a mind broadened by new experiences—and with a new name, El-Hajj Malik El-Shabazz. Thus his wife became Betty Shabazz. By 1965, she had given birth to four daughters: Attallah, Qubilah, Ilyasah, and Gamilah. It was not easy raising children whose father was away so often, and when the Nation of Islam turned against Malcolm, her job became much harder. On the evening of February 14, 1965, someone firebombed their house, and she and the four children narrowly escaped harm. Malcolm blamed the Nation of Islam.

Then just a week later, on February 21, he went to speak at the Audubon Ballroom. Shabazz was sitting near the front of the room, listening to her husband speak, when three gunmen—men later identified as members of the Nation of Islam—fired shots at him. She covered her children with her body; when the shooting stopped, she rushed to the stage to help Malcolm. But sixteen bullets had found their mark, and by the time she got to him, he was already dead.

Raising their children alone

Shabazz had trouble sleeping for three weeks after the assassination. She had frequent nightmares in which she saw Malcolm being shot all over again. But she had to get back on her feet again. She had four young daughters, and two more on the way: at the time of her husband's death, Shabazz was pregnant with twin girls, Malaak and Malikah, born seven months later.

Before his death, Malcolm had been invited to make another hajj to Mecca. Shabazz was now asked to go in his place. "Going to Mecca," she said later, "was very good for me because it made me think of all the people in the world who loved me and were for me, who prayed that I would get my life back together. I stopped focusing on the people who were trying to tear me and my family apart."

After that, she concentrated her attention on two things: raising her daughters and furthering her own education. As Malcolm would have wished, she made sure that the six children gained wide exposure to African American culture and history—but also to that of the world at large. So they studied French, Arabic, and ballet, and traveled throughout Africa, the West Indies, and the Middle East. As for her own education, she obtained a master's degree in public education from Jersey City State College in New Jersey in the early 1970s, then went on to earn her Ph.D. in education administration at the University of Massachusetts at Amherst in 1975. The next year, she became a member of the faculty at Medgar Evers College in Brooklyn, where she remained for the rest of her life. Popular with students, Shabazz became known as "Dr. Betty."

The thirty years between her husband's death and the mid-1990s were peaceful ones for Shabazz. She received a number of awards, hosted a radio talk show, made a few public appearances, and promoted several charities. She fought to protect her husband's name from commercialization, some of which resulted from the making of the 1992 film *Malcolm X*, directed by Spike Lee (1957– ; see entry in volume 3). Shabazz served as a consultant on that film, in which Angela Bassett (1958–) played Shabazz—a role Bassett would revive in 1994's *Panther*.

A mother's heart to the end

In 1994, Shabazz herself shattered the tranquility of her life when she told the *New York Post* that she believed Minister Louis Farrakhan (1933– ; see entry in volume 2, and update on p. 71), the controversial Nation of Islam leader, had ordered the assassination of her husband. Her disagreement

Betty Shabazz wipes away a tear at a news conference announcing a fundraiser for her daughter, Qubilah, who was accused of trying to kill Louis Farrakhan.

with Farrakhan brought her scorn from many who supported his politics. The controversy grew in 1995 when her second daughter, Qubilah, was accused of trying to kill Farrakhan. The charges were dropped on the condition that Qubilah undergo drug and psychiatric treatment. In May of that year, Shabazz and Farrakhan underwent a public reconciliation at a fundraiser for Qubilah's legal defense. That October, Shabazz appeared at the Million Man March, a massive rally in Washington, D.C., organized by Farrakhan. As for Qubilah, she continued to experience troubles, including problems with her twelve-year-old son, who she had named Malcolm after his grandfather. In early 1997, hoping to straighten him out, she sent him to live with his grandmother in New York City.

What followed was a tragic and ironic set of events. The boy grew homesick for his mother in San Antonio, Texas, and hatched a plan that he thought would ensure his return. If he set his grandmother's apartment on fire, he thought, she would become angry with him and send him home. He doused her back hallway in gasoline, lit it, and ran away. But he did not count on the fact that his grandmother would have a mother's heart, even to the end of her life: instead of fleeing to safety, she spent crucial minutes searching the apartment for him. By the time ambulances arrived, she had third-degree burns over eighty percent of her body. For a sixty-one-year-old woman, there was not much hope that she could survive. Still, people throughout America conducted prayer vigils for her, and in New York, thousands stood in line to donate blood for her. Doctors at Jacobi Hospital in the Bronx tried desperately to save her, performing five skin-grafts (operations where skin is transplanted from one area to another), but it was no use. On June 23, 1997, she died.

Shabazz was mourned throughout the world. At New York's Riverside Church, a group of more than 2,000 people attended her funeral, and heard speeches by a number of dignitaries, including two other widows of civil rights leaders, Coretta Scott King and Myrlie Evers-Williams (1953–), whose husband Medgar Evers (1925–63; see entry in volume 2) had been assassinated like Dr. King and Malcolm X.

Shabazz might best be remembered in the observations of a long-time friend, civil rights activist Yuri Kochiyama: "She became more her own person. She was not afraid to speak out against those that she felt were Malcolm's enemies. She became, I think, a leader in her own right."

Sources for further reading

Baye, Betty Winston. "Speak Up for Dr. Betty." Gannett News Service, March 15, 1994.

Brown, Jamie Foster. *Betty Shabazz: A Sisterfriends' Tribute in Words and Pictures.* New York: Simon & Schuster, 1998.

Contemporary Black Biography, Volume 7. Detroit: Gale, 1994, pp. 245–47.

Edwards, Audrey. "The Fire This Time." *Essence,* October 1, 1997, pp. 74–78.

Hampson, Rick, and Martha T. Moore. "Betty Shabazz: Malcolm X Widow Leaves Legacy of Dignity, Strength." *USA Today,* June 24, 1997, p. 1-A.

Malcolm X (motion picture). Warner Brothers, 1992.

Malcolm X, with Alex Haley. *The Autobiography of Malcolm X.* New York: Ballantine, 1964.

Neeley, DeQuendre. "Rift Mended, Shabazz Ends Long Feud with Farrakhan." *Newsday,* May 8, 1995, p. A-8.

The Real Malcolm X: An Intimate Portrait of the Man (videorecording). CBS News/Fox Video, 1992.

Shabazz, Betty. "Loving and Losing Malcolm." *Essence,* February 1992, pp. 50–54+.

Shabazz, Betty. *The Sister's Been Doing Her Homework* (sound recording). Pacifica Tape Library.

Smith, Jessie Carney, ed. *Notable Black American Women, Book II.* Detroit: Gale, 1996, pp. 590–93.

Tupac Shakur

Born June 16, 1971
New York, New York
Died September 13, 1996
Las Vegas, Nevada
Rap singer and actor

Singer and actor Tupac Shakur became famous to rap music fans in 1991 with the release of his first solo album *2Pacalypse Now;* but he became known to most Americans after the April 1992 shooting of a Texas state trooper. The young man charged with the crime claimed that Shakur's song "Soulja's Story," which depicts the murder of a policeman, had encouraged him to commit the crime. This led Vice President Dan Quayle (1947–), and other politicians, to demand that *2Pacalypse Now* be removed from record stores. Of course the attention helped increase sales of Shakur's CDs, and made his name a household word.

Over the next four years, Shakur established a name for himself with his albums, and with his movies, most notably a performance alongside pop singer Janet Jackson (1966– ; see entry in volume 2) in the 1993 film *Poetic Justice*, directed by John Singleton (1968– ; see entry in volume 4). But what mainly kept Shakur's name in the headlines was the violence that seemed to

"Success killed [Tupac]. It made him feel like he was invincible, and nobody is invincible."

—A friend of Shakur's

Rap artist Tupac Shakur performs in-concert.

follow him everywhere he went, as in 1994, when he was charged with shooting two off-duty police officers in Atlanta, Georgia. Then, on September 7, 1996, when he was shot in Las Vegas, Nevada, the violence finally caught up with Shakur. After six days in a coma, the twenty-five-year-old artist died. To many both inside and outside the rap community, his death seemed to prove that "gangsta rap" had gone too far in its glorification of violence.

"In prison before I was born"

Shakur often said he was in prison before he was born. His mother, born Alice Faye Williams in 1947, began snorting cocaine at age fifteen. In 1964 she became involved with radical black politics in New York City. In 1968, she moved in with Lumumba Abdul Shakur, a member of the militant Black Panther movement, and changed her name to Afeni Shakur.

In 1969, Afeni and others were charged with conspiracy to bomb several public places. While she was out on bail in 1970, she had a relationship with a man named William Garland. By the time she went to prison for the bombing charges, she was pregnant, and Garland was gone. Released in her eighth month of pregnancy, Afeni gave birth in New York City's East Harlem district. She named the boy Tupac Amaru Shakur after an ancient Inca Indian prince.

A young poet, dancer, and actor

Shakur spent his early years in the poorest areas of Harlem and the Bronx, often sleeping in homeless shelters. Soon Afeni had a second child, a daughter, and the three struggled to get by. Shakur later recalled that in those days he felt "like my life could be destroyed at any moment." He found escape in writing poetry, and after his mother enrolled him in the 127th Street Ensemble, an acting troupe, he discovered another aspect of his talent. His first role was in the play *A Raisin in the Sun*.

In 1984, the family moved to Baltimore, Maryland, where Shakur studied acting and dance at that city's School for the Arts. He started writing rap lyrics, and he seemed happy. In spite of the apparent order in Shakur's family life, however, more problems emerged. His mother had switched from snorting cocaine to smoking crack. In 1988, Afeni moved the family to Marin City, California, in an attempt to get away from drugs.

Troubles with his mother

Afeni's drug problems continued, and after a year, her eighteen-year-old son moved to nearby Oakland. There, in

Rap and violence: A wake-up call?

Tupac Shakur was named after an ancient Inca Indian king, Tupac Amaru. During the 1970s and 1980s in Peru, home of the original Tupac Amaru, a terrorist organization by that name made headlines for bombings and kidnappings. As for Tupac Shakur, when a preacher once asked him what he wanted to be when he grew up, he replied, "A revolutionary." A revolutionary can refer to someone who, like Shakur's mother or the Peruvian terrorists, tries to bring about political change through violence. It can also refer to someone who causes a creative and nonviolent change in people's thinking. There was a little bit of both in Tupac Shakur.

Shakur helped popularize "gangsta rap," a style of music that, its critics charged, encouraged violence. Shakur's song "Soulja's Story," which describes the killing of a police officer, was blamed for inciting the murder of a Texas state trooper in April 1992. Politicians denounced Shakur; meanwhile, his record sales climbed. To some extent, gangsta rap was all about hype—the selling of a star by record publicity people. But gangsta artists knew what they were talking about when they described gunfights, police ambushes, and other gang activities. But while many of them were making successful careers as gangsta artists, many of them were also dying because of the gangsta lifestyle.

Shakur's violent death in September 1996 was a wake-up call to those who glorified that lifestyle. Sadly, Shakur didn't have to die. The previous year, he had a renewed seriousness about the message his music was sending to kids. "If we really are saying rap is an art form," he said, "then we got to be true to it and be more responsible for our lyrics. If you see everybody dying because of what you saying, it doesn't matter that you didn't make them die, it just matters that you didn't save them." But after he got out of

1990, he got a job as a dancer and roadie for the rap group Digital Underground (DU). This led to a spot on *The Arsenio Hall Show,* and a tour of the United States and Japan. Meanwhile, his mother was wasting away.

In 1991, though, Afeni cleaned up her life while her son became a superstar with a bad reputation. She moved to New York City, began attending Narcotics Anonymous meetings, and was clean by the end of the year. Soon she and Tupac became close again, and remained close for the rest of his life.

prison, he went back into the world of gangstas, and when he finally left that world, it was in a coffin.

In life, Tupac had shared a not-so-friendly rivalry with the Notorious B.I.G., or "Biggie Smalls," as part of the "East Coast–West Coast" feud between rappers. Six months after Shakur's death, on March 25, 1997, Biggie was also shot to death. As a result, a number of rappers, including Snoop Doggy Dogg and Ice-T (1958– ; see entry in volume 2), began to fear for their lives.

Some asked "What did Tupac and Biggie achieve by dying?" Not much, in the view of rap veteran Chuck D (1960–) of Public Enemy (see entry in volume 3): "Tupac and Biggie are hot now," he said in 1997, "but three years from now, the new generation won't remember. That's the saddest part. These guys are dying for nothing." Many began to say that it was time to take some personal responsibility for the violence. After noting that much of gangsta rap's fan base is among white kids in the suburbs, *Time* magazine's Farai Chideya concluded, "The music may be in white America's homes, but the violence is in black America's neighborhoods. That's why we, the hip-hop generation, bear the ultimate responsibility for reshaping the art form we love."

That reshaping was already taking place in 1997 and 1998, and many considered Shakur's and Small's deaths a sign that the gangsta rap fad was coming to an end. Radio stations were increasingly turning toward R&B, and away from rap, while rap itself began turning away from violence. "Hip-hop used to lift us above the struggles we faced," wrote Chideya. "Now it's become one of the struggles we face. . . . We can do better than this."

In the meantime, Tupac had made his recording debut with the 1991 *This Is an EP Release* album by D.U., and followed this up with his solo debut, *2Pacalypse Now.* "Everyone's gonna know me," Shakur told *Vibe,* and soon it was true—but not necessarily for the best reasons.

Film stardom and run-ins with the police

In 1992, Shakur made his first movie appearance in *Juice.* The following year, he appeared with Jackson in *Poetic*

Justice. In both cases, critics gave Shakur high marks. But his relationship with the police was not as good. During a gunfight between members of Shakur's crew and a rival one in Marin City, a six-year-old boy was killed. In 1993 and 1994, Shakur had a series of run-ins with the law, most notably an arrest for allegedly shooting two off-duty policemen in Atlanta, where he had moved. He was acquitted, but in 1994, a woman took Shakur to court on claims that he and his friends had sexually abused her. In March of that year, Shakur spent fifteen days in jail for hitting a filmmaker.

Meanwhile, Shakur's albums sold in bigger and bigger numbers. *Strictly 4 My N.I.G.G.A.Z.* quickly went gold, and was followed by songs he and his group, Thug Life, contributed to the soundtrack of the 1994 film *Above the Rim*. Shakur also appeared in the movie, winning further praise from critics. Thug Life then released its first full-length album, *Volume One*. Soon afterward, Shakur was robbed and seriously wounded in a shooting. This happened during his trial for sexual abuse, in which he was found guilty and sentenced to a minimum of one and a half years in prison.

A kinder, gentler Tupac?

Shakur went into prison in 1995 with hopes that the experience would reform him. He had quit his marijuana habit of many years, he said, and with his newly cleared head, had some perspective about his violent lyrics (see accompanying sidebar). His album *Me Against the World* showed more signs of a less violent Tupac. In his hit single "Dear Mama," he paid tribute to Afeni: "Even as a crack fiend / Mama you was a black queen / . . . You always was committed / A poor single mother / on welfare / Tell me how you did it."

Despite being caught smoking marijuana in July 1995, Shakur claimed that he had changed. "The addict in Tupac is dead," he told *Vibe*. "The excuse maker in Tupac is dead. The vengeful Tupac is dead. The Tupac that would stand by and let dishonorable things happen is dead. God let me live for me to do something extraordinary, and that's what I have to do."

These were stirring words, but Shakur failed to live up to them—and it cost him his life.

Tupac's last ride

Released from prison, he returned to his old life, and became heavily associated with Marion "Suge" Knight (1966–), the controversial chief executive of Death Row Records. Shakur threw himself into the "East Coast vs. West Coast" feud, which pitted him and fellow Californians Knight and Snoop Doggy Dogg against New Yorkers Sean "Puffy" Combs (1969–) and Christopher Wallace, a.k.a. the Notorious B.I.G. (1973–97). Some believe that the infamous street gangs the Bloods and the Cripps were involved as well, respectively on the West and East Coast sides.

Many believe the rappers' feud was involved in the incident that took Shakur's life. On September 7, 1996, Shakur and Knight were driving on the Strip in Las Vegas when a white Cadillac pulled up beside them at a traffic light and began firing at their car. Knight suffered minor injuries, but Shakur was severely wounded. Shakur was rushed to the hospital, where doctors performed three emergency operations. But after six days in a coma, Shakur died on September 13.

A legacy of questions

Shakur's death left behind many unanswered questions, especially with regard to Knight's involvement. Las Vegas police had no leads and got little cooperation from Shakur's camp. One policeman said that despite ten cars of bodyguards and friends near Knight and Shakur, "they're telling us they didn't see anything and don't know anything." Some observers believed that Knight and his Death Row associates did not want to involve the police; others claimed that the flamboyant record executive knew more than he was saying. The mysteries surrounding the shooting even spawned rumors that Shakur was not really dead at all, but had simply faked his death in order to sell albums.

Shakur's mother, living on an estate her son had bought for her outside of Atlanta, continued to fight her son's battles. Following his death, she had his body cremated, and sprinkled his ashes over her garden, which suddenly bloomed. "Tupac made this garden go crazy," she told *People*. "Pac brought this place alive."

By the end of 1997, Afeni was embroiled in legal battles over Shakur's estate, which was valued as high as $100 million. Among those she fought in court were Knight, who had persuaded Shakur to sign a handwritten contract in prison. Several others were suing Shakur for the effects of his actions or—in the case of anti-rap activist C. DeLores Tucker (1927–), who Shakur had criticized in one of his songs—his words. Another particularly bitter legal battle was with William Garland, Shakur's biological father. Shakur never even knew his father, but after his death, Garland suddenly appeared and took Afeni to court for part of the estate. Afeni Shakur referred to him publicly as "garbage" and a "gold digger."

In September 1997, *Jet* reported that Shakur's poems would be studied in a college course at the University of California at Berkeley entitled "The Poetry and History of Tupac Shakur." Also in the fall of 1997, Shakur's last two films, *Gridlock'd* and *Gang Related,* were released. *Gang Related* co-star Jim Belushi (1954–) recalled that he and Shakur became friends on the set, and spent time singing and listening to music. Shakur was a born performer, Belushi said. "I loved him. Now it makes me smile when I watch him on the screen because the fortunate thing about being an artist is that your spirit can be captured and you're always alive."

Further Reading

Baker, Calvin, and Karen Brailsford. "Living Dangerously." *People,* September 23, 1996, pp. 75–76.

Castro, Peter, and Ken Baker. "All Eyes on Her." *People,* December 1, 1997, pp. 151–154.

Contemporary Black Biography, Volume 14. Detroit: Gale, 1997, pp. 198–201.

Contemporary Musicians, Volume 17. Detroit: Gale, 1997, pp. 228–31.

Corliss, Richard. "The Better Side of Tupac." *Time Australia,* August 4, 1997, p. 70.

Da 2Pac /makaveli Krib, da fattest 2Pac site. [Online] http://makaveli.simplenet.com/ (accessed on October 8, 1998).

Geier, Tom. "The Killing Fields of Rap's Gangsta Land." *U.S. News & World Report,* March 24, 1997, p. 32.

Gill, Mark Stuart, and Albert Kim. "Tupac's Missing Millions." *Entertainment Weekly,* July 25, 1997, pp. 22–24.

Harris, Lauren Lanzen, ed. *Biography Today: 1997 Annual Cumulation.* Detroit: Omnigraphics, 1998.

Leland, John. "Requiem for a Gangsta." *Newsweek,* March 24, 1997, pp. 74–76.

Newsmakers 1997, Issue 1. Detroit: Gale, 1997.

"Poems of Late Tupac Shakur to Be Studied at University of California at Berkeley." *Jet,* September 29, 1997, p. 22.

Roberts, Johnnie L. "Grabbing at a Dead Star." *Newsweek,* September 1, 1997, p. 48.

Rogers, Patrick, and Lorenzo Benet. "Prophecy Fulfilled." *People,* September 30, 1996, pp. 79-80.

Tupac Amaru Shakur, 1971-1996. New York: Crown, 1997.

Tupac Shakur: Thug Immortal, the Last Interview (videorecording). Santa Monica, CA: Xenon Entertainment Group, 1997.

O. J. Simpson

Born July 9, 1947
San Francisco, California
Football player,
sports commentator, actor

In many lives and histories, there is a "before and after moment" when everything changes. For O. J. Simpson, the "before and after moment" unquestionably came on the night of June 12, 1994, when his ex-wife Nicole Brown Simpson (1959–94) and her friend Ronald Goldman (1968–94) were brutally murdered by a knife-wielding assailant at Nicole's home in Los Angeles, California.

From the time Simpson emerged in the national spotlight as a football player in the late 1960s through his later career as a sports commentator and actor, he had seemed the ultimate all-American type. Handsome, athletic, funny, and well-mannered, to whites he appeared an exceedingly clean-cut example of black American manhood. Many black people, on the other hand, believed that Simpson wanted nothing to do with them—that he, in fact, wanted to "be white," symbolized by his marriage to a white woman, Nicole Brown. All of that would change in June 1994, when Simpson became the chief suspect in the murders.

> [Blacks' positive] reaction [to Simpson's not-guilty verdict] had more to do with anger at the system and the Whites who control it than love of O. J. himself. . . .
>
> Writer Isabel Wilkerson

"Pencil Legs" becomes a running back

Orenthal James Simpson's childhood in San Francisco, California, was not an easy one. One of four children raised by a single mother, Eunice Simpson, he suffered from a calcium deficiency that forced him to wear leg braces for several years. In an effort to strengthen his legs when the braces were removed, Simpson began running, and soon realized that he had great athletic ability.

Yet he still had, as he later recalled, "a lot of hatred and defiance in me," no doubt partly a result of his painful early years. He became involved in gangs, and "could easily have come to a bad end if I hadn't gotten a break." That "break" came in several forms: his mother's encouragement, an opportunity to spend a day with baseball legend Willie Mays (1931– ; see entry in volume 3), and Simpson's involvement with high-school football. By the time he entered high school in Oakland, California, Simpson had emerged as an outstanding running back and track star.

Despite his success on the field, Simpson—he had begun calling himself "O. J." because he didn't like his first name—had trouble with his classes. So instead of attending a four-year university, he enrolled at the City College of San Francisco in 1965. There he became one of the greatest running backs in junior college football history, scoring fifty-four touchdowns and rushing for 2,445 yards in just two seasons. Prestigious universities were now eager to snap him up, and Simpson chose to attend the University of Southern California (USC). He was about to become a superstar.

Wins Heisman Trophy

Simpson proved to be one of the greatest college football players of all time. In 1968, during his final year at USC, he ran for 1,709 yards—a single-season record. That was the year he also won the coveted Heisman Trophy (for most outstanding college player). In 1969, *Sport* magazine named him Man of the Year, the first time that award had gone to a college player.

The Buffalo Bills of the National Football League (NFL) drafted Simpson. He played eight years with them, breaking a number of records and making Buffalo the top rushing team in 1973 with more than 3,000 rushed yards. Because his initials were the same as those for "orange juice," he became known as simply "The Juice."

San Francisco 49ers running back O. J. Simpson takes a handoff.

Actor and sports commentator

Simpson left Buffalo in 1977, played one season for the San Francisco 49ers, then retired from football in 1979. During the next fifteen years, he devoted himself to careers as an actor and as a sports commentator. Simpson had begun acting in 1974, with the "disaster" movie *The Towering Inferno*, and appeared in a number of motion pictures, including the *Naked Gun* series of comic movies in the late 1980s and early 1990s.

Simpson's most famous "role," however, was as himself. In a series of commercials for the Hertz rental car agency, the ex-running back was shown sprinting through an airport toward a Hertz car. In addition to his acting, Simpson served as a football commentator for more than twenty-five years on ABC and NBC. His last commentator job began in 1989, when he became co-host of *NFL Live* on NBC. Simpson remained in that role until 1994, when his life changed forever.

Nicole Brown and Ron Goldman murdered

While he was at USC, Simpson married his high-school sweetheart, Marguerite Thomas, and the couple had three children: Arnelle, Jason, and Aaren. They divorced in 1979, and soon afterward, Aaren, not yet two years old, drowned. The newly single Simpson had a number of girlfriends, many of them white; one of them was Nicole Brown. Eighteen when she met Simpson, Nicole married him in 1982, and they had two children, Sydney and Justin. Simpson frequently beat Nicole, and in 1989 he pleaded "no contest" to charges that he had battered her. In 1992, they divorced, but Simpson continued to be obsessed with her. She told friends, "He's going to kill me someday . . . and he's going to get away with it."

At around 10:15 P.M. on June 12, 1994, somebody did kill her, along with Goldman, who had come to her house apparently to return a pair of glasses she had left at a restaurant earlier that night. The murderer stabbed the victims repeatedly and left them in a pool of blood. When concerned neighbors came to the house at a few minutes after midnight, they found Sydney and Justin asleep upstairs.

Tried for murder

When a person is murdered, the police usually consider the victim's spouse a prime suspect, but when the world learned that Simpson had been charged in the murder, it reacted in shock. Simpson's positive reputation made it hard for some to believe he could be capable of any crime, let alone this one. Suspicion grew when he and his friend Al Cowlings fled arresting police officers, leading their pursuers on a sixty-mile car chase at slow speeds. Even then, however, support for

Simpson was high: fans, many of them white, held up signs that said "Go, Juice, Go."

Simpson was captured and jailed, and a trial date was set. His defense team, dubbed "The Dream Team," included high-profile attorneys F. Lee Bailey (1933–), Robert Shapiro, and Johnnie Cochran. On the prosecution side were attorneys Marcia

Defense attorneys Robert Shapiro and Johnnie Cochran sit next to their client, murder suspect O. J. Simpson.

The "trial of the century": A thumbnail sketch

Virtually every fact surrounding the O. J. Simpson case has been discussed almost endlessly on television and in newspapers. Fifty or more books about the trial have been published. What follows are the condensed facts of the case.

Nicole Brown Simpson and Ron Goldman were murdered at about 10:15 P.M. on June 12, 1994. At 10:25 P.M., a limousine driver arrived at O. J. Simpson's house to take him to the airport. The driver received no response when he buzzed the intercom, but at 10:52 he saw a man who fit Simpson's description entering the house. Four minutes later, the driver again buzzed the intercom; this time Simpson answered, saying he had been napping. When Simpson got into the car, he appeared visibly agitated, according to the later testimony of the driver.

At 2:10 A.M., Los Angeles Police Department (LAPD) detective Mark Fuhrman was summoned to the crime scene. Three hours later, Fuhrman and several other officers went to Simpson's house to inform him of his ex-wife's murder. Finding that Simpson was not home, Fuhrman scaled the wall and opened the gate for the others. Fuhrman then discovered a right-hand glove on the premises; smeared with blood, it matched a left-hand glove lying next to the murder victims. The detectives also found a trail of blood from Simpson's white Ford Bronco to the house. When police questioned Simpson the next day, they noticed cuts and bruises on his hands. Four days later, Simpson was charged with the murders.

Leading up to the trial, opinions about Simpson's guilt or innocence were sharply divided along racial lines. However, the case did not immediately take on racial overtones, in part because Simpson had never made an issue of his race. Initially, Simpson's

Clark and Christopher Darden of the Los Angeles district attorney's office. (For details of the trial, see accompanying sidebar.)

From jury selection to verdict, the nationally-televised trial lasted 372 days. The Simpson case dominated headlines; a "media circus" had developed as every TV network and newspaper in the world, it seemed, attempted to capitalize on "The Trial of the Century." Judge Lance Ito was regularly criticized for his apparent inability to keep order in his courtroom, and people wondered what effect the drawn-out trial was having on the jury. In the course of the long months, numerous

most prominent lawyers were two whites, F. Lee Bailey and Robert Shapiro. But when African American attorney Johnnie Cochran emerged as the star of the "Dream Team," the case began to take on racial overtones.

In this regard, one of the most important turning points in the trial came when the defense discovered videotapes on which Fuhrman had repeatedly made insulting comments about blacks. This hurt the prosecution's case, particularly because Fuhrman had earlier testified that he had never made any racist statements in his life. Although he did not actually come out and say so, Cochran suggested that Fuhrman had planted the bloody glove at the crime scene.

Another significant moment in the trial came when Cochran asked Simpson to try on the glove. Simpson was already wearing a rubber glove, which he had not pushed down completely on his fingers. As he tried to put on the leather glove, he made faces to suggest that it was a difficult fit. Cochran would later utter one of the most famous statements of the case when, in referring to the glove, he told the jury, "If it doesn't fit, you must acquit."

The prosecution meanwhile concentrated on evidence involving DNA, or deoxyribonucleic acid, a sort of "fingerprint" that everyone carries in their blood. According to this evidence, the blood on the glove at Simpson's house, inside his Bronco, and at the crime scene all matched the victims' blood types. However, the jury found much of this testimony quite technical. In the end, the jurors said that the prosecution had simply not made as strong a case as the defense. The jury found Simpson not-guilty.

jurors had been dismissed, until the jury that remained was mostly African American and female. When the case finished it was expected that the jury would spend days and days deciding on a verdict. Instead it took them four hours. On October 3, 1995, their verdict was not guilty on all counts.

Divided reactions to the verdict

During the aftermath of the Simpson case, much of non-black America felt that the jurors' verdict was racially motivated. Many believed that rather than assessing the actual evidence before them, the jurors were attempting to make up for the many black men falsely convicted in the past by acquitting a man obviously guilty. Isabel Wilkerson in *Essence,* for instance, quoted a friend as saying that she felt "'satisfaction and revenge, perverse though it may be,' that a Black man had beaten Whites in their own coliseum—that Whites, for once, know how it feels to lose."

But this initial joy wore off, Wilkerson observed. Was Simpson's victory really a victory for black people, or simply a victory for Simpson? Having reached out to the African American community in his time of need, with the support of friends such as ex-football player and preacher Rosie Grier (1932–), Simpson had once again turned his back on the community. "As for O. J.," Wilkerson wrote in January 1996, "by now it is clear that he has no desire to become anybody's savior or even role model. Malcolm [X] and Martin [Luther King] would not have been down in Florida playing golf . . . on their daughters' birthdays. And whatever happened to O. J.'s sober vow that he would devote his life to finding Nicole's killer? No one said he had to do it, but since he brought it up. . . ."

Loses $33.5 million case

As it turned out, Simpson had his freedom, but little else. He faced serious financial problems when the Brown and Goldman families took him to court in a civil suit in 1996. Though they demanded a large sum of money from him, it was clear that they really wanted to prove Simpson's guilt—to get a measure of the justice they felt they had been denied.

In the civil trial, the African American community did not rally so forcefully to Simpson's defense. And unlike in the criminal trial, this time Simpson would be required to testify. The civil case revolved around an item of clothing, only it wasn't a glove that didn't seem to fit (as in the criminal trial). Here, the key piece of evidence was a pair of rare and expensive shoes matching those worn by the killer. Simpson claimed he didn't own them, but the plaintiffs' lawyers produced more than thirty photographs of him with the shoes on.

In the end, the jury ruled that Simpson owed the Browns and Goldmans (the plaintiffs) some $33.5 million in damages. This meant that he would be paying back money for a long, long time, especially because "The Dream Team" had cost a fortune, and because his possibilities for making money were now limited. On the positive side, the State of California—in a move that angered some people as much as the "not guilty" verdict—granted him custody of his and Nicole's children.

In September 1997, Simpson sold his Brentwood mansion for $3.95 million to pay off his debts. The house, reportedly purchased by investment banker Kenneth Abdalla, was torn down on July 29, 1998, so that the owner could build a new house—one presumably free from all the memories associated with Simpson. As for Simpson himself, he moved to a gated community about a mile from his old home, and has told CNN he is managing to survive on his NFL pension of $25,000 a month.

Sources for further reading

Aaseng, Nathan. *The O. J. Simpson Trial: What It Shows Us About Our Legal System.* New York: Walker, 1996.

Burchard, Marshall, and Sue Burchard. *Sports Hero, O. J. Simpson.* New York: Putnam, 1975.

"Can O. J. Simpson Win Again?" *Jet,* February 26, 1996, pp. 54–56.

CNN–O. J. Simpson Trial. [Online] http://www.cnn.com/US/OJ/index.html (accessed on October 8, 1998).

Court TV Casefiles: O. J. Simpson. [Online] http://www.courttv.com/casefiles/simpson (accessed on October 8, 1998).

Hewitt, Bill, et al. "Free, But Not Clear." *People,* November 13, 1995, pp. 58–61.

Hewitt, Bill, et al. "The Shoes Fit, So They Wouldn't Acquit." *People,* February 17, 1997, pp. 46–51.

Jackson, Jesse L., Jr. "Why Race Dialogue Stutters." *Nation,* March 31, 1997, pp. 22–24.

Loury, Glenn C. "Looking Beyond O. J." *U.S. News & World Report,* February 17, 1997, p. 13.

O. J. Central. [Online] http://pathfinder.com/@@6cr3b2GjUA-IAQFNw/pathfinder/features/oj/central1.html (accessed on October 8, 1998).

"O. J. Simpson Says He Will Live Off His $25,000-a-Month Pension." *Jet,* July 28, 1997, pp. 52–54.

Reilly, Rick. "Need a Fourth?" *Sports Illustrated,* March 31, 1997, pp. 42–45.

Rice, Earle, Jr. *The O. J. Simpson Trial.* San Diego, CA: Lucent Books, 1997.

Schmitz, Dorothy Childers. *O. J. Simpson: The Juice Is Loose.* Mankato, MN: Crestwood House, 1977.

Seter, Jennifer, Timothy M. Ito, and Robin M. Bennefield. "Simpson Trial & Trivia." *U.S. News & World Report,* October 16, 1995, pp. 42–43.

Stewart, James B. "Race, Science, and 'Just-Us': Understanding Jurors' Reasonable Doubt in the O. J. Simpson Trial." *Black Scholar,* Fall 1995, pp. 43–45.

Wilkerson, Isabel. "O. J.: Having Our Say." *Essence,* January 1996, pp. 82–84+.

Tina Turner

Born November 26, 1939
Brownsville, Tennessee
Singer, actress

With her 1984 album *Private Dancer*, which sold over 11 million copies, singer Tina Turner staged one of the greatest comebacks in music history; yet her "comeback" was actually much bigger than her original success. In the 1960s, she and her husband at the time, Ike Turner (1931–), had a number of minor hits, most notably a cover of Creedence Clearwater Revival's "Proud Mary."

Their popularity was greater in Europe, but even there, something seemed to be placing a limit on Tina's potential. Eventually she realized what it was. In 1976, she ended a stormy seventeen-year relationship with the abusive Ike. Years of struggle lay ahead for her, but in 1984 she enjoyed the payoff with a string of hits that included "You Better Be Good to Me," "Private Dancer," and "What's Love Got to Do with It." The latter became the title of an acclaimed 1993 film in which Angela Bassett (1958–) played Tina and Laurence Fishburne (1962–) portrayed Ike.

"I was a victim; I don't dwell on it. I stood up for my life."

From church choir to nightclub

Turner was born Anna Mae Bullock, the daughter of a Baptist deacon, in Brownville, Tennessee, in 1939. Hers was not a happy home life, and her parents fought constantly. When the United States entered World War II (1939–45) in December 1941, her parents went to work in the defense industry in nearby Knoxville. They left Turner and her sister Alline with their strict Baptist grandmother, Mama Roxanna, who became a strong influence.

After the war, the family moved to Spring Hill, where Turner—not yet eleven years old—became the youngest member of the church choir. In 1950, her parents divorced, and for the next six years she lived with one family member after another. In 1956 she joined her mother and Alline in St. Louis, Missouri.

This was a turning point for her. Though she had been a cheerleader in high school, Turner—who would later become known as one of the sexiest women in rock 'n roll—did not consider herself attractive. She was also shy, and therefore when Alline took her to a nightclub where people were drinking and dancing, she was a bit shocked by what she saw. Yet she was intrigued by a group called the Kings of Rhythm, and by their lead musician, Ike Turner.

"Tina Turner" is born

Ike had a tremendous stage presence, and a reputation for treating women terribly. He also had no shortage of female admirers, and took no immediate notice of Anna Mae Bullock, as she was still called. Alline was dating the band's drummer, who noticed that Anna Mae could sing. He persuaded her to take the stage, where she brought the house down with a rendition of a song by B. B. King (1925– ; see entry in volume 3). That got Ike's attention.

At that point, Ike's attentions were still platonic—that is, he treated Turner more like a sister or daughter than like a lover. She became involved with Raymond Hill, a saxophone player for the band, and had a child with him, a son named

Raymond Craig, in 1958. But by 1959 she was Ike's lover, and in 1960 she bore him a son named Ronald Renelle. Two years later, the couple were married in Mexico City, Mexico, though it is unlikely that the ceremony was legally binding since Ike did not divorce his previous wife until 1974.

In the summer of 1960, the two released their first single, "A Fool in Love," and with the record came a new name for Anna Mae Bullock. Ike was intrigued by the jungle queen "Sheena" from the 1940s movies, and he decided he liked the name "Tina" because it rhymed with "Sheena." Years later, long after she had left Ike, Tina Turner kept the name he had given her.

Emerging from Ike's shadow

During the early 1960s, the Ike and Tina Turner Revue began to make a name for themselves and attract a racially mixed audience. Their hits included "It's Going to Work Out Fine," "I Pity the Fool," "I Idolize You," and "Tra La La La La." They began playing at more prestigious venues, including the Apollo Theatre in New York's Harlem district, and appeared on the popular TV program *American Bandstand*. But Turner was not happy: Ike beat her frequently, and cheated on her with other women, including the group's backup singers, the Ikettes.

Ike "kept control of me with *fear*," Turner later recalled in her autobiography, but several events in the mid-1960s influenced her desire to escape from the unhealthy relationship. At that time, one of the most respected figures in soul music was a white man, producer Phil Spector (1940–), who had created such memorable hits as "He's So Fine" by the Chiffons and "Be My Little Baby" by the Ronettes. Now Spector wanted to make a superstar of Turner, and he presented her with a song called "River Deep, Mountain High." He requested, however, that Ike not be involved in the recording in any way.

Ike agreed to Spector's request, no doubt seeing the financial potential that the connection with Spector offered.

The song was released in 1966 with a huge promotional effort, but it failed to make a dent in the U.S. charts; in Europe, however, it was a smash. Turner recalls that the 1966 European tour, in which she and Ike opened for the Rolling Stones, was "the beginning of my escape from Ike Turner."

Declares her independence

The Stones tour led to enormous exposure and to a lifelong friendship with Stones lead singer Mick Jagger (1944–). Numerous hits followed, including covers of "I've Been Loving You Too Long" by Otis Redding (1941–68) in 1969; "Come Together" by the Beatles in 1970; and "I Want to Take You Higher" by Sly & the Family Stone, also in 1970. "Proud Mary" sold over a million copies and "Nutbush City Limits" (written by Turner herself) was a huge hit in both the United States and England in 1973.

Meanwhile, Turner was becoming more and more unhappy with her marriage and her life. In the late 1960s, she attempted suicide by taking fifty Valium tablets, and had to have her stomach pumped. She continued to develop a life separate from the one with Ike, appearing without him as the Acid Queen in the 1975 film of the rock opera *Tommy* by the Who. During the filming of the movie, she became friends with actress Ann-Margret (1941–), a longtime fan. Also in 1975, Ike and Tina had their last hit together, "Baby—Get It On."

Problems with the relationship came to a head in 1976, while the band was on tour in Texas. Taking just thirty-six cents and a gas station credit card, Tina left Ike for good. The day on which she declared her independence was July 1, just three days short of the Bicentennial, the 200th anniversary of the signing of the Declaration of Independence.

From welfare to superstardom

The next few years were hard ones. Turner earned money cleaning houses, and went on government food stamps for awhile. Meanwhile, Ike continued to harass her. In order to finalize the divorce with him, she gave up any financial claims

Mel Gibson and Tina Turner in a scene from Mad Max: Beyond Thunderdome.

she had on him, and even paid the debt incurred because of cancelled shows after her departure. In 1978, she released her first solo album, *Rough,* and it flopped.

Then Ann-Margret introduced Turner to Australian manager Roger Davies, who helped her redesign her stage act. Davies orchestrated her 1980–81 European tour, and began booking engagements for her in the United States, including a

Rock 'n' roll: What's color got to do with it?

There are many unusual things about rock star Tina Turner, not the least of which is the fact that she's a *black* rock star. Even though rock 'n' roll developed out of the blues, a style of music created by blacks, most African American performers are not rock musicians. Some of the most popular black vocalists are soul or R&B singers such as Aretha Franklin (1942– ; see entry in volume 2) and Stevie Wonder (1950– ; see entry in volume 4); or pop singers such as Diana Ross (1944– ; see entry in volume 3) and Whitney Houston (1963– ; see entry in volume 2); or rap and hip-hop artists such as Sean "Puff Daddy" Combs (1969–) and Tupac Shakur (1971–96; see entry).

But the very expression "rock 'n' roll" was created by blacks, and the first rock hit, "Sh-Boom," was recorded by a black group in 1954. Yet even as music was bringing young people together in the 1950s, racial prejudice pulled them apart. "Sh-Boom" only became a hit after it was recorded by a white group.

Elvis Presley (1935–77) used styles he had learned from black musicians, but he was more popular than contemporaries such as Fats Domino (1928–), Chuck Berry (1926– ; see entry in volume 1), and Little Richard (1932- ; see entry in volume 3). One reason was because Presley was white. But black rock and pop singers continued to score hits throughout the late 1950s and early 1960s, and in the mid-1960s, black music emerged in the mainstream of American popular culture.

well-publicized show at the Ritz in New York City and a spot on *Saturday Night Live* with Rod Stewart (1945–). Davies negotiated a deal with Capitol Records, and forced them to agree to release her album in both the United States and Europe. Turner and Davies together selected the songs for the album, including one written by Dire Straits lead vocalist Mark Knopfler entitled "Private Dancer."

The result, in the words of co-author Kurt Loder in Turner's autobiography, was that "after a quarter of a century, Tina Turner was an overnight sensation." Her album was a smash hit, earning her two American Music awards and two Grammys. A string of successes followed. She appeared on the cover of *Rolling Stone;* acted opposite Mel Gibson in *Mad Max:*

British rock stars such as Eric Clapton (1945–), Mick Jagger, and Led Zeppelin's Jimmy Page (1944–) were heavily influenced by American blues performers such as Muddy Waters (1915–83), B. B. King, and Howlin' Wolf (1910–76). Starting in 1964, first the Beatles and then a succession of British groups became a sensation in America, and they helped make white American kids aware of the great musical traditions in their midst.

Then in 1967, a true rock 'n' roll immortal appeared on the scene—and he was a black man, Jimi Hendrix (1942–70; see entry in volume 2). A true guitar genius, he played at the famous 1969 Woodstock festival, as did Sly & the Family Stone, and folk musician Richie Havens (1941–). Other popular black artists in the 1970s and 1980s included Billy Preston (1946–), George Clinton (1941–), the artist then known as Prince (1958–), and of course Tina Turner.

By the late 1980s and 1990s, more African Americans were hitting it big in the world of rock. These musicians included the group Living Color, singer Tracy Chapman (1964–), and Lennie Kravitz (1964–). By the late 1990s, music became more interracial, and one of the central figures in this movement was Puff Daddy. In 1998, he and Jimmy Page recorded a new danceable version of Led Zeppelin's 1975 classic, "Kashmir." It was clear that music—and relationships between people—had come a long way since the 1950s.

Beyond Thunderdome (1985), and sang the theme song, "We Don't Need Another Hero"; sang on the 1985 all-star charity recording "We Are the World"; and published her autobiography in 1986. Her albums *Break Every Rule* (1986), *Tina Live in Europe* (1988), and *Foreign Affair* (1989) were hugely popular.

Continued success in the 1990s

In 1991 Turner and her ex-husband were inducted into the Rock 'n' Roll Hall of Fame. In 1993, Fishburne and Bassett portrayed the former husband-and-wife singing duo in "What's Love Got to Do with It." Turner is "this beautiful, gorgeous woman with incredible energy," said Bassett. "When she came to the set, she just came and did things she didn't have to do. She could have sat back, but she helped with my make-up. She took the wigs, cut them for me, went to the store and bought shoes for me. She's so generous and loyal." In addition to her work with Bassett, Turner re-recorded some of her hits for the movie's soundtrack album.

In 1995, Turner sang the theme song for the James Bond movie *Goldeneye,* and in 1996 scored another big hit with the album *Wildest Dreams*. By then she had become involved with German record executive Erwin Bach, and she divided her time between houses in France and Zurich, Switzerland. She called Zurich "a very small, conservative city, but believe me, I'm waking them up!"

At almost sixty years old, Turner remains a sex symbol, and one of the most inspiring performers in rock music. "I never think of myself as sexy," she told *Jet* in August 1997. "I think I'm a lot of fun."

Sources for further reading

Busnar, Gene. *The Picture Life of Tina Turner.* New York: F. Watts, 1987.

Collier, Aldore. "What's Love Got to Do With It." *Ebony,* July 1993, pp. 110–112.

Gregory, Deborah. "People: Tina Turner." *Essence,* October 1996, p. 50.

Hirshey, Gerri. "Tina Turner." *Rolling Stone,* November 13, 1997, pp. 117–21.

Koenig, Teresa. *Tina Turner.* Mankato, MN: Crestwood House, 1986.

"Tina Turner Returns to U.S. with 'Wildest Dreams' World Tour." *Jet,* March 17, 1997, pp. 32–35.

"Tina Turner Succeeded as Singer Despite Having Insecurities About Her Voice." *Jet,* April 14, 1997, p. 62.

Turner, Tina, with Kurt Loder. *I, Tina.* New York: Morrow, 1986.

Tuskegee Airmen

First flight in 1943
Last flight in 1945
First African American World War II pilots

Officially they were graduates of the 66th Air Force Contract Flying School at the Tuskegee Institute in Tuskegee, Alabama, and their leading military unit was the 99th Squadron. In World War II (1939–45), they gained the nickname "Red-Tailed Angels." But thanks in part to a 1995 movie starring Laurence Fishburne (1962–), they are best known to the world as "the Tuskegee Airmen."

In the Second World War, the United States fought against racist superpowers in Nazi Germany and Japan, but ironically, "the land of the free and the home of the brave" was itself a country that practiced official policies of discrimination. The U.S. military remained segregated, and blacks eager to take part in the war effort found that the only jobs available to them were in non-combat positions such as cook and supply clerk.

But Colonel Benjamin Davis (1912–) and others, both black and white, believed that African Americans were capable of at least as great a degree of military heroism as their

> *"The lack of recognition of the black Americans who first struggled for the right to train as pilots, then for the right to fly in combat, is one of the saddest lapses in U.S. military history—an important saga missing from most textbooks."*
>
> —Time magazine, *August 28, 1995*

white counterparts. After a bitter struggle, they established the school at Tuskegee. Starting in 1943, Tuskegee graduates began flying in North Africa and later Italy, where they earned great distinction. As escorts, their job was to ensure that bomber planes made it to their targets without getting shot down. In more than 1,500 missions, the Tuskegee Airmen never lost a single bomber. In part because of the distinguished record of service established by the all-black flying units, President Harry S Truman (1884–1972) ordered the full integration of the armed forces in 1948.

Treated worse than prisoners

During World War II, American troops overseas were fighting in the name of freedom and democracy against fascism (pronounced "FASH-ism"), a type of dictatorship that promotes the nation or race over the individual. But it is a sad and ironic fact that freedom and democracy simply did not exist for most African Americans at the time.

Blacks were second-class citizens at best, and even those who tried to participate in the war effort found themselves treated disgracefully. For example, African Americans were forced to sit in the front railcars of trains, where soot from the engine poured in the window; German and Italian prisoners of war got better seats. Blacks were also not allowed to eat in the white section of the cafeteria at the military base; German prisoners of war, however, were free to dine there.

Given the environment in which they lived, the Tuskegee Airmen were particularly heroic for their desire to serve a country that treated them poorly. There were many all-black units serving with distinction during the war, but as Ray Mahon noted in *American Legion* magazine, "more than any unit or any one person, it was the Tuskegee Airmen who symbolized the hopes and aspirations of 13 million black Americans."

Racking up victories

The 66th Air Force Contract Flying School was established at Tuskegee in early 1941, and received hundreds of applications from some of the most well-educated black men in America. On March 21 of that year, the 99th Squadron was activated, and training of the first thirteen pilots began in the summer. By graduation day on March 7, 1942, after months of grueling training, only five of the original thirteen remained: Davis, Lemuel R. Curtis, Charles Debow, George S. Roberts, and Mac Ross.

Ultimately 992 African American pilots would graduate from the school, including future Detroit mayor Coleman Young (1918–97; see entry in volume 4). At first, it appeared that all their training would be in vain—that the military still wouldn't trust black pilots to fly planes. But first lady Eleanor Roosevelt (1884–1962) did a courageous thing: on a visit to the school, she went up in a plane with a Tuskegee pilot behind the wheel. "It was a well-publicized vote of confidence in the program," wrote Christopher John Farley and Margot Hornblower in *Time* magazine fifty years later. Soon thereafter, the 99th Fighter Squadron was dispatched to North Africa.

In 1942, Nazi Germany under Adolf Hitler (1889–1945), along with Italy and other nations that had joined in the Axis Pact, controlled most of Europe. The closest the Allies, chiefly the United States and Britain, could come to attacking the Axis position was in North Africa. That location is where the 99th Fighter Squadron first served in combat. On July 2, 1943, Lt. Charles B. Hall of Indiana became the first Tuskegee flyer to shoot down a German aircraft.

Soon the Allies crossed the Mediterranean Sea and began approaching Europe. They invaded the island of Sicily off the coast of Italy, where the 99th began to rack up victories. On one January day in 1944, Tuskegee pilots downed eight German aircraft—five in a matter of five minutes.

Officers reprimanded

Another saga almost as heroic as that of the 99th was unfolding as Art Carter and other journalists for the *Afro-American* became the first black American war correspondents. In their dispatches, published in 1944 as *This Is Our*

Seven members of the Tuskegee Airmen arrive at Laguardia Airport in New York on July 20, 1945, after flying in from Casablanca, North Africa.

War (and available for viewing online—see sources at the end of this entry), Carter faithfully reported on "Colonel Davis's Flyers in Italy." Twenty-two-year-old Lieutenant Lewis C. Smith, for instance, remembered: "The sky was full of planes, but I picked out one FW-190 and chased him to the outskirts of Rome, firing all the way. The plane burned and smoked profusely and I knew I had got[ten] him. It's a good feeling."

In October 1943, the 99th was briefly combined with an all-white squadron, the 79th Fighter Group, and it continued to serve with distinction despite a commander, Colonel William Momyer, who endangered the black flyers' lives by refusing to include them in key briefings before bombing runs. On July 4, 1944, the 99th ceased to exist, when it was combined with three other squadrons—the 100th, 301st, and 302nd, all trained at Tuskegee—to become the 332nd Fighter Group. Initially there was friction, because the other units lacked the combat experience gained by the flyers of the 99th, but ultimately the combined unit earned an outstanding record. In 1,578 missions, they won 150 Distinguished Flying Crosses and 744 air medals, which made them some of the most decorated flyers of the war. They also destroyed 261 German planes and damaged 159 others, while hitting some 950 enemy supply and transport targets.

By war's end, sixty-six Tuskegee pilots had died in combat, and thirty-three more had been shot down and become prisoners of war. The Tuskegee Airmen became legendary figures, not unlike the almost mythical all-black 54th Massachusetts Regiment during the Civil War (1861–65), later immortalized in the 1990 film *Glory*. The Tuskegee Airmen, too, would have their own film, with Andre Braugher (1962–), who had also appeared in *Glory,* playing the part of Davis. But that was half a century later, in 1995—in 1945, all that their heroism earned them was a reprimand, and for one pilot, a court-martial.

While attending training at the ironically named Freeman Field in Seymour, Indiana, in April 1945, a group of Tuskegee-trained officers were denied entry to the white officers' club. When they demanded to be admitted, 104 of them were arrested. Most received official reprimands, which stayed on their permanent records; one officer, Lieutenant Roger Terry, was court-martialed (convicted of violating military law and thrown out of the service).

Honors long overdue

The disgraceful treatment of the Tuskegee Airmen did not end in 1945. Whereas white flyers trained during the war found a world of opportunities as airline pilots in peacetime, such opportunities were not available to black airmen. Tuskegee graduate LeRoy Eley was one of the lucky ones: he got a job as a flight instructor, in which he trained sixty-eight white pilots. But all of the flyers he trained got jobs; Eley, himself, could not.

And yet changes were happening . . . slowly. With the support of Col. Noel Parrish, the white commanding officer at

Tuskegee, a small group of military leaders began urging the War Department (later renamed the Department of Defense) to reconsider its policy on segregation. President Truman was all for it, but Congress refused to pass legislation integrating the armed forces. So Truman exercised his power as president to issue two executive orders. The orders said in part, "It is hereby declared to be the policy of the President that there shall be equality of treatment and opportunity for all persons in the armed services without regard to race, color, religion or national origin." On June 1, 1949, the Air Force began deactivating its all-black squadrons and assigning members to integrated units.

Starting in 1952, Tuskegee graduate Robert Williams (1922–) began trying to sell the story of the Tuskegee Airmen to Hollywood. After a series of false starts, including a planned 1977 version, Home Box Office (HBO) in 1995 presented *The Tuskegee Airmen*. Among its stars, besides Fishburne and Braugher, were future Oscar winner Cuba Gooding, Jr. (1968–), Courtney B. Vance (1960–), Allen Payne (1962–), and Malcolm-Jamal Warner (1970–), who told *Time* magazine, "It's a crime, literally, that people don't know who [the Tuskegee Airmen are, and] that it takes a television movie to legitimize them."

Of course movies are not the same thing as history, as Stanley Sandler pointed out in an *American Historical Review* article. For instance, "We see a raving racist major (Chris McDonald) welcoming the black rookie cadets. . . . But he never existed. In reality, the racists at Tuskegee had to mute their feelings. Official policy was that the Tuskegee airmen were to receive training, treatment, and equipment identical to that of white cadets. This position . . . protected the military; if the Tuskegee 'experiment' failed, then the fault must lie with the cadets, not their treatment." Sandler concluded that "this film is no substitute for a sober presentation of the historical facts, which on their own are inspiring enough."

In 1994 Davis, now *General* Davis, was inducted into the Aviation Hall of Fame in Dayton, Ohio. "It means just about everything to me," he told *Jet*. "I never expected it to happen."

And in 1995, at a Tuskegee Airmen banquet in Atlanta, the Air Force announced that letters of reprimand were being removed from the permanent records of officers involved in the Freeman Field incident. The conviction of the court-martialed Terry was reversed and he received an apology for "a terrible wrong in the annals of U.S. military history."

The Tuskegee Airmen worked to create changes in America, and many lived to see the fruits of their labors. Some ex-airmen managed to visit schools and tell a new generation about their exploits as flyers. In March 1998, for instance, two Tuskegee pilots, Eugene Guyton and Buddy Johnston, visited a school near Cleveland, Ohio. Discussing the discrimination they had experienced, Guyton said, "Laws are just words written on paper and that's all they will ever be, until they are written in people's hearts." Said one high-school junior, "They are excellent examples of true Americans."

Sources for further reading

AFRO-Americ@. *The Tuskegee Airmen.* [Online] http://www.afroam.org/history/tusk/tuskmain.html (accessed on October 8, 1998).

Farley, Christopher John, and Margot Hornblower. "Winning the Right to Fly." *Time,* August 28, 1995, pp. 62–64.

"General Benjamin Davis, Jr., Tuskegee Airmen Founder, Inducted into Aviation Hall of Fame." *Jet,* August 15, 1994, p. 36.

Harris, Jacqueline L. *The Tuskegee Airmen: Black Heroes of World War II.* Parsippany, NJ: Dillon Press, 1996.

Howell, Ann Chandler. *Tuskegee Airmen: Heroes in Our Fight for Dignity, Inclusion, and Citizenship Rights.* Chicago: Chandler/White Publishing, 1994.

Kadlcek, Tina. "Tuskegee Airmen's Patriotism Overcame Bias." *Cleveland Plain Dealer,* March 18, 1998, p. 3-E.

McKissack, Patricia, and Frederick McKissack. *Red-Tail Angels: The Story of the Tuskegee Airmen of World War II.* Walker, 1995.

Mahon, Ray. "Color Them Courageous." *American Legion,* September 1995, pp. 72, 110.

Markowitz, Robert, director. *The Tuskegee Airmen* (motion picture). Home Box Office/Price Entertainment, 1995.

Newborn, Steve. "Pilots Fought a War on 2 Fronts." *Tampa Tribune,* April 24, 1998, p. 1.

Sandler, Stanley. "The Tuskegee Airmen." *American Historical Review,* October 1996, pp. 1171–73.

Tuskegee Airmen. Peterborough, NH: Cobbleston Publishing, 1997.

"Tuskegee Airmen Absolved of 50-Year-Old Reprimands at Atlanta Dinner." *Jet,* October 16, 1995, pp. 58–60.

Venus Williams

*Born June 17, 1980
Lynnwood, California
Tennis player*

In March 1998, Venus Williams won her first Women's Tennis Association (WTA) tournament when she defeated Joanette Kruger. Standing more than six feet tall and wearing her trademark beads in her hair, Williams makes an unusual figure on the court; but these are not the only unusual facts about her.

At the time of her first tournament win—she had played in several others and lost—Williams was not yet eighteen years old. The fact that she is black makes her a standout in a sport traditionally dominated by players of European heritage. And Williams did not get her start playing in elegant country clubs, as many players do: her first tennis court was on the mean streets of Compton, in South Central Los Angeles, California—one of the toughest neighborhoods in America.

Gunshots on the tennis court

Williams was born on June 17, 1980, the fourth child of Richard and Oracene Williams. The Williamses were firm in

"In the past, I really didn't worry about what other people thought because it was important what I thought, what my family thought. There's a lot of myths floating around. I knew one day people would see. It would just be a little bit of time. . . ."

their plans for their five children, all of whom are girls: they were to be brought up in the Jehovah's Witnesses faith, and they would be successful. One daughter studied to be a doctor, another a lawyer. As for the last two, Venus and her baby sister Serena, both would ultimately become tennis stars.

Richard Williams had taught himself tennis, and tried to teach his girls, but only Venus and Serena were interested. Venus took to the game at the age of four. She and her father first played on the public courts of Compton. "We've been shot at on the tennis court," Richard later told *Sports Illustrated*. "But now gang members know us and protect us when the shooting starts."

Called "the Cinderella of the Ghetto" by her father, Williams soon excelled at tennis. By the age of seven, she had attracted the attention of tennis legends John McEnroe (1959–) and Pete Sampras (1971–). When she was ten years old, she was ranked the top tennis player in the highly competitive under-12 division in southern California. Once Venus grew into the next division, Serena took the under-12 title.

Taken out of the game

Williams was becoming a star, soon attracting attention from fans and the media. She had to change elementary schools three times to get away from reporters. All this fame began to bother her parents. Even though their father allowed Venus and Serena to attend Ric Macci's tennis academy in Del Ray Beach, Florida, he decided in 1991 that they would not play in any junior tennis tournaments. Instead, they would try to have a normal experience in middle school and junior high, and return to tennis when they were old enough to become professionals.

At that time, WTA rules allowed a player to turn pro at fourteen, which for Williams would be in 1994. But a rule change had been passed, and the minimum age would soon be raised to fifteen, meaning that if Venus planned to turn pro before she was fifteen, she had to act quickly. Although her father didn't want her to go pro, he allowed her to make the decision herself—as long as she kept up her grades. By then the entire family had moved to Florida, and he had enrolled her in a private school, where she maintained an impressive 3.8 grade point average. She decided to turn pro.

Loses first two Grand Slam tournaments

In her first professional game, Williams defeated Shaun Stafford (1968–) at the Bank of the West Classic, but was in turn beaten by top-seeded Arantxa Sanchez Vicario (1971–). In 1995 and 1996, she did not play many tournaments; following her graduation from high school in 1997, however, she joined the WTA Tour full-time.

Professional tennis is dominated by four Grand Slam tournaments, which are played in four different countries on three continents: Wimbledon in Great Britain, the French Open, the U.S. Open, and the Australian Open. Williams played her first Grand Slam tournament at the 1997 French Open. After an initial win against Naoko Sawamatsu (1973–), she lost to France's Natalie Tauziat.

Williams looked like a favorite to win at her next Grand Slam tournament, Wimbledon, in July 1997. "She was like nothing Wimbledon had ever seen," wrote S. L. Price in *Sports Illustrated,* recounting the response of the British press to the six-foot-tall black tennis player, who wore green, purple, and white beads in her hair. Serena was so confident of her sister's abilities that while Venus played Magdalena Grazybowska of Poland, she sat in the stands reading *A Tale of Two Cities* by Charles Dickens (1812–70). Serena told a reporter that she had also read Dickens's *Great Expectations,* "but I like this one better."

As it turned out, the Williams family's great expectations were in vain. "Venus fell apart," wrote Price, who like many other sportswriters and fans had criticized her for behaving arrogantly toward her opponents. Williams was "a huge talent with little idea of how to adjust to an opponent or adversity."

With her braids flying, Venus Williams attacks a volley at the U.S. Open.

Surprises at the U.S. Open

But it was much too early to count Williams out. She knew that, and so did Althea Gibson (1927– ; see entry in volume 2), who had become the first African American female tennis champion at Wimbledon in 1956. When the two met, Gibson gave Williams this advice: "Play aggressively and with spirit."

As the seventeen-year-old prepared for her first U.S. Open in the fall of 1997, her prospects did not appear high. She was ranked 66th in the world, and to many, seemed to have an attitude problem. But things started to change. At the U.S. Open, Williams complimented an opponent, and gave fans a collection of blue beads that had fallen out of her hair. "My goal coming in was not to lose one bead during a match," admitted Williams, who, in honor of the U.S. Open, had spent nine hours stringing 1,800 red, white, and blue beads in her braids.

Williams did not win at the U.S. Open, despite an initial victory over Irena Spirlea (1974–) of Romania. But she became only the second female in history, after Pam Shriver (1962–) in 1978, to reach the tournament's semifinal on her first appearance. After she lost to Martina Hingis (1980–), Williams was philosophical, and told reporters that even though she hadn't won, "I guess this is a great tournament for me."

Great victories before eighteenth birthday

Williams's breakthrough year was 1998. In the Australian Open, she defeated Hingis—and then faced her own sister. After she defeated Serena, Venus said, "I told her, 'Serena, I'm sorry I took you out. I didn't want to, but I had to do it.'" She ended up losing the singles tournament, but winning the mixed doubles title alongside Justin Gimelstob.

In March 1998, Williams won her first WTA tournament, defeating Joanette Kruger at the IGA Tennis Classic. She then won the Lipton International, defeating Hingis yet again in the semifinals, and Anna Kournikova of Russia in the final. Accepting the $27,000 prize, she told reporters, "This is one I will probably always remember."

Despite her successes and such financial rewards as a $12 million endorsement deal with Reebok, which she signed in 1995, Venus has a down-to-earth side as well. She enjoys games and movies, but rarely watches TV except to see tennis matches. In high school, she was a good student, and she also prepared for the future by taking business classes at a local college. Her father, who has sometimes been criticized by the media for his training methods, has said, "She needs time to get her education, because all these girls who come along chewing gum and not being able to speak that well, what happens to them when their careers are over?"

Venus has said that she hopes one day to be an architect, or to run a clothing store with her mother and Serena. She also told *People* magazine that she might pursue a career as a paleontologist (one who studies dinosaur bones) or an archeologist (one who studies the remains of past civilizations). "I like digging into the past. Maybe because I wasn't there. But I need to catch up on biology first."

Sources for further reading

Bowers, Faye. "Rising Star in Women's Tennis: Venus." *Christian Science Monitor,* September 4, 1997, p. 1.

Buxton, Angela, and Sanford Baruch. "Advice from a Legend." *Tennis,* August 1997, p. 16.

Contemporary Black Biography, volume 17. Detroit: Gale, 1998.

Fiske, Susan Festa, and Joel Drucker. "Working Out with Venus Williams." *Tennis,* February 1998, p. 84.

Montville, Leigh. "Slice Girls." *Sports Illustrated,* February 2, 1998, pp. 66–70.

Neill, Michael, and Fannie Weinstein. "Venus Rising." *People,* October 27, 1997, pp. 103-6.

O'Brien, Richard, and Hank Hersch. "Venus Writing." *Sports Illustrated,* November 17, 1997, p. 31.

Price, S. L. "In Her Long-Delayed Debut, Venus Williams Couldn't Live Up to Her Own Billing." *Sports Illustrated,* July 7, 1997, p. 26.

"Williams Sisters Display Loving Sibling Rivalry at Australia Open." *Jet,* February 9, 1998, pp. 49–50.

Eldrick "Tiger" Woods

Born December 30, 1975
Long Beach, California
Professional golfer

He was born with the name Eldrick, but the world knows him as Tiger Woods. He is not only the most successful African American professional golfer of all time—particularly notable because blacks have historically been unrepresented in that sport—he is one of the most successful golfers in history. Period. As an amateur, he was the youngest golfer—and the only African American—to ever win the U.S. Junior Amateur title. He is also the only player to win the title three times.

And that is only one of Tiger Woods's many accomplishments. In 1994 he again became the youngest golfer and the only African American to win the U.S. Amateur title match. He successfully defended his crown in 1995 and 1996. Up to this time, Woods was a sensation in the golf community, but his name became a household word after his record-breaking performance at the 1997 Masters tournament in Augusta, Georgia. His score of 270, or 18 under par, was remarkable for a golfer of any race. But Woods has been reluctant to allow

"I did the same things every kid did. I studied and went to the mall. I [liked] wrestling, rap music, and **The Simpsons.** *I got into trouble. . . . I loved my parents. . . . The only difference is I can sometimes hit a little ball into a hole in [fewer] strokes than some other people."*

himself to be classified as "a black golfer," and this, along with his reputation for cockiness, has often led to controversy. Woods has made it clear that his ambition is to be the greatest golfer, not simply the greatest *black* golfer, of all time.

How Tiger got his name

One reason Woods does not always speak of himself as black is that only one of his parents, his father Earl, is an African American. As an Army lieutenant colonel with the elite Green Berets stationed in Southeast Asia, Earl met Woods's mother, Kultida, a native of Thailand. Another Asian who became close to Earl Woods in the Vietnam War (1954–75) was a South Vietnamese soldier named Nguyen "Tiger" Phong, who saved his life. Later Earl named his son after his brave Vietnamese friend.

Earl Woods was an athlete in college, the first African American player on the Kansas State University baseball team. But he decided that his only child would learn golf at an early age. So at the age of ten months, Tiger began getting golf lessons from his father! Earl would hit golf balls into a net in the family garage, and Tiger would watch him; later, the father shortened a putter for him, and Tiger carried it everywhere.

By the time he was three, Woods could already play golf as well as many adults. At that age he shot 48 for nine holes, a respectable score, and before he was five he had appeared on the TV shows *That's Incredible* and *The Mike Douglas Show,* on which he won a putting contest against comedian and amateur golfer Bob Hope (1902–). Woods, who had not yet even learned to read and write, was already signing autographs by printing his name.

Makes history in Junior Amateurs

At the age of eight, Woods won the ten-and-under division of the Junior World Golf Championship. Three years later, the eleven-year-old was undefeated in more than thirty southern California junior tournaments. But his father had his sights set on higher goals, and he worked constantly with Woods to improve his concentration—a key element of suc-

A jubilant Tiger Woods celebrates success on the golf course.

cess in golf. "I wanted to make sure he'd never run into anybody who was tougher mentally than he was," Earl Woods told *Sports Illustrated*.

In 1991, Woods, at fifteen, became the youngest player—and the only African American—ever to win the U.S. Junior Amateur championship. He won the championship the next two years, adding another record to his accomplishments by becoming the first golfer ever to win the Junior Amateur title three times.

Though he remained an amateur, Woods played in his first Professional Golfers' Association (PGA) tournament when he was sixteen years old. He failed to qualify for the last two rounds, but he impressed the pros. Then in 1994, he became the first African American to win the U.S. Amateur Golf Championship. At eighteen, he was also the youngest player ever to win the title, edging out legendary golfer Jack

Nicklaus (1940–), who had been nineteen when he won the Amateur title.

College and a difficult decision

Woods made international headlines later in 1994, when he and his teammates gave the United States its first win in six years at the World Amateur golf championships in Europe. French newspapers began calling him "Tiger La Terreur" (Tiger the Terror). But just like many other young people finishing high school, he had to make a decision regarding college. A number of schools wanted him to play for them, but Woods chose California's Stanford University. "I'm not a celebrity at Stanford," he told *Sports Illustrated*. "Everybody's special. You have to be to get in here. That's why I love the place."

Woods won several college tournaments in 1995, and not surprisingly, was ranked the nation's number-one collegiate player. He also successfully defended his U.S. Amateur title, which qualified him to play in the Masters at Augusta National Golf Club. Though he finished 41st at the Masters, he was the only amateur to qualify to play in the final two rounds.

Throughout 1995 and 1996, Woods had a series of successes, including winning a third straight U.S. Amateur Championship in August 1996, another record. Now, with several companies ready to offer him million-dollar endorsement contracts, he faced the decision of turning pro. The problem was that he was happy in college. "Stanford is like utopia," he said in an interview, using a word that refers to a sort of paradise. "It's not the real world, which I guess is why I want to spend more time here. Maybe my game is ready, but the question is, am I ready mentally and emotionally to live the life of a pro?"

Eventually, he did decide to turn pro, but he continued to think back on college life as a lost paradise. "You know what I miss?" he told Jonathan Abrahams of *Golf Magazine* in 1998. "College. Not so much the work, but living in the dorms. The atmosphere was so relaxed. We were on equal terms, doing something that we've never done before, and we had the greatest talks. We would just talk about anything. . . . Golf

Tiger Woods looks on after hitting a tee shot.

carts or the evolution of Mongolian tribes. It didn't matter. It was so invigorating."

A record-smashing performance at the Masters

Woods won his first two tournaments as a professional at the end of 1996, and became the first player since 1982 to fin-

Is Tiger Woods "really" black?

The fact that Tiger Woods is young and black meant that his win at the 1997 Masters gained far more attention than it normally would outside of golf circles. On the minus side, though, racial controversy has surrounded him.

Members of the African American community were outraged by Woods's reluctance to refer to himself as "black." He calls himself by a racial name he invented, "Cablinasian" (Caucasian, Black, Indian, Asian). When federal government officials began discussing the addition of a "new" racial category for the Year 2000 Census, which would allow people of mixed racial heritage to identify themselves as such, the label soon acquired the nickname "the Tiger Woods category."

Isabel Wilkerson in *Essence* described the excitement with which she and other African Americans greeted Woods. "We had [grown] tired of O. J. [Simpson (1947– ; see entry]," she wrote, "and were still missing a hero. . . ." It was thrilling to see Woods "all but [laughing] at the records set by White men twice his age." But then he disappointed her and others by announcing "that he considered himself 'only one-fourth black.'"

Wilkerson noted that Woods's style of clothing was not "black" enough: "He is the very opposite of the gangsta boyz 'n the hood who wear their pants hanging down like the prisoners in the penitentiary. Next to them, he's prep school and Pepsodent. He puts a pretty face on Blackness."

ish in the top five of five consecutive tournaments. Nike signed him to a $40 million, five-year contract, and other companies also offered him contracts for endorsements (advertisements in which a person promotes a company's products).

As Woods began 1997, his reputation soared. He won another championship, and gained the praise of no less than Nicklaus himself. He said, "This kid is absolutely the most fundamentally sound golfer that I've seen at almost any age." With his performance at the Masters, Woods set a number of records. His twelve-stroke lead was the largest margin in tour history, and he set a record with his score of 270 for four rounds. He

On Woods's treatment of the media, Jonathan Abrahams of *Golf Magazine* said an African American journalist told him, "As a person of color, Tiger should know . . . not to see the media as just the media, but a group of individuals." The idea behind this remark was that people who have been subjected to discrimination should not themselves discriminate, and as Abrahams reported, Woods has a reputation for sometimes being unfriendly toward reporters.

As for his role as a black golfer, Woods has admitted, "There's no doubt I arrived at the right time." Referring to early African American golfing pioneers, Woods said, "When you look at the accomplishments of a Lee Elder [1934–] or a Charles Sifford [1922–], you realize that if I had come along in the '60s or '70s I wouldn't have had a chance. Those guys have knocked down the doors for me to play. And I plan to take full advantage of it."

In a more direct statement about his race, Woods issued a press release in the mid-1990s. He said, "The media has portrayed me as African-American; sometimes, Asian. In fact, I am both. . . . Truthfully, I feel very fortunate, and EQUALLY PROUD, to be both African-American and Asian! The critical and fundamental point is that ethnic background and/or composition should NOT make a difference. It does NOT make a difference to me. The bottom line is that I am an American . . . and proud of it! That is who I am and what I am. Now, with your cooperation, I hope I can just be a golfer and a human being."

was the youngest Masters winner, only the third player to win the tournament in his first try as a professional–and, of course, he was the first black player to win the Masters.

Superstardom

His Masters win led to controversy about Woods's race (see accompanying sidebar), but it also led to almost unbelievable success and fame. Between 1996 and 1998, nearly fifty different books were published about him. Books were published in Braille; and Chinese, French, and Japanese translations were available, too.

In 1997, Woods was the number-one ranked player in the world; then he experienced a slump, but he came back with a win at the May 1998 BellSouth Classic. He continued to compete with success in 1998, but his eye was also on the future. Woods and his father oversee Eldrick Tiger Woods Inc., the company that manages some $80 million in endorsements from Nike, American Express, and others. They also operate a nonprofit organization to promote golf among inner-city youth.

Late in 1997, the Woods family had a tearful meeting with a woman who had never even heard of Tiger Woods. Her name was Lythi Bich Van, the widow of "Tiger" Phong. For years, Earl Woods had said that he hoped his old friend would hear about his son and contact him. But he learned that Phong had died of starvation in a concentration camp in September 1976, about a year and a half after the Communist North Vietnamese took over South Vietnam in April 1975. Tom Callahan, a *Golf Digest* writer, managed to get into Communist-held Vietnam in the mid-1990s to research the story, and arranged for the Woods family to meet Phong's widow. "It was very sweet," Callahan reported. "They just sat on the couch and talked for hours. Tiger was very much into it." Woods said, "I never knew him as Tiger Phong. He was Tiger One—the first Tiger."

Sources for further reading

Abrahams, Jonathan. "Golden Child or Spoiled Brat?" *Golf Magazine,* April 1998, pp. 56–69.

Golf.com—Eye on the Tiger. [Online] http://www.golf.com/tiger/ (accessed on October 8, 1998).

Joseph, Paul. *Tiger Woods.* Minneapolis: Abdo & Daughters, 1998.

Mark, Steve. "Golf Is Cool." *Boys' Life,* August 1997, pp. 6–7.

Mattern, Joanne. *Tiger Woods: Young Champion.* Mahwah, NJ: Troll, 1998.

Nicklaus, Jack. "Jack Nicklaus to Golf's Young Tigers: 'Have a Life.'" *USA Weekend,* July 10–12, 1998, pp. 12-13.

The Original Tiger Woods Web Page. [Online] http://www.geocities.com/Colosseum/2396/tiger.html (accessed on October 8, 1998).

Rambeck, Richard. *Tiger Woods.* Chanhassen, MN: Child's World, 1998.

Rosaforte, Tim. *Tiger Woods: The Makings of a Champion* (sound recording). Newport Beach, CA: Books on Tape, 1997.

Smith, Eric L. "Eye of the Tiger." *Black Enterprise,* September 1997, pp. 90–91.

Stewart, Mark. *Tiger Woods: Driving Force.* New York: Children's Press, 1998.

"Tiger Woods." *People,* December 30, 1996–January 6, 1997, p. 110.

Tiger Woods—CBS SportsLine. [Online] http://www.tigerwoods.com/ (accessed on October 8, 1998).

Wilkerson, Isabel. "The All American." *Essence,* November 1997, pp. 99–100+.

Williams, Brian, producer. *Tiger Woods: Son, Hero & Champion* (videorecording). New York: CBS Video, 1997.

Woods, Tiger, and David LaFontaine, ed. *Tiger: Reflections of a Champion.* Beverly Hills, CA: Dove Books, 1997.

Andrew Young

Born March 12, 1932
New Orleans, Louisiana
Politician, civil rights activist

Andrew Young has served the African American community—and the United States—in a number of positions. During the course of a career that has found him in a variety of roles, Young has emerged as a significant figure in international circles, and has become highly respected among business and government leaders throughout the world.

During the 1960s, Young worked in the Southern Christian Leadership Conference (SCLC) in Atlanta, Georgia, under the leadership of Dr. Martin Luther King, Jr. (1929–68; see entry in volume 3). In 1972 he became the first African American elected to Congress from the South since 1901, and in 1977 he was appointed U.S. ambassador to the United Nations (UN) under President Jimmy Carter (1924–). Later Young became mayor of Atlanta, serving from 1982 to 1990, and helped lead the effort to stage the 1996 Olympics in that city.

"We created more than 85,000 jobs in Atlanta from the Olympics. No white people complained because everybody was working [and] making money. If we had all been fighting black against white, we would have had nothing."

Civil rights involvement

Young grew up in a mostly Irish and Italian neighborhood in New Orleans, Louisiana. He experienced some racial conflict, but his parents were educated people—a doctor and a teacher—and they emphasized negotiation, rather than violence, as a solution to problems. Young was extremely bright, and graduated from high school at the age of fifteen. At Howard University in Washington, D.C., he initially majored in biology, but he soon became interested in the ideas of Mohandas K. Gandhi (1869–1948). Gandhi, who led the effort to end British rule in his native India during the 1930s and 1940s, advocated a philosophy of nonviolent resistance. Gandhi's ideas had a profound effect on Young.

Young decided to become a minister, and enrolled at the Hartford Theological Seminary in Hartford, Connecticut. Ordained as a United Church of Christ pastor in 1955, when he was twenty-three, Young pastored churches in Marion, Alabama, and the south Georgia towns of Thomasville and Beachton. During this time, he was inspired by the efforts of King and other civil rights leaders, especially the bus boycott they organized in Montgomery, Alabama. (A boycott is a nonviolent protest in which people refuse to buy a certain product or service as a way of putting economic pressure on a company or government; in the case of Montgomery, African Americans were protesting the rules that required black passengers to ride in the backs of buses.)

In spite of threats from the Ku Klux Klan (white supremacists), Young began organizing his local community and encouraging blacks to exercise their voting rights. In 1957, he became associate director of the Department of Youth Work for the National Council of Churches in New York City. Four years later, when the United Church of Christ launched a voter-education program for Southern blacks in 1961, Young was appointed to lead it. His new role took him back to Atlanta, where he became involved with King and the SCLC.

In 1962, King asked Young to serve as his administrative assistant, and in 1964 Young became SCLC's executive director. In this capacity, he worked closely with King as the civil rights leader led marches and other civil rights protests. It was a dangerous position to be in, because King had angered many people who opposed the changes he wanted to bring about. On April 4, 1968, King was assassinated in Memphis, Tennessee. Young was standing nearby, in the courtyard of the Lorraine Motel, when he heard the gunshots.

First Southern black congressman since 1901

In 1970, Young moved into politics, announcing his candidacy for Congress from Georgia's Fifth District. He did not win, but he used a subsequent appointment to Atlanta's Community Relations Commission (CRC) to establish himself as a significant voice in Georgia politics. Around this time, he also got to know Georgia's new governor, Jimmy Carter.

In 1972, Young ran for Congress again, and this time he was elected, with much support from white voters. As he took his seat in Congress in 1973, he became the first black representative elected from the South since 1901, and the first from Georgia since the Reconstruction (an era following the Civil War [1861–65] when the federal government made an ultimately unsuccessful attempt to enforce rapid racial change in the South). Reelected to Congress again in 1974 and 1976, Young proved an outspoken advocate of affirmative action and other programs.

Controversial UN ambassador

Meanwhile, Carter was elected president in 1976, and soon appointed Young the nation's ambassador to the UN. As such, he would articulate U.S. foreign policy to the more than 150 countries who were members of the UN. As ambassador, Young was often involved in controversy. He expressed support for troops from Cuba helping to wage a civil war in the African nation of Angola; he sharply criticized South Africa for its policy of racial segregation called apartheid (pronounced "uh-PAR-tide"); and he generally seemed to praise America's enemies while attacking the United States and its

With his late first wife, Jean, at his side, Andrew Young announces his candidacy for Georgia governor in 1990. He lost to Lt. Governor Zell Miller.

allies. On the positive side, he emerged as an admired and respected leader with representatives of Third World nations in Africa, Asia, and Latin America.

The controversy surrounding Young came to a head in August 1979, when he conducted a meeting with a representative of the terrorist Palestine Liberation Organization (PLO). The United States supported Israel, the PLO's enemy, and Young's action was a violation of State Department directives. Young was asked to resign. "I really don't feel a bit sorry for anything that I have done," he told *Time* magazine. "And I could not say to anybody that given the same situation I wouldn't do it again almost exactly the same way."

Helps bring Olympics to Atlanta

For two years, Young worked chiefly in his consulting firm, Young Ideas. But in 1981, he ran for mayor of Atlanta and won. He become the city's second black chief executive;

Maynard Jackson (1938–) was the first. Although the issue of race occasionally crept into the campaign, once Young was in office he attempted to create racial harmony in Atlanta. (The leadership in Georgia's capital city was divided between the predominantly white business community and the mostly black city government.) Young was an able mayor, and presided over a period of rapid growth as Atlanta evolved from a small Southern city to a fast-paced international business center.

Following his two terms as mayor, Young in 1990 made a bid to become Georgia's first black governor, but was defeated by Lieutenant Governor Zell Miller. He then turned his attention to an effort dear to his heart: Atlanta's bid to host the 1996 Summer Olympics. Since 1987, Young had worked closely with Atlanta lawyer Billy Payne, head of the Atlanta Organizing Committee. Atlanta had to prove to the Olympic governing body, the International Olympic Committee (IOC), that it could host the Games. It was at this juncture that Young became a vital player: through his international connections, he acquired widespread support for the Atlanta effort, which resulted in Atlanta being chosen as the host city in September 1990. Over the next six years Young worked with what was now the Atlanta Committee for the Olympic Games (ACOG) and helped bring together the largest Olympic Games in history.

Widowed and remarried

Young and his wife Jean had raised four children, and when she died in 1994, he was devastated. Carolyn Watson, a schoolteacher, had lived next to the Youngs for twenty years, and after Jean died she proved a comforting friend in Young's time of need. "I think the first date we had," she later told *People,* "was when we went to South Africa to get married." The two were wed on March 24, 1996, by Archbishop Desmond Tutu (1931–), a well-known leader in the movement that helped bring about the downfall of apartheid in 1990.

In 1997, Young wrote *An Easy Burden: The Civil Rights Movement and the Transformation of America,* a book that combined elements of his life story with a history of the civil rights movement. Later that year, his name was once again associated with controversy. As a paid consultant for shoe manufacturer Nike, he travelled to Nike factories in Asia to investigate claims that workers there were underpaid and mistreated. Young, as the head of the consulting firm Good Works, reported that conditions looked good in the factories he visited. Then it was discovered that the translators he used were paid by Nike. A *Village Voice* article reported that Young's "account of the working conditions, including pay, was shockingly [different from] research by human rights monitors" in the same countries. A group of former members of the Student Nonviolent Coordinating Committee (SNCC), another 1960s civil rights organization, wrote Young a public letter of protest to which he did not respond.

Young had mixed feelings about the October 1995 Million Man March. He said that such an event would not have been possible without the groundbreaking leadership of civil rights figures such as King, whose message of racial harmony was very different from that of organizer Louis Farrakhan (1933– ; see entry in volume 2, and update on p. 71): "I thought [the March] was wonderful. [But] those people were there not because they were angry but because they were successful. They came because of jobs generated by the civil rights movement. See, what we in the movement are about in the 1990s is integrating The Money. We have a group of men here in Atlanta called 100 Black Men, and some of them went to the Million Man March. But what [100 Black Men is] doing [in Atlanta] is more significant. They adopted an eighth-grade class from a school with one of the highest dropout rates in the state. . . . It's much better to put your money into sending a kid to college than going to Washington and staying in a hotel."

In 1997, *Modern Maturity* writer Claudia Dreifus interviewed Young. Young discussed his feelings about his first wife's death, and his sense of letdown when the Olympics were over. He talked philosophically about how, as UN ambassador, he would be walking out of the exclusive Waldorf-Astoria Hotel in New York City "and a guy would come out, see the only black person around, and hand me his car keys. . . . I took them over to the guy who parks the cars and said, 'The man over there needs some help.'"

Sources for further reading

"Andrew Young and Bride Carolyn Wed Again in Atlanta." *Jet,* June 3, 1996, p. 6.

"Andrew Young and Carolyn Watson." *People,* February 10, 1997, p. 149.

Baldwin, Lewis V. "An Easy Burden: The Civil Rights Movement and the Transformation of America." *America,* July 5–12, 1997, pp. 23–24.

Dreifus, Claudia. "Andrew Young: On Life, Sin, and the Murder of Friends." *Modern Maturity,* March 1997, pp. 52–59+.

Chappell, Kevin. "The 3 Mayors Who Made It Happen." *Ebony,* July 1996, pp. 66–72.

Glass, Stephen. "The Young and the Feckless." *New Republic,* September 8–15, 1997, pp. 20–24.

Hentoff, Nat. "The Ghosts of Andrew Young's Past." *Village Voice,* April 7, 1998, p. 22.

Potter, Joan, and Constance Claytor. *African Americans Who Were First: Illustrated with Photographs.* New York: Cobblehill Books, 1997.

Roberts, Naurice. *Andrew Young, Freedom Fighter.* Chicago: Childrens Press, 1983.

Simpson, Jan. *Andrew Young: A Matter of Choice.* St. Paul, MN: EMC, 1978.

Westman, Paul. *Andrew Young, Champion of the Poor.* Minneapolis, MN: Dillon Press, 1983.

Young, Andrew. *An Easy Burden: The Civil Rights Movement and the Transformation of America.* New York: HarperCollins, 1997.

Bibliography

Dorothy Dandridge

Books

Aaseng, Nathan. *Florence Griffith Joyner: Dazzling Olympian.* Minneapolis: Lerner Publications Co., 1989.

Aaseng, Nathan. *The O. J. Simpson Trial: What It Shows Us About Our Legal System.* New York: Walker, 1996.

African American Almanac. Detroit: Gale, 1997.

American Decades, 1970–1979. Detroit: Gale Research, 1995.

Applegate, Katherine. *The Story of Two American Generals, Benjamin O. Davis, Jr., Colin L. Powell.* New York: Dell Publishing, 1992.

Banta, Melissa. *Colin Powell.* New York: Chelsea House, 1995.

Bedini, A. Silvio. *The Life of Benjamin Banneker.* New York: Scribner's, 1972.

Blue, Rose. *Barbara Jordan.* Broomall, PA: Chelsea House, 1992.

Bogle, Donald. *Dorothy Dandridge.* New York: Boulevard, 1997.

Brown, Jamie Foster. *Betty Shabazz: A Sisterfriends' Tribute in Words and Pictures.* New York: Simon & Schuster, 1998.

Brown, Les. *Les Brown's Encyclopedia of Television,* third edition. Detroit: Gale, 1992.

Brown, Tracey L. *The Life and Times of Ron Brown.* New York: William Morrow, 1998.

Bryant, Ira B. *Barbara Charline Jordan: From the Ghetto to the Capitol.* Houston: D. Armstrong Co., 1977.

Burchard, Marshall, and Sue Burchard. *Sports Hero, O. J. Simpson.* New York: Putnam, 1975.

Burton, Elizabeth, with Lynn Offerdahl. *Cinderfella & the Slam Dunk Contest* (fiction; illustrated). Boston: Branden Pub. Co., 1994.

Busnar, Gene. *The Picture Life of Tina Turner.* New York: F. Watts, 1987.

Cable, Mary. *Black Odyssey: The Case of the Slave Ship* Amistad. New York: Penguin USA, 1998.

Coffey, Wayne. *Wilma Rudolph.* Woodbridge, CT: Blackbirch Press, 1993.

Commire, Anne, ed. *Historic World Leaders.* Detroit: Gale, 1994.

Conord, Bruce W. *Bill Cosby.* New York: Chelsea Juniors, 1993.

Contemporary Black Biography, various volumes. Detroit: Gale.

Contemporary Musicians, Volume 17. Detroit: Gale, 1997.

Cosby, Bill. *The Best Way to Play.* New York: Scholastic, 1997.

Cosby, Bill. *Childhood.* New York City: Putnam, 1991.

Cosby, Bill. *Fatherhood.* Garden City, NY: Doubleday, 1986.

Cosby, Bill. *Love and Marriage.* New York: Doubleday, 1989.

Cosby, Bill. *The Meanest Thing to Say.* New York: Scholastic, 1997.

Cosby, Bill. *Money Troubles.* New York: Scholastic, 1997.

Cosby, Bill. *Shipwreck Saturday.* New York: Scholastic, 1997.

Cosby, Bill. *Super-Fine Valentine.* New York: Scholastic, 1997.

Cosby, Bill. *Time Flies.* New York: Doubleday, 1987.

Cosby, Bill. *The Treasure Hunt.* New York: Scholastic, 1997.

Cummings, Judith, and Stefan Rudnicki. *Colin Powell and the American Dream.* Beverly Hills, CA: Dove Books, 1995.

Delany, Sarah, and A. Elizabeth Delany, with Amy Hill Hearth. *Delany Sisters' Book of Everyday Wisdom.* New York: Kodansha International, 1994.

Delany, Sarah, and A. Elizabeth Delany, with Amy Hill Hearth. *Having Our Say: The Delany Sisters' First 100 Years.* New York: Kodansha International, 1993.

Delany, Sarah, with Amy Hill Hearth. *On My Own at 107: Reflections on Life Without Bessie.* New York: HarperSanFrancisco, 1997.

Dictionary of Twentieth Century Culture, Volume 5: *African American Culture.* Detroit: Gale, 1996.

Dolan, Sean. *Michael Jordan* (introductory essay by Coretta Scott King). New York: Chelsea House, 1994.

Ferris, Jerri. *What Are You Figuring Now? A Story About Benjamin Banneker.* New York: Scholastic, 1988.

Fidelman, Geoffrey Mark. *First Lady of Song: Ella Fitzgerald for the Record.* New York: Citadel Press, 1996.

Finlayson, Reggie. *Colin Powell.* Minneapolis: Lerner Publications, 1997.

Foreman, George, and Cherie Calbom. *George Foreman's Knock-Out-the-Fat Barbeque and Grilling Cookbook.* New York: Villard, 1996.

Foreman, George, and Joel Engel. *By George, The Autobiography of George Foreman.* New York: Villard, 1995.

Frank, Steven. *Magic Johnson.* New York: Chelsea House Publishers, 1995.

Gaston, A. G. *Green Power, the Successful Way of A. G. Gaston.* Birmingham: Southern University Press, 1968.

Gourse, Leslie. *The Ella Fitzgerald Companion: Seven Decades of Commentary.* New York: Schirmer Books, 1998.

Graham, Maryemma, and Amritjit Singh, eds. *Conversations with Ralph Ellison.* Jackson, MS: University of Mississippi, 1995.

Harris, Jacqueline L. *The Tuskegee Airmen: Black Heroes of World War II.* Parsippany, NJ: Dillon Press, 1996.

Harris, Lauren Lanzen, ed. *Biography Today: 1997 Annual Cumulation.* Detroit: Omnigraphics, 1998.

Harris, Laurie Lanzen, ed. *Biography Today: Sports Series, Vol. 1, 1996.* Detroit: Omnigraphics, 1996.

Harris, Laurie Lanzen, ed. *Pocket Profiles: Tiger Woods.* Detroit: Omnigraphics, 1997.

Haskins, James. *Sports Great Magic Johnson.* Hillside, NJ: Enslow Publishers, 1992.

Haskins, Jim. *Bill Cosby: America's Most Famous Father.* New York: Walker, 1988.

Haskins, Jim. *Louis Farrakhan and the Nation of Islam.* New York: Walker, 1996.

Haskins, Jim. *One More River to Cross: The Stories of Twelve Black Americans.* New York: Scholastic, 1992.

Howell, Ann Chandler. *Tuskegee Airmen: Heroes in Our Fight for Dignity, Inclusion, and Citizenship Rights.* Chicago: Chandler/White Publishing, 1994.

Hudson, Wade, and Valerie Wilson Wesley. *Afro-Bets Book of Black Heroes From A to Z: An Introduction to Important Black Achievers for Young Readers.* East Orange, NJ: Just Us Books, 1997.

Hughes, Libby. *Colin Powell: A Man of Quality.* Parsippany, NJ: Dillon Press, 1996.

In Black and White. Detroit: Gale, 1980.

International Dictionary of Films and Filmmakers, Volume 3: *Actors and Actresses.* St. James Press, 1986.

Jeffrey, Laura S. *Barbara Jordan: Congresswoman, Lawyer, Educator.* Springfield, NJ: Enslow, 1997.

Johnson, Earvin "Magic." *What You Can Do to Avoid AIDS.* New York: Times Books, 1992.

Johnson, Earvin "Magic," with Richard Levin. *Magic.* New York: Viking Press, 1983.

Johnson, Earvin "Magic," with Roy S. Johnson. *Magic's Touch.* Reading, MA: Addison-Wesley, 1989.

Johnson, Earvin "Magic," with William Novak. *My Life.* New York: Random House, 1992.

Johnson, Linda Carlson. *Barbara Jordan: Congresswoman.* Woodbridge, CT: Blackbirch, 1997.

Jones, Howard. *Mutiny on the* Amistad. New York: Oxford University Press, 1997.

Jordan, Barbara, and Shelby Hearon. *Barbara Jordan, A Self-Portrait.* Garden City, NY: Doubleday, 1979.

Jordan, Michael. *I Can't Accept Not Trying: Michael Jordan on the Pursuit of Excellence.* San Francisco: HarperSanFrancisco, 1994.

Jordan, Michael. *Rare Air: Michael on Michael.* San Francisco: HarperSanFrancisco, 1993.

Joseph, Paul. *Tiger Woods.* Minneapolis: Abdo & Daughters, 1998.

Jurmain, Suzanne. *Freedom's Sons: The True Story of the* Amistad Mutiny. New York: Lothrop Lee & Shepard, 1998.

Kessler, James H., et al. *Distinguished African American Scientists of the 20th Century.* Phoenix, AZ: Oryx Press, 1996.

Keyes, Alan. *Masters of the Dream: The Strength and Betrayal of Black America.* New York: Morrow, 1995.

Keyes, Alan. *Our Character, Our Future: Reclaiming America's Moral Destiny.* Grand Rapids, MI: Zondervan, 1996.

Kleinbaum, Nancy H. *The Magnificent Seven: The Authorized Story of American Gold.* New York: Bantam, 1996.

Kliment, Bud. *Ella Fitzgerald (Black Americans of Achievement).* Broomall, PA: Chelsea House, 1988.

Knapp, Ron. *Michael Jordan: Star Guard.* Hillside, NJ: Enslow Publishers, 1994.

Koenig, Teresa. *Tina Turner.* Mankato, MN: Crestwood House, 1986.

Koral, April. *Florence Griffith Joyner: Track and Field Star.* Danbury, CT: Franklin Watts, 1992.

Kornbluth, Jesse. *Airborne Again!: The Triumph and Struggle of Michael Jordan.* New York: Aladdin Paperbacks, 1996.

Krulik, Nancy E. *Space Jam*. New York: Scholastic Inc., 1996.

Krull, Kathleen. *Wilma Unlimited: How Wilma Rudolph Became the World's Fastest Woman*. San Diego: Harcourt Brace, 1996.

Lazenby, Roland. *Yo, Baby, It's Attitude!: The New Bad Boyz of the NBA Take the Jordan Test*. Lenexa, KS: Addax Pub. Group, 1997.

Magida, Arthur J. *Prophet of Rage: A Life of Louis Farrakhan and His Nation*. New York: Basic Books, 1996.

Malcolm X, with Alex Haley. *The Autobiography of Malcolm X*. New York: Ballantine, 1964.

Mattern, Joanne. *Tiger Woods: Young Champion*. Mahwah, NJ: Troll, 1998.

McKissack, Patricia, and Frederick McKissack. *Red-Tail Angels: The Story of the Tuskegee Airmen of World War II*. Walker, 1995.

Metcalf, Doris Hunter. *Portraits of Exceptional African American Scientists*. Carthage, IL: Good Apple, 1994.

Naden, Corinne. (Introductory essay by Coretta Scott King). *Ronald McNair*. New York: Chelsea House, 1990.

Newsmakers, various volumes. Detroit: Gale.

Nicholson, Stuart. *Ella Fitzgerald: A Biography of the First Lady of Jazz*. New York: Scribner, 1994.

The Olympics Factbook: A Spectator's Guide to the Winter and Summer Games. Detroit: Visible Ink Press, 1992.

Owens, Thomas S. *Michael Jordan: Legendary Guard*. New York: PowerKids Press, 1997.

Owens, William A. *Black Mutiny: The Revolt of the Schooner* Amistad. New York: Plume, 1997.

Pascarelli, Peter F. *The Courage of Magic Johnson: from Boyhood Dreams to Superstar to His Toughest Challenge*. New York: Bantam Books, 1992.

Patrick-Wexler, Diane. *Barbara Jordan*. Austin, TX: 1995.

Pinckney, Andrea Davis. *Dear Benjamin Banneker*. San Diego, CA: Harcourt Brace, 1994.

Potter, Joan, and Constance Claytor. *African Americans Who Were First: Illustrated with Photographs*. New York: Cobblehill Books, 1997.

Powell, Colin. *In His Own Words: Colin Powell*. New York: Berkley, 1995.

Powell, Colin L., with Joseph E. Persico. *My American Journey*. New York: Random House, 1995.

Powerful Black Women. Detroit: Visible Ink, 1996.

Rambeck, Richard. *Tiger Woods*. Chanhassen, MN: Child's World, 1998.

Rhodes, Lisa Renee. *Barbara Jordan: Voice of Democracy*. Danbury, CT: Franklin Watts, 1998.

Rice, Earle, Jr. *The O. J. Simpson Trial*. San Diego, CA: Lucent Books, 1997.

Roberts, Maurice. *Andrew Young, Freedom Fighter*. Chicago: Childrens Press, 1983.

Roberts, Maurice. *Barbara Jordan, The Great Lady from Texas*. Chicago: Childrens Press, 1984.

Rock, Chris. *Rock This!* New York: Hyperion, 1997.

Rogers, Mary Beth. *Barbara Jordan: American Hero*. New York: Bantam Doubleday Dell, 1998.

Roth, David. *Sacred Honor: A Biography of Colin Powell*. Grand Rapids, MI: Zondervan, 1993.

Rothaus, James R. *Magic Johnson*. Mankato, MN: Child's World, 1991.

Schmitz, Dorothy Childers. *O. J. Simpson: The Juice Is Loose*. Mankato, MN: Crestwood House, 1977.

Schraff, Anne. *Colin Powell: Soldier and Patriot*. Springfield, NJ: Enslow Publishers, 1997.

Schuman, N. J. *Bill Cosby: Actor and Comedian*. Springfield, NJ: Enslow Publishers, 1995.

Schwabacher, Martin. *Magic Johnson*. New York: Chelsea Juniors, 1994.

Shaw, Dena. *Ronald McNair*. New York: Chelsea House, 1994.

Sherrow, Victoria. *Wilma Rudolph: Olympic Champion*. New York: Chelsea House, 1995.

Simpson, Jan. *Andrew Young: A Matter of Choice*. St. Paul, MN: EMC, 1978.

Smith, Jessie Carney, ed. *Notable Black American Men*. Detroit: Gale, 1998.

Smith, Jessie Carney, ed. *Notable Black American Women*. Detroit: Gale, 1992.

Smith, Jessie Carney, ed. *Notable Black American Women, Book II*. Detroit: Gale, 1996.

Stewart, Mark. *Florence Griffith Joyner*. Danbury, CT: Children's Press, 1996.

Stewart, Mark. *Tiger Woods: Driving Force*. New York: Children's Press, 1998.

Strauss, Larry. *Magic Man*. Los Angeles: Lowell House Juvenile, 1992.

Strazzabosco, Jeanne. *Learning About Responsibility from the Life of Colin Powell*. New York: Rosen, 1996.

Super Stars of Gymnastics. Burbank, CA: Laurel Canyon Productions, 1995.

Tupac Amaru Shakur, 1971-1996. New York: Crown, 1997.

Turner, Tina, with Kurt Loder. *I, Tina*. New York: Morrow, 1986.

Tuskegee Airmen. Peterborough, NH: Cobblestone Publishing, 1997.

Westman, Paul. *Andrew Young, Champion of the Poor*. Minneapolis, MN: Dillon Press, 1983.

Woods, Tiger, and David LaFontaine, ed. *Tiger: Reflections of a Champion*. Beverly Hills, CA: Dove Books, 1997.

Wyman, Carolyn. *Ella Fitzgerald: Jazz Singer Supreme*. Danbury, CT: Franklin Watts, 1993.

Young, Andrew. *An Easy Burden: The Civil Rights Movement and the Transformation of America.* New York: HarperCollins, 1997.

Zeinert, Karen. *The* Amistad *Slave Revolt and American Abolition.* North Haven, CT: Linnet Books, 1997.

Zilboorg, Caroline, ed. *Women's Firsts.* Detroit: Gale, 1997.

Magazines and newspapers

Able, James A. "The Story of Benjamin Banneker." *Cricket,* February 1994, pp. 21–25.

Abrahams, Jonathan. "Golden Child or Spoiled Brat?" *Golf Magazine,* April 1998, pp. 56–69.

"Actress Halle Berry Reveals How She Copes with Diabetes." *Jet,* June 20, 1994, p. 37.

"America's Oldest Best-Selling Author, Sadie Delany, Is on Her Own at 107." *Tennessee Tribune,* January 29, 1997.

"Andrew Young and Bride Carolyn Wed Again in Atlanta." *Jet,* June 3, 1996, p. 6.

"Andrew Young and Carolyn Watson." *People,* February 10, 1997, p. 149.

Apple, R. W., Jr. "In Book, Powell Says a 3d Party May Be Needed." *New York Times,* September 10, 1995, p. 1.

Baines, Gwendolyn. "The Matthew Walker New Birthing Center to Honor Wilma Rudolph." *Tennessee Tribune,* November 23, 1995.

Baker, Calvin, and Karen Brailsford. "Living Dangerously." *People,* September 23, 1996, pp. 75–76.

Baldwin, Lewis V. "An Easy Burden: The Civil Rights Movement and the Transformation of America." *America,* July 5–12, 1997, pp. 23–24.

"Bannekers Break Ground." *Jet,* September 30, 1996, p. 23.

Baye, Betty Winston. "Speak Up for Dr. Betty." Gannett News Service, March 15, 1994.

Bellow, Saul. "Ralph Ellison in Tivoli." *Los Angeles Times Book Review,* May 10, 1998, p. 5.

"Bessie Delany, Candid Witness to a Tumultuous Century, Dies at 104." *People,* October 9, 1995, pp. 48–49.

"Black Caucus Asks U.S. to Check Reports that Secretary Ron Brown Died from Gunshot." *Jet,* January 12, 1998, pp. 39–40.

"Black Celebrities Who Are Also Ministers." *Jet,* December 18, 1995, pp. 54–57.

Bourne, Stephen. "Obituary: Alice Childress." *Independent,* April 30, 1994, p. 12.

Bowers, Faye. "Rising Star in Women's Tennis: Venus." *Christian Science Monitor,* September 4, 1997, p. 1.

"Boxer Larry Holmes Wants to Fight Soon, Maybe Against Foreman." *Jet,* April 6, 1998, p. 50.

Boyd, Herb. "Andrew Young Finds Nike Factories without Abuses." *Amsterdam News,* June 28, 1997, p. 5.

Brailsford, Karen. "Don't Give Up the Ship." *People,* December 22, 1997, p. 22.

Braxton, Greg. "Time's Up for 'Magic Hour'." *Los Angeles Times,* August 7, 1998, business section, p. 2.

Brown, John L. "The Collected Essays (Book Reviews)." *World Literature Today,* September 22, 1997, p. 786.

Browne, J. Zamgba. "Conservatives Gain NAACP Backing in Call for Ron Brown Inquiry." *Amsterdam News,* February 19, 1998, pp. 1–2.

Browne, J. Zamgba. "Tracey Brown Remembers Lion of a Man in a Tribute to Her Father." *Amsterdam News,* April 23, 1998, p. 8.

Brownlee, Shannon. "And Her Last Name Is Not Moceanu." *U.S. News & World Report,* June 10, 1996, pp. 67–68.

Butgereit, Betsy. "A. G. Gaston Dies: 103-Year-Old Businessman Broke Barriers." *Birmingham News,* January 19, 1996.

Buxton, Angela, and Sanford Baruch. "Advice from a Legend." *Tennis,* August 1997, p. 16.

"Camille Cosby Stands by Husband, Bill, Who Admitted He Had a 'Rendezvous' Years Ago." *Jet,* February 17, 1997, p. 18.

"Can O. J. Simpson Win Again?" *Jet,* February 26, 1996, pp. 54–56.

Carter, Janelle. "Barry Rails Against White House, Congress." Associated Press, August 6, 1997.

Castro, Peter, and Ken Baker. "All Eyes on Her." *People,* December 1, 1997, pp. 151–54.

Castro, Peter, et al. "Goodbye, Friend: Slain Son Ennis Inspired His Colleagues, His Students, But Most of All His Family." *People,* February 3, 1997, p. 68.

Cavendish, Dominic. "Theatre: Debut." *Independent,* July 1, 1998, p. 11.

Chappell, Kevin. "The 3 Mayors Who Made It Happen." *Ebony,* July 1996, pp. 66–72.

Chicago Tribune, July 22, 1988.

"Chris Rock Talks About His Comedy, New Wife and Fame." *Jet,* October 20, 1997, pp. 32–36.

Climer, David. "Wilma Rudolph Dead at 54." Gannett News Service, November 12, 1994.

"Clinton Leads Final Tribute to Brown: 'This Man Loved Life and All Things in It.'" *Detroit News,* April 11, 1996.

"Clothes Ignite, Butterfly McQueen Dies." *USA Today,* December 26, 1995.

Cohen, Gary. "Labor Secretary on the Griddle." *U.S. News & World Report,* January 26, 1998, p. 41.

"Colin Powell's Wife Reveals She Got Hate Mail During Time He Considered Bid for President." *Jet,* May 6, 1996, p. 12.

Collier, Aldore. "What's Love Got to Do With It." *Ebony,* July 1993, pp. 110–12.

"Cookie Johnson Says 'The Lord Has Healed Earvin' in April's *Ebony.*" *Jet,* April 7, 1997, p. 50.

Corliss, Richard. "The Better Side of Tupac." *Time Australia,* August 4, 1997, p. 70.

Corliss, Richard. "Lady Screens the Blues." *Time,* September 1, 1997, p. 73.

Corliss, Richard. "Obituary: Invincible Man Ralph Ellison 1914–1994." *Times,* April 25, 1994, p. 90.

"Cosby Asks California State Officials to Take Back Reward Money Offered to Catch Son's Killer." *Jet,* February 17, 1997, p. 17.

"Cosby Makes First Return to Concert Stage Since Son's Death." *Jet,* February 17, 1997, p. 17.

Dauphin, Gary. "Dorothy's Day." *Village Voice,* June 24, 1997, p. 84.

"David Justice Seeks Alimony from Estranged Wife Halle Berry." *Jet,* July 29, 1996, p. 18.

Detroit Free Press, November 30, 1995, p. D2.

Detroit News, October 23, 1998.

Dieffenbach, Dan. "Sport Lifestyle: Sparring with George Foreman." *Sport,* June 1995, pp. 80–81.

Dixon, Oscar. "Greg Gumbel Agrees to Deal with CBS." *USA Today,* January 22, 1998, p. 3C.

Dixon, Otis. "Admirers Gather to Honor Rudolph." *USA Today,* November 18, 1994, p. 2.

Dixon, Otis. "Mentor: 'I Knew That She Was Going to Be Great.'" *USA Today,* November 14, 1994, p. 2.

"Dr. Betty Shabazz, Minister Farrakhan Mend 30-Year Rift During Fund-Raiser." *Jet,* May 22, 1995, p. 12.

Dowling, Claudia. "Ten Years Ago Seven Brave Americans Died As They Reached for the Stars." *Life,* February 1996, pp. 38–43.

Dreifus, Claudia. "Andrew Young: On Life, Sin, and the Murder of Friends." *Modern Maturity,* March 1997, pp. 52–59+.

Edwards, Audrey. "The Fire This Time." *Essence,* October 1, 1997, pp. 74–78.

Edwards, Tamala M. "Labor of Love." *Essence,* March 1998, pp. 86–90+.

Ellis, David, Linda Kramer, and Brant Clifton. "Justice Delayed: The Alleged Killers of James Jordan Still Await Arraignment." *People,* August 22, 1994, p. 77.

Elvin, John. "Yet Another Independent Counsel." *Insight on the News,* June 22, 1998, p. 33.

Evans, Howie. "Venus Wins First Title as Tiger Loses in Playoff." *Amsterdam News,* March 3, 1998, p. 49.

Farley, Christopher John, and Margot Hornblower. "Winning the Right to Fly." *Time,* August 28, 1995, pp. 62–64.

Feldman, Linda. "Alan Keyes." *Christian Science Monitor,* January 11, 1996, p. 10.

"The 50 Most Beautiful People in the World." *People,* May 8, 1995, p. 68.

"Fired NAACP Chief Still Backs Farrakhan." *Chicago Tribune,* August 29, 1994, p. 4.

"First Tunes: A Sweet Set from Ella." *Fortune,* January 13, 1997, p. 28.

Fiske, Susan Festa, and Joel Drucker. "Working Out with Venus Williams." *Tennis,* February 1998, p. 84.

Fix, Janet. "When Social Security Might Not Be Enough." *Detroit Free Press,* June 22, 1998, p. 4F.

Forte, Roland. "Cleveland's Grand Dame, Zelma George, Dies at Age 90." *Call and Post,* July 7, 1994.

Franks, Jeff. "Barbara Jordan Remembered as 'American Original'." Reuters, January 20, 1996.

Fretts, Bruce. "Chris Rock." *Entertainment Weekly,* December 26, 1997–January 2, 1998, p. 20.

"Friends, Fans Salute Michael Jordan During Chicago Tribute at New Stadium." *Jet,* November 21, 1994, p. 54.

Garner, Jack. "'Gone with the Wind' Deserves This Re-Release." Gannett News Service, June 24, 1998.

Gee, Denise. "The Gospel According to George." *Southern Living,* February 1997, pp. 94–95.

Geier, Tom. "The Killing Fields of Rap's Gangsta Land." *U.S. News & World Report,* March 24, 1997, p. 32.

"General Benjamin Davis, Jr., Tuskegee Airmen Founder, Inducted into Aviation Hall of Fame." *Jet,* August 15, 1994, p. 36.

"Gen. Powell Praises Plans for First Memorial Honoring Black Civil War GIs." *Jet,* September 30, 1996, p. 51.

"Generation Next." *People,* November 18, 1996, pp. 50–53.

Gill, Mark Stuart, and Albert Kim. "Tupac's Missing Millions." *Entertainment Weekly,* July 25, 1997, pp. 22–24.

Glass, Stephen. "The Young and the Feckless." *New Republic,* September 8–15, 1997, pp. 20–24.

Goldberg, Jeffrey. "Marion Barry Confronts a Hostile Takeover." *New York Times,* October 29, 1995, Section 6, p. 39.

Gordon, Larry. "Last Reprise: Antique Store Offers Everyday Items From Ella Fitzgerald's Life." *Los Angeles Times,* September 21, 1997, Metro section, p. 1.

Gottesman, Jane. "The Two Dominiques." *Women's Sports & Fitness,* February 1996, p. 29.

Grace, Kevin Michael. "The Reverend and the Gangsta." *Alberta Report,* September 23, 1996, p. 25.

"The Greatest Love Stories of the Century: Colin Powell & Alma Johnson." *People,* February 12, 1996, p. 168.

"Green Sentenced to Life in Prison for Murder of James Jordan." *Jet,* April 1, 1996, p. 36.

Greenlee, Craig T. "Rekindling Wilma's Legacy: Tennessee State University Struggles to Revive Olympic Tradition." *Black Issues in Higher Education,* August 8, 1996.

Gregory, Deborah. "People: Tina Turner." *Essence,* October 1996, p. 50.

Grove, Lloyd. "Chris Rock: Stone Cold Funny." *Washington Post,* April 10, 1997, p. B1.

"Growing Up with a Famous Father." *Ebony,* June 1996, pp. 122–25.

Hadnot, Ira J. "Jazz's Queen Treated All Like Royalty: Busy Miss Ella Always Found Time for Her Many Admirers." *Dallas Morning News,* June 18, 1996, p. 21A.

"Halle Berry, Mariah Carey, Vanessa L. Williams Talk About Their Careers After Marital Breakups." *Jet,* March 2, 1998, p. 58.

"Halle Berry Must Choose Between a Black Man and White Man in TV Movie 'The Wedding.'" *Jet,* February 16, 1998, p. 54.

"Halle Berry Portrays Georgia Hairdresser Who Moves to Beverly Hills to Make Her Dreams Come True in Comedy 'B.A.P.S.'" *Jet,* April 7, 1997, p. 22.

"Halle Berry Stars in Murder Mystery 'The Rich Man's Wife'." *Jet,* September 2, 1996, p. 32.

Hampson, Rick, and Martha T. Moore. "Betty Shabazz: Malcolm X Widow Leaves Legacy of Dignity, Strength." *USA Today,* June 24, 1997, p. 1-A.

Hearth, Amy Hill. "The American Century of Bessie and Sadie Delany." *American Heritage,* October 1993, pp. 68–79.

Hentoff, Nat. "The Abolitionist: Sam Cotton." *Village Voice,* August 6, 1996, p. 10.

Hentoff, Nat. "Farrakhan's World Friendship Tour." *Village Voice,* April 23, 1996, p. 10.

Hentoff, Nat. "The Ghosts of Andrew Young's Past." *Village Voice,* April 7, 1998, p. 22.

Hentoff, Nat. "Here's the Proof, Mr. Farrakhan!" *Village Voice,* August 20, 1996, p. 10.

Herman, Don. "Jazz: The 'Complete Singer' Remembered." *Los Angeles Times,* June 26, 1997, p. F20.

Hewitt, Bill, et al. "Free, But Not Clear." *People,* November 13, 1995, pp. 58–61.

Hewitt, Bill, et al. "The Shoes Fit, So They Wouldn't Acquit." *People,* February 17, 1997, pp. 46–51.

Hines, Cragg. "Barbara Jordan Lived as Pioneer and Prophet." *Houston Chronicle,* January 17, 1996.

Hirshey, Gerri. "Tina Turner." *Rolling Stone,* November 13, 1997, pp. 117–21.

Hoover, Ala. "Jordan Will Take Another Swing: Mr. Basketball Finds Fulfillment as Baseball's Mr. Average." *Washington Post,* August 31, 1994, p. B-1.

Hoover, Kent. "Attention Conspirators: Alan Keyes Is on to Us." *Orlando Business Journal,* November 24, 1995, p. 42.

Hosenball, Mark, and Gregory L. Vistica. "The Life and Times of a Rumor." *Newsweek.* January 9, 1998, p. 31.

"House Passes Bill to Honor Former Sec'y Ron Brown." *Amsterdam News,* September 25, 1997, p. 4.

"How Blacks Participated in the Republican Convention." *Jet,* September 2, 1996, p. 4.

Hubbard, Kim, and Penelope Rowlands. "On Top of Her Game: A New Book and a New Guy Have Terry McMillan Breathing Easy." *People,* April 29, 1996, p. 111.

Ireland, Doug. "Alan Keyes Does the Hustle." *Nation,* October 30, 1995, pp. 500–503.

Jackson, Jesse L., Jr. "Why Race Dialogue Stutters." *Nation,* March 31, 1997, pp. 22–24.

"Janet, Magic, and Jheryl Busby Buy Majority Stake in Los Angeles Bank." *Jet,* May 18, 1998, p. 14.

Janofsky, Michael. "Washington's Mayor Is Back and Says He's Going to Stay." *New York Times,* May 14, 1996, p. A-14.

"Jet Milestones: 1951-1997." *Jet,* November 3, 1997, pp. 10–19.

Jones, Howard. "All We Want Is Make Us Free!" *American History,* February 1998, pp. 22–29.

Jones, Syl. "Despite Hating Her Big Film, Blacks Owe a Debt to McQueen." *Star Tribune,* December 31, 1995, p. 19A.

"Jordan Takes Piano Over Golf for Relaxation." *Jet,* June 22, 1998, p. 50.

Judson, David. "Clinton Picks Daley for Commerce." Gannett News Service, December 13, 1996.

"Justice Is Served: As Their Divorce Turns Nasty, Halle Berry Plays Court-Order Hardball with Baseball's David Justice." *People,* October 21, 1996, p. 64.

Kadlcek, Tina. "Tuskegee Airmen's Patriotism Overcame Bias." *Cleveland Plain Dealer,* March 18, 1998, p. 3-E.

Kakutani, Michiko. "'Flying Home'—Ralph Ellison As a Young Author." *Star Tribune,* January 16, 1997, p. 5E.

Kane, Gregory P. "'Gone with the Wind': Racism Just One of Its Faults." *Star Tribune,* July 9, 1998.

Kanfer, Stefan. "*Having Our Say* (play review)." *New Leader,* May 8–22, 1995, pp. 22–23.

Katz, Lee Michael. "U.N. Honors Magic Johnson." *USA Today,* April 17, 1998, p. 3-C.

Kelly, Michael. "TRB from Washington: Banality and Evil." *New Republic,* May 5, 1997, p. 6.

Kempton, Murray. "Coda for Ralph Ellison." *Newsday,* May 27, 1994, p. A13.

Kojima, Emi, "Activist Rosa Parks Graces Annual Marathon Reading." *University Wire,* May 18, 1998.

Kram, Mark. "The Burger King." *Esquire,* February 1995, pp. 98–102.

Landrum, Armetta. "Dr. Zelma Watson George." *Call and Post,* July 14, 1994.

Lane, Randall. "Mickey Mouse, Meet George Foreman." *Forbes,* December 18, 1995, p. 210.

Leland, John. "Requiem for a Gangsta." *Newsweek,* March 24, 1997, pp. 74–76.

"Like Father, Like Son." *Jet,* January 27, 1997, p. 32.

"A Literary Knockout–*By George, the Autobiography of George Foreman* by George Foreman and Joel Engel." *Sport,* September 1995, p. 6.

Loeb, Vernon. "A Turbulent Era That Defined D.C. Comes to an End." *Washington Post,* May 22, 1998, p. A-1.

Los Angeles Times, July 22, 1997.

"Louis Farrakhan." *Time,* June 17, 1996, p. 67.

"Louis Farrakhan Tells Black Journalists They're Afraid to Write the Truth." *Jet,* September 9, 1996, pp. 8–10.

Loury, Glenn C. "Looking Beyond O. J." *U.S. News & World Report,* February 17, 1997, p. 13.

Macintyre, Ben. "Left Right Left Right." *Times* (London), August 26, 1995.

"Magic Johnson and Wife Cookie Adopt Baby Girl." *Jet,* February 6, 1995, p. 53.

"Magic Johnson Enters the Talk Show Arena with 'The Magic Hour.'" *Jet,* June 22, 1998, p. 58.

"Magic Johnson Retires Again, Saying It's on His Own Terms This Time." *Jet,* June 3, 1996, p. 46.

"Magic Makes Comeback with L.A. Lakers." *Jet,* February 19, 1996, p. 52.

Mahon, Ray. "Color Them Courageous." *American Legion,* September 1995, pp. 72, 110.

Mandulor, Rhea. "Sharing Our Best with Others: An Interview with Dr. Betty Shabazz." *City Sun,* June 9–15, 1993.

Mark, Steve. "Golf Is Cool." *Boys' Life,* August 1997, pp. 6–7.

Martzke, Rudy. "Gumbel Primed 'To Put the Lights Out' for NBC." *USA Today,* January 23, 1998, p. 18E.

Martzke, Rudy. "Return of NFL Lights a Fire at CBS." *USA Today,* May 21, 1998, p. 2C.

Martzke, Rudy. "Same Opportunity, Different Network for Greg Gumbel." *USA Today,* July 20, 1996, p. 2C.

McCallum, Jack, and Hank Hersch. "A Gentle Warrior Says Goodbye." *Sports Illustrated,* December 1, 1997, pp. 22–24.

McCarthy, Rebecca. "Remains of Actress's Estate a Mystery: Tracking Down GWTW Player's Belongings Futile." *Atlanta Journal and Constitution,* December 18, 1996, p. D7.

McCarthy, Rebecca. "Some Fear McQueen's Home Looted After Death." *Atlanta Journal and Constitution,* December 30, 1995, p. A1.

"Media Focuses on Conservative GOPer Alan Keyes in 1996 Presidential Race." *Jet,* April 17, 1995, p. 6.

Mendelsohn, Jennifer. "Rock of Pages." *People,* December 1, 1997, p. 53.

Meyers, Kate. "The Humble Gumbel." *Entertainment Weekly,* February 18–25, 1994, p. 102.

"Michael Jordan Has $10 Billion Impact on U.S. Economy." *Jet,* June 22, 1998, p. 48.

"Michael Jordan Reveals He Gives Advice to Golf Sensation Tiger Woods." *Jet,* May 5, 1997, p. 50.

"Michael Jordan Says His Ultimate Dream Is to Spend More Time 'Watching My Kids Grow Up.'" *Jet,* March 9, 1998, p. 34.

"Michael Jordan Says 'I'm Back for the Love of the Game!'" *Jet,* April 10, 1995, p. 51.

"Michael Jordan Talks About Playing Reggie Miller, Family, and the End of His NBA Career." *Jet,* April 20, 1998, p. 51.

"Million Man March Draws More Than 1 Million Black Men to Nation's Capital." *Jet,* October 30, 1995, p. 5.

Mitchell, Ralph E. "TSU Names Building in Honor of Olympic Great Wilma Rudolph." *Tennessee Tribune,* August 8, 1995.

Montville, Leigh. "Slice Girls." *Sports Illustrated,* February 2, 1998, pp. 66–70.

"Monument Honoring Memory of Space Shuttle Astronaut Dr. Ronald McNair Unveiled in Refurbished Brooklyn Park." *Jet,* July 11, 1994, p. 26.

Moorer, Talise D. "'Gang Related' Features Tupac Shakur in Final Starring Role." *Amsterdam News,* October 2, 1997, p. 21.

Morehouse, Macon. "Butterfly McQueen Dies of Burns." *Atlanta Journal and Constitution,* December 23, 1995, p. A1.

Murray, Barbra. "Interpreting the Atonement." *U.S. News & World Report,* October 27, 1997, p. 44.

"Nation's Capital 'Getting Better,' According to Mayor Marion Barry." *Jet,* April 28, 1997, p. 25.

Neeley, DeQuendre. "Rift Mended, Shabazz Ends Long Feud with Farrakhan." *Newsday,* May 8, 1995, p. A-8.

Neill, Michael, and Fannie Weinstein. "Venus Rising." *People,* October 27, 1997, pp. 103–6.

Nelson, Jill. "Alternative Rock." *USA Weekend,* July 10–12, 1998, pp. 4–5.

New York Times Magazine, July 21, 1993.

New York Times, September 22, 1998, p. C26.

Newborn, Steve. "Pilots Fought a War on 2 Fronts." *Tampa Tribune,* April 24, 1998, p. 1.

Newsday, July 24, 1988; September 7, 1988; September 30, 1988.

Newsweek, August 1, 1988.

Nicklaus, Jack. "Jack Nicklaus to Golf's Young Tigers: 'Have a Life.'" *USA Weekend,* July 10–12, 1998, pp. 12–13.

Noble, Kenneth B. "Magic Johnson Finds Success in a New Forum." *New York Times,* January 8, 1996, p. 8.

Noel, Peter. "Farrakhan Hires a Convicted Killer of Malcolm X." *Village Voice,* March 31, 1998, pp. 39–41.

"O. J. Simpson Says He Will Live Off His $25,000-a-Month Pension." *Jet,* July 28, 1997, pp. 52–54.

O'Brien, Richard, and Hank Hersch. "Venus Writing." *Sports Illustrated,* November 17, 1997, p. 31.

O'Neill, Ann. "The Court Files." *Los Angeles Times,* September 14, 1997, p. B1.

"One Man March." *Economist,* March 2, 1996, p. 30.

Overbea, Luix Virgil. "'Hi-De-Ho' Man Cab Calloway Touched a World with His Music." *Bay State Banner,* November 24, 1994.

"Poems of Late Tupac Shakur to Be Studied at University of California at Berkeley." *Jet,* September 29, 1997, p. 22.

Polner, Rob. "Tangible Glimpse of 'Invisible Man.'" *Newsday,* April 18, 1994, p. A13.

"Powell Gives Opening Keynote Speech at GOP Convention." *Jet,* September 2, 1996, p. 12.

Powell, Michael. "Control Board Picks Management Chief: Appointee to Oversee Major D.C. Agencies." *Washington Post,* December 23, 1997, p. A-1.

"Powell, Woods, Jordan Most Popular Americans." *Jet,* May 19, 1997, p. 5.

Price, S. L. "In Her Long-Delayed Debut, Venus Williams Couldn't Live Up to Her Own Billing." *Sports Illustrated,* July 7, 1997, p. 26.

Price, Susan. "Cosby Leads Tribute for Calloway." *Newsday,* November 30, 1994, p. A52.

Puente, Maria. "Familiar Voice Leads Way in Reform Effort." *USA Today,* July 14, 1994, p. 5.

Pusey, Allen. "Darkness Visible: Tales Prefigure 'Invisible Man.'" *Dallas Morning News,* January 5, 1997, p. 8J.

"Ralph Ellison's Second Novel to Be Published." *Star Tribune,* July 14, 1995, p. 7A.

Randolph, Laura B. "A Black-and-White Alabama Homecoming." *Ebony,* November 1997, pp. 124–32.

Reilly, Rick. "Need a Fourth?" *Sports Illustrated,* March 31, 1997, pp. 42–45.

"Relieving O'Hare." *Economist,* January 10, 1998, pp. 22–23.

"Reward Tip Leads to Arrest of 18-Year-Old Russian Immigrant in Murder of Ennis Cosby. . . ." *Jet,* March 31, 1997, p. 12.

Richardson, Gwen Daye, and Robert Stanton, et al. "20 Most Influential Black Conservatives." *Headway,* September 1997, pp. 6–16.

Richardson, Kevin R. "Jesse Jackson, Jr." *Elle,* September 1996, p. 318.

Roberts, Johnnie L. "Grabbing at a Dead Star." *Newsweek,* September 1, 1997, p. 48.

Roberts, Steven V. "The Death of a Salesman." *U.S. News & World Report,* April 15, 1996, pp. 38–39.

"Rock to Launch Comedy Magazine at Howard." *Black Issues in Higher Education,* February 19, 1998, p. 8.

Rogers, Patrick, and Lorenzo Benet. "Prophecy Fulfilled." *People,* September 30, 1996, pp. 79–80.

Rubin, Steve. "Black America's Political Action Committee." *Human Events,* May 17, 1996, p. 16.

Russell, Yvette. "Jonesin' for Dandridge." *Essence,* May 1997, p. 114.

St. Louis Post-Dispatch, July 5, 1994, p. 4B.

"Samuel Pieh Applauds 'Amistad' Movie About His Ancestor, Slave Revolt Leader Joseph Cinque." *Jet,* February 23, 1998, p. 39.

Sandler, Stanley. "The Tuskegee Airmen." *American Historical Review,* October 1996, pp. 1171–73.

Schneider, Karen S., Johnny Dodd, and Paula Yoo. "Hurts So Bad: Actress Halle Berry Planned Her Success Carefully, But She Didn't Foresee the End of Her Marriage." *People,* May 13, 1996, p. 102.

Scruby, Jennifer. "Halle's Comet." *Elle,* February 1998, pp. 78–80.

Seter, Jennifer, Timothy M. Ito, and Robin M. Bennefield. "Simpson Trial & Trivia." *U.S. News & World Report,* October 16, 1995, pp. 42–43.

Seymour, Gene. "Cab Calloway Dies: 'Hi-De-Ho Man' a Pop Music Icon." *Newsday,* November 20, 1994, p. A7.

Shabazz, Betty. "Loving and Losing Malcolm." *Essence,* February 1992, pp. 50–54+.

Smith, Eric L. "Blazing a Path for 100 Years: A. G. Gaston, [*Black Enterprise*'s] 'Entrepreneur of the Century,' Set the Tone for a Generation to Follow." *Black Enterprise,* March 31, 1996.

Smith, Eric L. "Eye of the Tiger." *Black Enterprise,* September 1997, pp. 90–91.

"Smithsonian Displays Just a Little Bit of Ella." *Dallas Morning News,* March 23, 1998, p. 6C.

"Son's Life Was Basis for Theo Huxtable." *USA Today,* January 17, 1997, p. 3-A.

Sporting News, October 10, 1988; October 17, 1988; February 23, 1989.

Stambler, Lyndon, and Julia Campbell. "In Search of Justice: Ennis's Accused Killer Goes on Trial in L.A., as the Cosbys Struggle to Rebuild Their Shattered Lives." *People,* July 6, 1998, p. 80.

Stearns, Daniel Patrick. "Honoring the Art and Soul of Ella Fitzgerald." *USA Today,* July 11, 1996, p. 9D.

Stein, Joel. "Q & A." *Time Canada,* February 9, 1998, p. 75.

Stewart, James B. "Race, Science, and 'Just-Us': Understanding Jurors' Reasonable Doubt in the O. J. Simpson Trial." *Black Scholar,* Fall 1995, pp. 43–45.

"Talking with . . . Terry McMillan." *People,* February 5, 1996.

"Ten Sexy Men." *People,* November 17, 1997, p. 97.

"This Weekend" *Newsday,* April 10, 1998, p. B2.

"Ties to Michael Jordan Still Remain in His Hometown of Wilmington, NC." *Jet,* June 23, 1997, p. 50.

"Tiger Woods." *People,* December 30, 1996–January 6, 1997, p. 110.

"Tina Turner Returns to U.S. with 'Wildest Dreams' World Tour." *Jet,* March 17, 1997, pp. 32–35.

"Tina Turner Succeeded as Singer Despite Having Insecurities About Her Voice." *Jet,* April 14, 1997, p. 62.

Townsel, Lisa Jones, and Kevin Chappel. "Cheryl McNair: Transcending the *Challenger* Disaster." *Ebony,* May 1996, p. 94.

Tucker, Ken. "Rocking Late Night." *Entertainment Weekly,* November 28, 1997, p. 61.

"Tuskegee Airmen Absolved of 50-Year-Old Reprimands at Atlanta Dinner." *Jet,* October 16, 1995, pp. 58–60.

"12-Year-Old Admits Trying to Kill Betty Shabazz." *Washington Afro-American,* June 7, 1997.

"The 25 Most Intriguing People '97: Bill Cosby: Struck by Loss and Scandal, He Gallantly Soldiers On." *People,* December 29, 1997–January 5, 1998, p. 54.

"Ukrainian Immigrant Mikail Markhasev Found Guilty of Murdering Ennis Cosby." *Jet,* July 27, 1998, p. 24.

"U.S. Denies Farrakhan's Request for Libyan Gift." *Christian Century,* September 11–18, 1996, p. 846.

Vognar, Chris. "Different Road to the 'Hood: First-Time Filmmaker Is a Talkative, Ambitious Auteur." *Dallas Morning News,* April 2, 1998, p. 1C.

Warner, Jack. "Actress McQueen's Charred Belongings Go on Sale at Hotel." *Atlanta Journal and Constitution,* April 13, 1996, p. E4.

Weinraub, Bernard. "At Work with Cookie Johnson: Moving Forward, with Hope." *New York Times,* May 2, 1996, p. C-1.

Weinstein, Henry. "Ella Fitzgerald, Jazz's First Lady of Song, Dies." *Los Angeles Times,* June 16, 1996, p. A1.

Weir, Tom. "Olympic Congress Opens with Tribute to Rudolph." *USA Today,* November 11, 1994, p. 7.

Whitcomb, Dan. "Music World Mourns Loss of Jazz Legend Fitzgerald." Reuters, June 16, 1996.

White, Jack E. "An Empty Seat at the Table: Ronald Harmon Brown: 1941–1996." *Time,* April 15, 1996, p. 72.

"Whitney Houston, Angela Bassett, Lela Rochon, Loretta Devine Star in 'Waiting to Exhale.'" *Jet,* December 25, 1995–January 1, 1996, p. 22.

Wilkerson, Isabel. "The All American." *Essence,* November 1997, pp. 99–100+.

Wilkerson, Isabel. "O. J.: Having Our Say." *Essence,* January 1996, pp. 82–84+.

"Williams Sisters Display Loving Sibling Rivalry at Australia Open." *Jet,* February 9, 1998, pp. 49–50.

Women's Sports + Fitness, September 1995, pp. 44–45.

Wong, Kimberly. "Hopelessly Devoted." *Sports Illustrated,* December 30, 1996–January 6, 1997, p. 20.

Wright, James. "A. G. Gaston Worked Hard for His Millions; Was an Inspiration." *Washington Afro-American,* January 27, 1996.

Wright, Sarah E. "Celebrities Remember Alice Childress with Love." *New York Amsterdam News,* November 19, 1994.

"Year-End Culmination of Ron Brown Salutes." *Amsterdam News,* January 1, 1998, p. 4.

York, Byron. "Ron Brown's Body." *American Spectator,* February 1998, pp. 50–53.

Other

African-American Playwrights. "Alice Childress." [Online] http://www.scilsrutgers.edu/~cybers/child.html (accessed on October 8, 1998).

AFRO-Americ@. *The Tuskegee Airmen.* [Online] http://www.afroam.org/history/tusk/tuskmain.html (accessed on October 8, 1998).

Amazing Grace: Black Women in Sport (videorecording). Philadelphia: Black Women in Sport Foundation, 1993.

Amistad: An Extraordinary Tale of Courage, Justice, and Humanity. [Online] http://www.penguinputnam.com/amistad/ (accessed on October 8, 1998).

Amistad Trial Home Page. [Online] http://www.law.umkc.edu/faculty/projects/ftrials/amistad/amistd.htm (accessed on October 8, 1998).

Barbara Jordan. [Online] http://www.rice.edu/armadillo/ Texas/jordan.html (accessed on October 8, 1998).

"Benjamin Banneker to the Secretary of State." [Online] http://www.lib.virginia.edu/etext/readex/24073.html (accessed on October 8, 1998).

"Betty Shabazz Legacy." *Good Morning America.* ABC-TV, June 24, 1997.

"Butterfly McQueen Remembered." *Freethought Today,* January/February 1996. [Online] http://www.infidels.org/org/ ffrf/fttoday/jan_feb96/butterfly.html (accessed on October 8, 1998).

CNN–O. J. Simpson Trial. [Online] http://www.cnn.com/US/ OJ/index.html (accessed on October 8, 1998).

Congressman Jesse Jackson, Jr. Web Site. [Online] http:// www.jessejacksonjr.org/about.cgi (accessed on October 8, 1998).

Costa, Richard. "The Short Happy Afterlife of Charles Gordone." *The Touchstone,* February/March 1996. [Online] http://www.rtis.com/reg/bcs/pol/touchstone/February96/costa.htm (accessed on October 8, 1998).

Court TV Casefiles: O. J. Simpson. [Online] http://www.courttv.com/casefiles/simpson (accessed on October 8, 1998).

Da 2Pac /makaveli Krib, da fattest 2Pac site. [Online] http://makaveli.simplenet.com/ (accessed on October 8, 1998).

Dominique Dawes. [Online] http://www.dominiquedawes.com (accessed on October 8, 1998).

The Ella Fitzgerald Homepage. [Online] http://www.seas.columbia.edu/~tts6/ella.html (accessed on October 8, 1998).

Golf.com—Eye on the Tiger. [Online] http://www.golf.com/ tiger/ (accessed on October 8, 1998).

Gumbel, Greg (host). *Stride to Glory: The History of African American Achievement in the Olympic Games* (videorecording). Santa Monica, CA: Trans World International/ Xenon Entertainment Group, 1997.

Halle Berry. [Online] http://www.geocities.com/Hollywood/Set/1592/ (accessed on October 8, 1998).

Having Our Say. [Online] http://havingoursay-theplay.com/ (accessed on October 8, 1998).

HBO: The Chris Rock Show. [Online] http://www.hbo.com/ rock/ (accessed on October 29, 1998).

How Stella Got Her Groove Back (motion picture). 20th Century Fox, 1998.

Magic Johnson Foundation. [Online] http://www.magicjohnson.org (accessed on October 8, 1998).

Malcolm X (motion picture). Warner Brothers, 1992.

Markowitz, Robert, director. *The Tuskegee Airmen* (motion picture). Home Box Office/Price Entertainment, 1995.

Maryland's African American Heritage. "Benjamin Banneker." [Online] http://tqd.advanced.org/3337/banneker.html (accessed on October 8, 1998).

The Michael Jordan Ring. [Online] http://www.bomis.com/rings/bulls_jordan/ring_home.html (accessed on October 8, 1998).

The Nation of Islam Online. [Online] http://www.noi.org (accessed on October 8, 1998).

O. J. Central. [Online] http://pathfinder.com/@@6cr3b2GjUAIAQFNw/pathfinder/features/oj/central1.html (accessed on October 8, 1998).

The Official Michael Jordan Web Site–CBS SportsLine. [Online] http://jordan.sportsline.com (accessed on October 8, 1998).

The Original Tiger Woods Web Page. [Online] http://www.geocities.com/Colosseum/2396/tiger.html (accessed on October 8, 1998).

"Ralph Ellison (1914-1994)." [Online] http://www.levity.com/corduroy/ellison.htm (accessed on October 8, 1998).

The Real Malcolm X: An Intimate Portrait of the Man (videorecording). CBS News/Fox Video, 1992.

Rosaforte, Tim. *Tiger Woods: The Makings of a Champion* (sound recording). Newport Beach, CA: Books on Tape, 1997.

Shabazz, Betty. *The Sister's Been Doing Her Homework* (sound recording). Pacifica Tape Library.

"Shabazz Memorial Service." *Morning Edition.* National Public Radio, June 30, 1997.

"Shabazz Obituary." *All Things Considered,* National Public Radio, June 26, 1997.

Smalls, Robert, producer. *Benjamin Banneker* (filmstrip). Chicago, IL: Society for Visual Education, 1964.

Stamp on Black History Month. "Benjamin Banneker." [Online] http://library.advanced.org/10320/Banneker.htm (accessed on October 8, 1998).

Tiger Woods—CBS SportsLine. [Online] http://www.tigerwoods.com/ (accessed on October 8, 1998).

Tupac Shakur: Thug Immortal, the Last Interview (videorecording). Santa Monica, CA: Xenon Entertainment Group, 1997.

Waiting to Exhale (motion picture). 20th Century Fox, 1995.

When We Were Kings (motion picture). PolyGram Filmed Entertainment/Gramercy Pictures, 1996.

Williams, Brian, producer. *Tiger Woods: Son, Hero & Champion* (videorecording). New York: CBS Video, 1997.

Picture Credits

Chris Rock

The photographs appearing in *African American Biography, volume 5,* were reproduced by permission of the following sources:

Fisk University Library: p. 1; **CorbisBettman:** pp. 2, 5, 140, 243; **AP/Wide World Photos:** pp. 9, 41, 47, 53, 55, 71, 83, 89, 93, 97, 101, 105, 109, 121, 133, 147, 149, 155, 159, 171, 185, 189, 197, 209, 217, 239, 241; **AP/Wide World Photos/Michael Caulfield:** 13; **AP/Wide World Photos/Danny Johnston:** p. 17; **AP/Wide World Photos/Chris Morris:** p. 19; **Library of Congress/Carl Van Vechten:** p. 23; **Jerry Bauer:** p. 27; **Library of Congress:** 31, 33, 249; **NYT Pictures/Suzanne De Chillo:** p. 59; **Archive Photos:** pp. 67, 165, 207; **Archive Photos/Mike Theiler:** p. 74; **Archive Photos/American Stock:** p. 77; **AP/Wide World Photos/Itsuo Inouye:** p. 81; **AP/Wide World Photos/Patrick Pagnano:** p. 112; **AP/Wide World Photos/Joe Marquette:** p. 115; **AP/Wide World/Ruth Fremson:** p. 117; **AP/Wide World Photos/Bebeto Matthews:** p. 124; **Bettman Archive/News-**

photos, Inc.: pp. 127, 139; **AP/Wide World Photos/Michael Caulfield:** p. 131; **The Kobal Collection:** pp. 142, 221; **UPI/CorbisBettmann/Bill Mitchell:** p. 161; **AP/Wide World Photos/Richard Drew:** p. 177; **AP/Wide World Photos/Kevork Djansezian:** p. 182; **CorbisBettmann/Mike Segar:** p. 194; **Michael Ochs Archives/Raymond Boyd:** p. 198; **Archive Photos/Rick Meyer:** p. 211; **UPI/CorbisBettmann:** pp. 225, 228; **AP/Wide World Photos/Ron Fehm:** p. 233; **Archive Photos/Agence France Presses:** p. 236; **UPI/Corbis-Bettmann/David Tulis:** p. 252.

Index

Italic type indicates volume number; **boldface** indicates main entries and their page numbers; (ill.) indicates photos and illustrations. For a listing of fields of endeavor, see p. ix.

Alan Keyes

A

A. Philip Randolph Institute, *3:* 640, 642
Aaron, Hank, *1:* **1–3,** 1 (ill.); *2:* 313
ABC News, *4:* 670, 671
ABC Sports, *5:* 210
Abdalla, Kenneth, *5:* 215
Abdul-Jabbar, Kareem, *1:* **3–5,** 4 (ill.); *2:* 401; *5:* 143
Abernathy, Ralph David, *1:* **5–8,** 6 (ill.); *3:* 457, 483, 545
Abolitionists, *5:* 31, 34
Absence (dance), *2:* 411, 412
Acquired Immune Deficiency Syndrome (AIDS), *1:* 27; *2:* 400, 402, 412; *5:* 128, 129
Adams, John Quincy, *5:* 31, 36, 38, 39
Advocates Scene, *4:* 659
African Journey, 3: 619, 620
African Liberation Support Committee, *2:* 276
Afro-American Association (AAA), *4:* 657
Afro-American, 5: 227–28
Afrocentric movement, *1:* 23, 25
Afrocentricity: The Theory of Social Change, 1: 25
AIDS. *See* Acquired Immune Deficiency Syndrome (AIDS)
Ailey, Alvin, *1:* **8–11,** 9 (ill.)
"Ain't Misbehavin'," *1:* 22
Al-Amin, Jamil Abdullah. *See* Brown, H. Rap
Alcindor, Lew. *See* Abdul-Jabbar, Kareem
Ali, Muhammad, *1:* 5, **11–14,** 12 (ill.) 76; *5:* 81, 84
All Afrikan People's Revolutionary Party, *1:* 119
All American Women: Lines that Divide, Ties that Bind, 1: 152

All God's Chillun Got Wings, 3: 622
All Hail the Queen, 3: 606
Allen, Debbie, *5:* 39
Alliance Against Racism and Political Repression, *1:* 183
Alpha Suffrage Club, *1:* 43
"Ambassador of Love," *1:* 29
Ambush, Kathy, *4:* 711
American Bandstand, 1: 168, 169
American Committee on Africa, *3:* 641
An American Dilemma, 1: 105
American Equal Rights Association, *4:* 730
American Federation of Labor and Congress of Industrial Organizations (AFL-CIO), *3:* 611
American Jewish Congress, *3:* 642
American Legion Boys Nation, *5:* 148
American Library Association, *3:* 629
American Medical Association, *2:* 230, 231
American Muslim Mission, *2:* 239
American Negro Theater, *3:* 581, 582
American Political Science Association, *1:* 106
American Red Cross, *1:* 208
American Society for the Prevention of Cruelty to Animals, *5:* 168
American Spectator, 5: 21
American Tennis Association, *2:* 267
American Theater for Poets, *1:* 39
Amistad (ship) *5:* 31, 32, 33, 33 (ill.), 34
And the Walls Came Tumbling Down, 1: 6
Anderson, Marian, *1:* **14–17,** 102; *3:* 590
Anderson, Myers, *4:* 710–11
Angela Davis, 1: 183

Angelou, Maya, *1:* **17–20,** 18 (ill.)
Ann-Margret, *5:* 220, 221
Annan, Kofi, *5:* 131
Annie Allen, 1: 86
Ansen, David, *2:* 278
Anthropology for the Nineties, 1: 152
Anti-Semitism, *5:* 72, 73
Apartheid, *5:* 149, 251
Arafat, Yasir, *2:* 381
Argaiz, Pedro Alcantara de, *5:* 35
Arkansas State Press, 1: 51
Armstrong, Louis, *1:* **20–23,** 22 (ill.), 189; *2:* 383; *4:* 757
Asante, Molefi Kete, *1:* **23–25,** 24 (ill.)
Ashe, Arthur, *1:* **25–28,** 26 (ill.)
Ashford, Evelyn, *5:* 104
Association for the Study of Afro-American Life and History, *4:* 799
Association for the Study of Negro Life and History, *4:* 798, 799–800
Association for Theatre in Higher Education, *5:* 28
Association of Black Anthropologists, *1:* 198
Atlanta Committee on Appeal for Human Rights (COHAR), *1:* 69
Atlanta, Georgia, *5:* 249, 252, 253, 254
Atlantic Monthly, 1: 134
Atlantic Records, *2:* 246
Atomic bomb, *3:* 603
Atomic reactor, *3:* 603
Ausbie, Geese, *2:* 320
Austin, Clyde, *2:* 320
The Autobiography of Malcolm X, 2: 302
The Autobiography of Miss Jane Pittman, 2: 253, 255
Avalon Community Center, *2:* 264
Aykroyd, Dan, *5:* 24
Aziz, Muhammad Abdul, *5:* 76

B

Bach, Erwin, *5:* 224
Bailey, F. Lee, *5:* 211, 213
Bailey, Joy, *2:* 313
Bailey, Pearl, *5:* 24, **28–30,** 29 (ill.)
Bailey's Cafe, 3: 559
Baker, Augusta, *1:* **30–32,** 30 (ill.)
Baker, Josephine, *1:* **32–34,** 33 (ill.)
Baldwin, James, *1:* **34–37,** 36 (ill.), 143; *4:* 687, 688, 800
Baldwin, Roger S., *5:* 34
Ballard, Florence, *3:* 630
Baltimore Elite Giants, *1:* 114
Banneker, Benjamin, *5:* **1–7,** 1 (ill.), 2 (ill.), 5 (ill.)
Baraka, Amiri, *1:* **37–40,** 39 (ill.); *2:* 276; *3:* 609; *4:* 650
Barker, Danny, *4:* 678
Barnard, James, *4:* 706
Barnett, Camille C., *5:* 12
Barnett, Charlie, *2:* 358
Barnett, Ida B. Wells, *1:* **40–43,** 41 (ill.)
Barnett, Marguerite Ross, *1:* **43–45,** 44 (ill.)
Barrow, Joseph Louis. *See* Louis, Joe
Barry, Marion, *1:* **45–47,** 47 (ill.); *2:* 330; *3:* 448; *5:* **9–12,** 9 (ill.), 182
Baryshnikov, Mikhail, *2:* 351
Baseball Hall of Fame, *1:* 116, *3:* 575, 626
Basketball Hall of Fame, *1:* 67
Basie, Count, *1:* 28, **48–50,** 49 (ill.); *4:* 680
Bassett, Angela, *5:* 155, 167, 193, 217, 223–24
Bates, Daisy, *1:* **50–53,** 51 (ill.)
Battle, Kathleen, *1:* **53–55,** 54 (ill.)
Baumfree, Isabella, *4:* 728
Beastie Boys, *2:* 314
Beat cultural revolution, *1:* 38
Beatles, *1:* 22; *2:* 337; *5:* 220, 223

Beatty, Warren, *5:* 15
Beauvoir, Simone de, *4:* 803
Beckham, William, *4:* 805
Beckwith, Byron de la, *2:* 236
Bedford, David, *4:* 790
Before Columbus Foundation, *3:* 616
Behind the Scenes, Or, Thirty Years a Slave and Four Years in the White House, 3: 443
Belafonte, Harry, *1:* **55–58,** 56 (ill.); *5:* 48, 49
Beloved, 3: 543
Belushi, Jim, *5:* 204
Belushi, John, *5:* 24
Ben Folds Five, *5:* 28
Benjamin Banneker Historical Park and Museum, *5:* 6
Bennett College, *4:* 654
Bennett, Ned, *4:* 743
Bennett, Rolla, *4:* 743
Bennett, Tony, *5:* 78
Benny Goodman Quartet, *2:* 316
Benson, George W., *4:* 729
Bensonhurst shooting, *4:* 666
Benton, Robert, *2:* 277
Berlin, Germany, *3:* 571
Berlin, Irving, *2:* 244; *5:* 78
Bernstein, Leonard, *4:* 766, 768
Berry, Chu, *5:* 24
Berry, Chuck, *1:* **58–61,** 59 (ill.); *5:* 24, 222
Berry, Halle, *1:* **61–63,** 62 (ill.); *5:* **13–16,** 13 (ill.), 47, 52
Berry Park, *1:* 60
Bethune-Cookman College, *1:* 64
Bethune, Mary McLeod, *1:* 43, **63–65,** 63 (ill.); *2:* 334
The Beulah Show, 3: 517
Beverly Hills Cop, 3: 554
"Bhahiana," *1:* 216
Biafra, Jello, *2:* 372
Bicentennial Nigger, 3: 598
Bing, Dave, *1:* **65–67,** 66 (ill.)
Bird, Daniel W., Jr., *4:* 775
Bird, Larry, *2:* 400–401; *5:* 128
Birmingham Barons, *5:* 141
Birmingham Black Barons, *3:* 510

Birth of a Nation, 5: 166
Bizet, Georges, *5:* 49
Black America's Political Action Committee (BAMPAC), *5:* 154
Black Arts Movement, *1:* 37
Black Arts Repertory Theater School, *1:* 39
Black Boy, 4: 802–3
Black History Month, *4:* 800
Black Horizons Theater Company, *4:* 791
Black Judgement, 2: 272
"Black" language, *4:* 651
Black Magic, *1:* 156
Black Muslims, *4:* 650; *5:* 72
The Black Muslims in America, 3: 550
Black nationalism, *1:* 39, 119; *2:* 256, 374
Black Panthers, *1:* 100, 119, 120, 143–46, 182; *3:* 560, 561, 562; *4:* 657–59; *5:* 199
Black Patti. *See* Jones, Sissieretta
Black Patti's Troubadors, *2:* 421
Black Periodical Literature Project, *2:* 262
Black Power: The Politics of Liberation in America, 1: 120
Black Press Hall of Fame, *2:* 406
Black Street Hawkeyes, *2:* 279–80
Black Student Alliance (BSA), *4:* 701
Black supremacy, *5:* 73
Black Thunder, 1: 75
Black Wings, 1: 160
Black Writers Conference, *1:* 88
The Blackboard Jungle, 3: 582
Blackburn, Jack, *3:* 479
Blacklock, Jimmy, *2:* 320
Blacks in America: With All Deliberate Speed, 1: 79
Blackthink, 3: 572
Blood, *1:* 207, 208
Bloodchild, 1: 109
Bloom, Allan, *5:* 148
Blouis, James, *4:* 705
Blow, Kurtis, *2:* 371

The Blues Brothers, 1: 113; *5:* 24
The Bluest Eye, 3: 542
Bluford, Guy, *5:* 159
Boghetti, Giuseppe, *1:* 15
Bogle, Donald, *2:* 278
Bond, Julian, *1:* **67–71,** 68 (ill.)
The Bonds: An American Family, 1: 69
Bonilla, Bobby, *1:* **71–73,** 72 (ill.)
Bontemps, Arna, *1:* **73–75,** 74 (ill.), 151, 180; *4:* 715
The Book of American Negro Poetry, 2: 405
Booker T. Washington (BTW) Burial Insurance Company, *2:* 259; *5:* 89
Booker T. Washington (BTW) Business College, *2:* 260
Booker T. Washington (BTW) Insurance Company, *2:* 258
Books about Negro Life for Children, 1: 31
Borg, Bjorn, *1:* 27
Bork, Robert, *4:* 669
Bosnia, *5:* 18
Boston Celtics, *2:* 401; *3:* 638, 639; *5:* 128
Boukmann, *4:* 719
Bowe, Riddick, *1:* **75–78,** 76 (ill.)
Boycotts, *3:* 455, 457, 482, 579, 612, 641
"The Boys of Summer," *1:* 115
Boyz N the Hood, 4: 675–76
Bradley, Ed, *1:* **78–80,** 80 (ill.)
Bradshaw, Terry, *5:* 111
Braugher, Andre, *5:* 229, 230
Braun, Carol Moseley, *1:* **80–83,** 82 (ill.)
Brawley, Tawana, *4:* 666
Breaking Barriers: A Memoir, 3: 634
Bridges, Richard, *4:* 686
Briggs, Bunny, *2:* 351
Bring the Pain, 5: 180
Broadside Press, *3:* 607, 608
Broadus, Doc, *5:* 82, 83
Brontë, Emily, *5:* 67

Brooke, Edward W., III, *1:* **83–85,** 84 (ill.)
Brooklyn Dodgers, *1:* 114; *3:* 625
Brooks, Gwendolyn, *1:* **86–88,** 87 (ill.); *3:* 609, 629
Brother Ray, *1:* 130
Brotherhood of Sleeping Car Porters, *3:* 611
Brown, Bobby, *2:* 362
Brown, Claude, *1:* **88–91,** 90 (ill.)
Brown Girl, Brownstones, 3: 502
Brown, H. Rap, *1:* **91–93,** 92 (ill.); *3:* 449
Brown, James, *1:* **93–95,** 94 (ill.), 169; *2:* 312; *4:* 665
Brown, Jim, *5:* 82
Brown, Ron, *1:* **95–99,** 98 (ill.); *5:* **17–22,** 17 (ill.), 19 (ill.), 116
Brown, Tracey, *5:* 19
Brown v. Board of Education, 3: 504, 505, 545, 633; *4:* 777
Bryant, William Cullen, *5:* 35
Buchanan, James, *4:* 653
Buckley, Tom, *4:* 807
Buffalo Bills, *5:* 208–9
Bugs Bunny, *5:* 141, 142 (ill.)
Bullins, Ed, *1:* **99–101,** 100 (ill.)
Bullock, Anna Mae, *5:* 218
Bumbry, Grace, *1:* **101–4,** 103 (ill.)
Bunche, Ralph, *1:* **104–6,** 105 (ill.)
Burke, Yvonne Brathwaite, *1:* **106–9,** 108 (ill.)
Burns, Kephera, *4:* 704
"Burrell House," *1:* 216
Burrell, Stanley, *2:* 312
Burrill, Mamie, *2:* 293
Burroughs, James, *4:* 758
Bus boycotts, *1:* 7; *5:* 250
Busby, Jheryl, *5:* 130
Bush, George, *2:* 356, 402; *4:* 671, 710, 712, 713, 805; *5:* 18, 128, 172, 173, 174
Bush, George W., *5:* 175
Butler, Octavia E., *1:* **109–11,** 110 (ill.)
Butterfly Ballet, 3: 526

C

"Cablinasian," *5:* 244
Caldwell, Erskine, *5:* 97
California General Assembly, *1:* 107, 108
California State University, *1:* 148
Call & Post, 3: 540
Callahan, John F., *5:* 68–69
Callahan, Tom, *5:* 246
Calloway, Cab, *1:* **111–14,** 113 (ill.); *5:* **23–25,** 23 (ill.)
Calloway, Nuffie, *5:* 25
Campaign for Nuclear Disarmament, *3:* 641
Campanella, Roy, *1:* **114–16,** 115 (ill.)
Campbell, Naomi, *1:* **116–18,** 117 (ill.)
Cancer research, *1:* 148
Cane, 4: 713, 715–16
Cantor, Mickey, *5:* 19
Capitol Records, *1:* 157
Carlucci, Frank, *5:* 172
Carmen Jones, 5: 49, 52
Carmichael, Stokely, *1:* **118–21,** 120 (ill.)
Carnegie, Andrew, *4:* 760
Carnegie Hall, *1:* 102, 155; *2:* 270; *3:* 453
Carson, Benjamin, *1:* **121–24,** 122 (ill.)
Carson, Johnny, *2:* 304–5, 306
Carter, Art, *5:* 227–28
Carter, Greg, *5:* 99
Carter, Jimmy, *1:* 70; *2:* 329, 392, 432; *4:* 656, 805; *5:* 116, 135, 174, 249, 251
Cartwright, Marguerite, *4:* 649
Carver Club, *1:* 198
Carver, George Washington, *1:* 75, **124–27,** 124 (ill.); *4:* 760
Casey, Robert P., *4:* 693
Castro, Fidel, *1:* 145, 2: 381
Catherine Carmier, 4: 254
Catholic Church, *4:* 683–86
CBS Radio, *1:* 79
CBS Sports, *5:* 111, 112, 113
CBS This Morning, 5: 111

CBS-TV, *1:* 79
Challenge of Change, 1: 85
Challenger Center for Space Science Exploration, *5:* 163
Challenger (space shuttle), *2:* 396; *5:* 159, 162, 163
Chamberlain, Wilt, *1:* 5, **127–29,** 127 (ill.); *3:* 639; *5:* 143
Chambre Syndicale du Prêt-à-Porter, *3:* 445
Chapin, Katherine Garrison, *4:* 691
Chapman, Tracy, *5:* 223
Charles, Ray, *1:* **130–32,** 131 (ill.); *2:* 417; *5:* 24
Charleston, South Carolina, *4:* 742–44
Chase, Richard, *4:* 717
Chattanooga Lookouts, *3:* 573
Chavis, Benjamin, *5:* 73
Chesnutt, Charles Waddell, *1:* **132–35,** 133 (ill.)
Chicago Bulls, *2:* 427, 428–29; *5:* 140–41
Chicago Business Hall of Fame, *2:* 406
Chicago Conservator, 1: 42
"Chicago Eight," *4:* 658
Chicago, Illinois, *5:* 124–25, 140
Chicago White Sox, *5:* 141
Chiffons, *5:* 219
The Children of Ham, 1: 89, 90
Children's Defense Fund (CDF), *2:* 223, 224
Childress, Alice, *1:* **135–38,** 136 (ill.); *5:* **27–29,** 27 (ill.)
Chisholm, Shirley, *1:* **138–40,** 139 (ill.)
Chopin, Frédéric, *4:* 766
The Chosen Place, the Timeless People, 3: 502
Christophe, Henri, *4:* 720–21
Chuckie D, *3:* 599–602; *5:* 201
Church of the Advocate, *2:* 324
Cinque, *5:* **31–40,** 31 (ill.), 33 (ill.)
Citadel (magazine), *1:* 100

Citizens Against Government Waste, *5:* 153
Citizens Federal Savings Bank, *2:* 258
Civil Rights Act (1964), *3:* 578
Civil Rights movement, *5:* 37, 63, 151
Civil War, *5:* 60, 151, 166
Claessen, David, *2:* 281
Clapton, Eric, *5:* 223
Clara's Ole Man, 1: *100*
Clark, Dick, *1:* 168, 169
Clark, Joe, *1:* **140–43,** 141 (ill.)
Clark, John L., *4:* 695
Clark, Marcia, *5:* 211
Clark, Ramsey, *4:* 808
Clay, Cassius. *See* Ali, Muhammad
Clay's Ark, 1: 111
Clayton, E., *4:* 648
Cleaver, Eldridge, *1:* 37, 120, **143–46,** 144 (ill.); *3:* 561
Clements, George, *1:* **146–48;** 147 (ill.)
Cleveland Call, 3: 538, 540
Cleveland Job Corps Center for Women, *5:* 94–95
Clinton, Bill, *1:* 5, 20, 96, 200; *3:* 567, 589; *5:* 17, 18, 19, 20, 21, 71, 79, 101, 106, 107, 115, 117–18, 134, 136, 148, 172–73, 174, 181
Clinton, George, *5:* 223
Clinton, Hillary Rodham, *5:* 64, 118
Cobb, Jewel Plummer, *1:* **148–50,** 149 (ill.)
Cochran, Johnnie, *5:* 211, 211 (ill.), 213
Cole, Johnnetta Betsch, *1:* 150, **151–53,** 151 (ill.)
Cole, Nat "King," *1:* **153–55,** 154 (ill.)
Cole, Natalie, *1:* **155–58,** 157 (ill.)
Coleman, Bessie, *1:* **158–60,** 159 (ill.)
Coleman, J. Marshall, *4:* 776
Coleridge-Taylor, Samuel, *4:* 689

Collier, Aldore, *2:* 377
Collins, Marva, *1:* **160–63,** 162 (ill.)
The Colonel's Dream, 1: 135
Color, 1: 179
Color Me Flo: My Hard Life and Good Times, 3: 448
The Color Purple, 2: 277–78, 280, 281; *4:* 749
Coltrane, John, *1:* **163–65,** 164 (ill.), 187; *3:* 495, 535
Columbia Records, *2:* 246, 383
Columbus, Christopher, *5:* 36
Combs, Sean "Puff Daddy," *5:* 180, 203, 222, 223
Comedy Central, *5:* 180
Comic Relief, *2:* 281
Commission on Immigration Reform (CIR), *5:* 135–36
Committee on Fair Employment Practice, *3:* 640
Committee on Un-American Activities, *3:* 620; *4:* 804
Committee to Support South African Resistance, *3:* 641
Communism, *3:* 623
Communist Party, *1:* 182; *4:* 801
Community Relations Commission (CRC), *5:* 251
Compton, Malaak, *5:* 177
Con Funk Shun, *2:* 313
Congress of African Peoples, *1:* 40; *3:* 538
Congress of Racial Equality (CORE), *1:* 119; *2:* 237, 238, 291, 374, 375, 376, 380; *3:* 520, 521, 522, 556, 640; *4:* 686
Congressional Gold Medal, *3:* 573
Conjure, 3: 617
The Conjure Woman, 1: 134
Connie's Hot Chocolates, 1: 112
Connors, Jimmy, *1:* 27
"Conservative," *5:* 150–51
Constitution, *4:* 653, 654; *5:* 38
Content, Marjorie, *4:* 715
Cookman Institute, *1:* 64
Cooney, Gerry, *5:* 85

Cooper, Anna J., *1:* **165–67,** 167 (ill.)
Cooper, Samuel, *4:* 773
Coppola, Francis Ford, *2:* 350
Cornelius, Don, *1:* **168–70,** 169 (ill.)
Cornell University, *5:* 148
Cornish, James, *4:* 781
Cosby, Bill, *1:* **170–73,** 172 (ill.), 188; *3:* 597; *5:* 25, **41–45,** 41 (ill.), 64
Cosby, Camille, *5:* 41, 42–43, 64
Cosby, Ennis, *5:* 41, 43, 44
The Cosby Show, 1: 171, 173; *5:* 42
Cosmetics, *4:* 674
Cosmopolitan, 1: 116
Cotten, Elizabeth, *1:* **173–75,** 174 (ill.)
"Cotten style," *1:* 173, 174
Cotton Club, *1:* 112; *2:* 228, 357; *5:* 48
"Cotton picking," *1:* 174
Council of Planned Parenthood Federation of America (PPFA), *4:* 763, 764–66
Council on African Affairs, *3:* 620
Counter, S. Allen, *2:* 341
Cowlings, Al, *5:* 210
Craft, Ellen, *1:* **175–78,** 177 (ill.)
Crawford, Cindy, *5:* 15
Creedence Clearwater Revival, *5:* 217
Creole Jazz Band, *1:* 21
Crisis, 1: 210, 212
Croatia, *5:* 17, 18
Crown Heights riots, *1:* 200
Crystal, Billy, *2:* 351
Cuba, *5:* 32
Cullen, Countee, *1:* 74, **178–80,** 179 (ill.)
Curtis, Lemuel R., *5:* 227

D

Da Gama, Vasco, *5:* 36
Dafoe, Willem, *2:* 351
Daily American, 2: 403

Daley, Richard, *4:* 649
Daley, William, *5:* 19, 20
Dandridge, Dorothy, *5:* 15, **47–52,** 47 (ill.), 50 (ill.), 167
Danforth, John, *4:* 711
Dante, Madam, *4:* 756
Darden, Christopher, *5:* 212
Daughters of the American Revolution (DAR), *1:* 16; *3:* 585
Davies, Roger, *5:* 221–22
Davis, Angela, *1:* **180–83,** 181 (ill.), 193
Davis, Benjamin, *5:* 225, 228, 229, 230–31
Davis, Benjamin O., Sr., *1:* **183–86,** 185 (ill.)
Davis, Clive, *2:* 361
Davis Cup, *1:* 26
Davis, Mike, *2:* 313
Davis, Miles, *1:* 164, **186–88,** 187 (ill.); *3:* 495; *4:* 662
Davis, Nelson, *4:* 733
Davis, Ossie, *1:* **188–91,** 190 (ill.)
Davis, Sammy, Jr., *1:* **191–93,** 192 (ill.); *2:* 351; *5:* 50 (ill.)
Dawes, Dominique, *5:* **53–57,** 53 (ill.), 55 (ill.)
Dawson, William, *4:* 649
A Day Late and a Dollar Short, 5: 157
"Day of Atonement," *5:* 76
Dayton Tattler, 1: 213
Daytona Normal and Industrial School for Negro Girls, *1:* 64
Dead Kennedys, *2:* 372
Death Row Records, *5:* 203
DeBarge, James, *2:* 377
Debow, Charles, *5:* 227
Declaration of Independence, *5:* 2, 4, 37
Def Jam, *3:* 600
Delany Sisters (Sadie and Bessie), *5:* **59–65,** 59 (ill.)
Delgado Museum, *2:* 367
Delta Sigma Theta, *2:* 334
Demery, Larry, *5:* 141

Democratic National Committee (DNC), *1:* 96, 97; *5:* 17, 18, 117
Democratic Party, *1:* 70, 108; *2:* 381; *3:* 445; *4:* 658; *5:* 108, 134, 150–51
DeNiro, Robert, *2:* 362
Denison, Jack, *5:* 51
Department of Peace, *5:* 6
Derricotte, Juliette, *1:* **193–96,** 194 (ill.)
Desert Shield/Storm, *3:* 586, 588, 589; *5:* 172
Dessa Rose, 4: 789
Dessalines, Jean Jacques, *4:* 721
Detroit, Michigan, *2:* 286; *3:* 607; *4:* 803–6
Detroit Pistons, *2:* 314
Devine, Loretta, *5:* 155
Dexter Avenue Baptist Church, *3:* 457
Dickens, Charles, *5:* 235
Die Nigger Die!, 1: 91, 92
Diggs, Irene, *1:* **196–98**
Digital Underground (DU), *5:* 200
Dillard, Annie, *4:* 687
Dinkins, David, *1:* 97, **198–200,** 199 (ill.); *2:* 376; *5:* 18
Dire Straits, *5:* 222
Disabled children, *2:* 298
Disappearing Acts, 3: 522, 524; *5:* 156, 158, 524
District of Columbia. *See* Washington, D.C.
Dixie Fliers, *1:* 33
Do the Right Thing, 3: 470
Dole, Bob, *5:* 154, 173
Domino, Fats, *5:* 222
Donahue, Phil, *4:* 794
Dorsey, Thomas A., *1:* **201–4,** 202 (ill.); *2:* 383
Dostoevski, Fedor, *4:* 687
Douglas, Michael, *2:* 402
Douglass, Frederick, *1:* 42, 75, 135, 181, **204–7,** 205 (ill.), 214; *4:* 653–54, 688, 729, 779, 781
Drayton, William, *3:* 600

Dred Scott v. John Sanford, 4: 653
Drew, Charles Richard, *1:* **207–9,** 208 (ill.)
Drug treatment programs, *2:* 251
Du Bois, William Edward Burgardt (W. E. B.), *1:* 190, 196, **209–12,** 211 (ill.); *2:* 257; *3:* 561, 610; *4:* 662, 724, 726, 777, 800
Dugan, Alan, *4:* 783
Dukakis, Michael, *2:* 382; *5:* 18, 123
Duke, David, *3:* 530
Dumont, John J., *4:* 728
Dunbar, Paul Laurence, *1:* 86, 180, **212–15,** 215 (ill.)
Dunham, Katherine, *1:* **215–17,** 216 (ill.)
Durocher, Leo, *3:* 511
Dutchman, 1: *39*
Duvalier, Jean-Claude "Baby Doc," *5:* 18
Dylan, Bob, *2:* 411
"Dynamite Hill," *1:* 181

E

Eakins, Thomas, *4:* 697
Earl, Nancy, *5:* 134
Eastwood, Clint, *4:* 738, 739
Ebony magazine, *2:* 405, *2:* 407; *4:* 649
Ebony Man magazine, *2:* 408
Eckford, Elizabeth, *1:* 52
Eckstine, Billy, *4:* 740–41
Economic Regulatory Administration, *3:* 566
Edelman, Marian Wright, *2:* **223–25,** 225 (ill.)
Edwards, Eli. *See* McKay, Claude
Eisenhower, Dwight D., *1:* 17, 52, 183; *2:* 265; *5:* 94
Elder, Lee, *5:* 245
Eldridge, Elleanor, 225–27
The Electronic Nigger, 1: 100
Eley, LeRoy, *5:* 229
Eliot, T. S., *5:* 67–68
Elizabeth, Queen, *1:* 16

Elle, 1: 116
Ellicott, Andrew, *5:* 4
Ellington, Duke, *1:* 112; *2:* **227–30,** 229 (ill.)
Ellington, Mercer, *2:* 228
Ellis, Effie O'Neal, *2:* **230–32,** 231 (ill.)
Ellison, Ralph, *2:* **232–34,** 233 (ill.); *4:* 716, 790, 800; *5:* 66, **67–70,** 67 (ill.), 99
Elma Lewis School of Fine Arts, *3:* 473, 474, 475
Emerson, John, *4:* 652
The Emperor Jones, 3: 622
ENABLE (Education and Neighborhood Action for a Better Living Environment), *2:* 390
Endeavour (space shuttle), *2:* 394, 397
Episcopal Church, *2:* 323, 324; *3:* 557
Equal Employment Opportunity Commission (EEOC), *2:* 341, 342; *4:* 711–12
Erwiah, Alex, *4:* 674
Eskimos, *2:* 339–40
ESPN (Entertainment and Sports Programming Network), *5:* 111
Essence magazine, *4:* 702–4
Ethiopian Orthodox Church of North and South America, *3:* 538
Evans, Robert, *2:* 350
Evening Shade, 1: 188
Evers, Medgar, *2:* **234–36,** 236 (ill.); *4:* 668; *5:* 195
Evers-Williams, Myrlie, *2:* 236; *4:* 668; *5:* 195
"Executive Order 8802," *3:* 612
Experimental Black Actors Guild, *4:* 722

F

Fagan, Eleanora. *See* Holiday, Billie
Faggs-Starr, Mae, *5:* 187

Fair Deal (production company), *1:* 94
Fair Employment Practice Committee, *3:* 612
Fard, Wallace D., *3:* 549
Farley, Chris, *5:* 183
Farmer, James, *2:*, **237–39,** 238 (ill.); *3:* 522; *4:* 807
Farrakhan, Louis, *2:* **239–42,** 241 (ill.); *3:* 549; *5:* 21, 37, **71–76,** 71 (ill.), 74 (ill.), 151, 193–94, 254
Farrell, Perry, *2:* 374
Fat Albert and the Cosby Kids, 5: 42
Federal Bureau of Investigation (FBI), *1:* 92, 144, 182; *2:* 236
Federal Committee on Fair Employment Practices, *1:* 65
Federal Communications Commission (FCC), *2:* 355
Federal Energy Administration, *3:* 566
Fellowship of Reconciliation, *3:* 640
Feminist Party, *3:* 449
Fenger, Christian, *4:* 781
Ferraro, Geraldine, *5:* 135
Field, Sally, *2:* 277
Fields, Freddie, *4:* 786
Findlay, Michael, *4:* 674
Finley, Charley, *2:* 312–13
The Fire Next Time, 1: 37
First African Methodist Episcopal Church, *3:* 507, 509
First World Festival of Negro Art, *1:* 217
Fishburne, Laurence, *5:* 217, 223, 225, 230
Fisher, Orpheus, *1:* 17
Fisk University, *1:* 193, 196
Fitzgerald, Ella, *1:* 156; *2:* **242–45,** 244 (ill.), 245; *4:* 740; *5:* **77–80,** 77 (ill.)
The Five Heartbeats, 4: 723–24
Flash Photography, 3: 57 /
Flavor Flav, *3:* 600
Fleisher, Leon, *4:* 768

Fletcher Henderson Band, *1:* 21
Floating Bear, 1: 39
Florence Griffith Joyner Youth Foundation, *5:* 107
Floyd, John, *4:* 736
Fokker airplane, *1:* 159
Folger, Ben, *4:* 729
Folies Bergère, *1:* 33
Folklore, *2:* 310, 368; *3:* 541
For Colored Girls Who Have Considered Suicide/When the Rainbow Is Enuf, 4: 662, 663–64
For Malcolm: Poems on the Life and Death of Malcolm X, 3: 609
Forbes, George Washington, *4:* 725
Ford, Gerald, *4:* 656; *5:* 174
Ford, Henry, II, *4:* 807
Ford-Taylor, Margaret, *5:* 95
Foreman, George, *1:* 13; *5:* **81–88,** 81 (ill.), 83 (ill.)
Forrester, William T., *4:* 754
48 Hours, 3: 554
Foster, Greg, *5:* 103
Foster, Vincent, *5:* 21
Fox Sports, *5:* 113
Fox Television Network, *4:* 769
Fox, Vivica, *5:* 182
Franklin, Aretha, *1:* 169, 201; *2:* **245–47,** 246 (ill.), 360; *4:* 793; *5:* 222
Franklin, John Hope, *2:* **247–50,** 248 (ill.)
Frazier, Joe, *1:* 13; *5:* 81, 84
Free D.C. Movement, *1:* 46
The Free-Lance Pallbearers, 3: 617
Free Speech, 1: 40, 41
Free Speech and Headlight, 1: 41
Freedman's Hospital, *4:* 781
Freedom, 2: 317
Freedom Farm, *2:* 308
Freedom from Religion Foundation, *5:* 168
Freedom rides, *2:* 237, 238; *3:* 641
Freeman Field, *5:* 229, 231

Freeman, Morgan, *1:* 142; *5:* 39
"Freight Train," *1:* 173
Frelinghuysen University, *1:* 167
French Resistance, *1:* 34
French Revolution, *4:* 719
Friedan, Betty, *2:* 342; *3:* 557
Frost, Robert, *4:* 791
Fruit of Islam, *2:* 240
Fugard, Athol, *2:* 277
Fugitive Slave Law *1:* 177; *4:* 733
Fuhrman, Mark, *5:* 212, 213
Futrell, Mary Hatwood, *2:* **250–53,** 252 (ill.)

G

G.A. Morgan Hair Refining Cream, *3:* 539
Gagarin, Yuri, *5:* 160
Gaines, Ernest J., *2:* **253–55,** 254 (ill.)
Gandhi, Mohandas K., *1:* 126; *5:* 250
"Gangsta rap," *5:* 197–204
Garland, William, *5:* 199, 204
Garrison, William Lloyd, *1:* 205, 206; *4:* 729
Garry, Charles, *4:* 658
Garvey, Marcus, *2:* **255–58,** 257 (ill.); *3:* 474, 536, 611
Gas mask, *3:* 538, 539
Gass, William, *4:* 687
Gaston, Arthur, *2:* **258–61,** 259 (ill.); *5:* **89–92,** 89 (ill.)
Gates, Henry Louis, Jr., *2:* **261–63,** 262 (ill.)
Gaye, Marvin, *2:* 378
Gee, Jack, *4:* 679–80
George, Clayborne, *5:* 94
George VI, King, *1:* 16
George, Zelma Watson, *2:* **263–66,** 265 (ill.); *5:* **93–95,** 93 (ill.)
Georgia Georgia, *1:* 19
Georgia Music Hall of Fame, *1:* 204
"Georgia on My Mind," *1:* 132
Giant Steps, *1:* 5

Gibbs, Marla, *4:* 661
Gibson, Althea, *2:* **266–68,** 267 (ill.); *5:* 236
Gibson, Mel, *2:* 278; *5:* 177, 221 (ill.), 222
Gilbert, Olive, *4:* 729
Gillespie, Dizzy, *1:* 186; *2:* **268–71,** 270 (ill.), 417; *3:* 495; *4:* 662, 741; *5:* 24
Gimelstob, Justin, *5:* 237
Giovanni, Nikki, *2:* **271–73,** 273 (ill.)
Girl Scouts, *4:* 654–57
Giuliani, Rudolph W., *1:* 199, 200
Givens, Robin, *2:* **273–76,** 275 (ill.)
Glamour magazine, *2:* 397, 398
Glenn, John, *5:* 160
Glover, Danny, *1:* 188; *2:* **276–78,** 277 (ill.); *5:* 177
Go Tell It on the Mountain, *1:* 36
Goldberg, Whoopi, *2:* 277, **278–81,** 280 (ill.); *5:* 182,
Golden Lynx, *1:* 30
Goldman, Ronald, *5:* 207, 210, 212
Gone with the Wind, *3:* 515, 525, 526, 527; *5:* 165, 166–67, 168
Goode, W. Wilson, *2:* **281–84,** 282 (ill.)
Gooding, Cuba, *5:* 230
Goodman, Benny, *2:* 316; *4:* 680
Goodwill Games, *2:* 434
Gordon, Franklin, *4:* 764, 765
Gordone, Charles, *2:* **284–86,** 285 (ill.); *5:* **97–99,** 97 (ill.)
Gordy, Berry, Jr., *2:* **286–89,** 287 (ill.); *3:* 630
Gospel Music Association, *1:* 204
Gould, Glenn, *4:* 767–68
Grabeau, *5:* 33
Grand Negro Jubilee, *2:* 420
Grand Ole Opry, *3:* 594
Grant, Ulysses S., *4:* 730
Gray, Thomas, *4:* 736
Grazybowska, Magdalena, *5:* 235
Great Depression, *5:* 61

The Greatest: My Own Story, *1:* 13
Greece, *5:* 36
Green, Charlie, *4:* 679
Green, Daniel, *5:* 141
Green, Mrs. Charles, *4:* 706
Gregory, Dick, *1:* 77; *2:* **289–91,** 290 (ill.); *3:* 597; *5:* 21
Grenada, *5:* 172
Grier, Rosie, *5:* 214
Griffin, Merv, *2:* 305
Griffith, D. W., *5:* 166
Griffith Joyner, Florence, *2:* 434; *5:* **101–8,** 101 (ill.), 105 (ill.)
Grimké, Angelina Weld, *2:* **291–94,** 293 (ill.)
Grimké, Archibald, *2:* 292
Grimké, Sarah, *2:* 292
"A Guide to Negro Music," *2:* 265
Gulf War, *5:* 18, 172. *See also* Operation Desert Shield/Storm
Gullah Jack, *4:* 743
Gumbel, Bryant, *2:* **294–96,** 295 (ill.); *5:* 109, 110
Gumbel, Greg, *5:* **109–13,** 109 (ill.), 112 (ill.)
Gunning, Lucille C., *2:* **297–99,** 297 (ill.)
Gurdjieff, George I., *4:* 715
Guyton, Eugene, *5:* 231

H

Hair straightener, *3:* 538
Hajj, *5:* 192, 193
Hale, Clara, *2:* 299–301, **300 (ill.)**
Hale House, *2:* 299, 301
Hale, Teddy, *2:* 349
Haley, Alex, *1:* 62; *2:* **301–4,** 303 (ill.)
Hall, Arsenio, *2:* **304–6,** 305 (ill.); *4:* 770; *5:* 179
Hall, Charles B., *5:* 227
Halley's comet, *5:* 62, 162

Hamer, Fannie Lou, *2:* **307–9,** 308 (ill.)
Hamilton, Virginia, *2:* **309–12,** 311 (ill.)
Hammer, *2:* **312–14,** 313 (ill.)
Hammond, John, *4:* 677, 680
Hampton, Lionel, *2:* **314–17,** 316 (ill.); *4:* 680
Hancock, Herbie, *5:* 14
Handy, W. C., *4:* 690
Hansberry, Lorraine, *2:* **317–19,** 318 (ill.)
A Hard Road to Glory, *1:* 27
Hardy, Thomas, *5:* 67
Harlem Art Workshop, *3:* 465
Harlem Globetrotters, *1:* 127, 128; *2:* **320–22,** 322 (ill.)
Harlem Renaissance, *1:* 73, 74, 178; *2:* 294, 362, 370; *4:* 713, 715
Harlem riots (1964), *3:* 641
Harlem Writers Guild, *3:* 523
Harpo Productions, *4:* 795
Harriet Tubman Association, *3:* 537
Harriet Tubman Society, *1:* 139
Harris, Barbara, *2:* **323–25,** 324 (ill.)
Harris, Frank, *3:* 519
Harris, Joel Chandler, *4:* 718
Harris, Marcelite J., *2:* **325–28,** 327 (ill.)
Harris, Patricia, 328–30, 328 (ill.)
Harrison, William Henry, *5:* 38
Hart, Moss, *5:* 97
Hartman, Phil, *5:* 183
Hartzell, Joseph, *4:* 697
Hatch, Orrin G., *4:* 669
Havens, Richie, *5:* 223
Hawkins, Yusef, *1:* 200
Hayden, Robert, Jr., *2:* **330–33,** 331 (ill.); *3:* 609
Hayes, Lester, *5:* 82
Haynes, Marques, *2:* 320
Hearth, Amy Hill, *5:* 59, 62, 63–64
Heavy D and the Boyz, *2:* 314

Height, Dorothy, *2:* **333–35,** 334 (ill.)
Heisman Trophy, *5:* 208
Hello Dolly!, 1: 22, 29
Helms, Jesse, *3:* 530
Hemingway, Ernest, *4:* 687, 700; *5:* 98
Hendrix, Jimi, *2:* **336–38,** 336 (ill.); *5:* 223
Henson, Matthew, *2:* **338–41,** 340 (ill.)
Here I Stand, 3: 622
Herman, Alexis, *5:* **115–19,** 115 (ill.), 117 (ill.)
Hernandez, Aileen, *2:* **341–43,** 343 (ill.)
A Hero Ain't Nothin' but a Sandwich, 1: 137
"Hero of the 80s," *3:* 596
Hertz Rental Car Agency, *5:* 209
Hewitt, Don, *1:* 79
"Hi-De-Ho Man," *5:* 24
Hickey, James A., *4:* 684
Hill, Anita, *1:* 81; *2:* **344–46,** 344 (ill.); *3:* 618; *4:* 710, 712–13
Hill, Kelli, *5:* 54
Hill, Raymond, *5:* 218
Himes, Chester, *2:* **346–49,** 347 (ill.)
Hines, Earl, *4:* 740
Hines, Gregory, *2:* **349–51,** 350 (ill.)
Hines, Maurice, *2:* 349, 350
Hingis, Martina, *5:* 237
Hitler, Adolf, *2:* 240; *3:* 480, 571; *5:* 227
HIV, *2:* 400, 402; *5:* 129
Hobley, Billy Ray, *2:* 320
Hoffman, Julius, *4:* 658–59
Holiday, Billie, *2:* **351–54,** 352 (ill.); *3:* 449; *4:* 677
Hollywood Shuffle, 4: 723
Holy Angels Church (Chicago), *1:* 146, 148
Holy Ghost Boys, *2:* 313
Holyfield, Evander, *5:* 81, 86
Hooks, Benjamin L., *2:* **354–57,** 356 (ill.); *4:* 668, 688

Hoover, J. Edgar, *1:* 144
Hope, Bob, *1:* 62; *5:* 14, 240
Hopkins, Anthony, *5:* 39
Hopwood Award, *2:* 331
Horne, Lena, *1:* 189; *2:* **357–59,** 359 (ill.); *5:* 24
The Hotel Messenger, 3: 611
Hounsou, Djimon, *5:* 39
The House Behind the Cedars, 1: 135
Houston, Charles Hamilton, *4:* 692
Houston, Whitney, *2:* **359–62,** 360 (ill.); *5:* 52, 155, 167, 222
How Stella Got Her Groove Back, 5: 155, 157
Howard Beach shooting, *4:* 666
Howard University, *5:* 183
Howlin' Wolf, *5:* 223
Huang, John, *5:* 20
Hue magazine, *2:* 408
Hughes, Langston, *1:* 74, 86; *2:* 233, 331, **362–65,** 363 (ill.), 370; *3:* 629; *4:* 690–91, 748, 790; *5:* 68
Humphrey, Hubert, *5:* 186
Hunter, Clementine, *2:* **366–68,** 367 (ill.)
Hurok, Sol, *1:* 16
Hurston, Zora Neale, *2:* **368–71,** 369 (ill.); *3:* 558; *4:* 748
Hussein, Saddam, *5:* 172
Hybl, Bill, *5:* 107
Hyde, Henry, *5:* 125

I

"I Have a Dream" speech, *3:* 458; *5:* 73
I Have Changed, 3: 572
I Know Why the Caged Bird Sings, 1: 19
I Shall Not Be Moved, 1: 19
I Spy, 1: 171; *5:* 41, 42
Ibsen, Henrik, *4:* 714
Ice Cube, *2:* 371
Ice-T, *2:* **371–74,** 373 (ill.); *5:* 201

"If We Must Die," *3:* 517, 519
I'm Gonna Git You Sucka!, 4: 769
Imani Temple African American Catholic Congregation, *4:* 683, 684
In Living Color, 4: 769, 770, 771; *5:* 179
Independent Old Catholic Church, *4:* 686
Independent Order of Saint Luke (IOSL), *4:* 753–54
Indiana State University *2:* 400; *5:* 128
Indianapolis Clowns Negro League, *1:* 1
The Inner Circle, *2:* 316
Innis, Roy, *2:* **374–76,** 375 (ill.)
Interracial Ministerial Alliance, *1:* 52
Interracial romance, *5:* 49–50
Invisible Man, 2: 232, 233, 234; *5:* 67, 68
Iran, *5:* 75
Iraq, *5:* 75, 172
Isaac, Lorrain, *4:* 783
Islam, *1:* 4, 93; *3:* 489
Italy, *5:* 227
Ito, Lance, *5:* 212
It's My Party, 2: 417

J

Jackson, Autumn, *5:* 43–44
Jackson Five, *2:* 288, 377, 384–86
Jackson, Jacqueline, *5:* 122
Jackson, Janet, *2:* 362, **376–78;** 377 (ill.); *5:* 25, 52, 130, 197, 201
Jackson, Jermaine, *2:* 361
Jackson, Jesse, *1:* 96, 200, 240, 378, 380 (ill.), 432; *2:* **378–82;** *4:* 666–67, 712, 770, 778–79; *5:* 18, 71, 72–73, 116, 121, 124 (ill.), 149, 151, 153, 160, 182
Jackson, Jesse, Jr., *5:* **121–26,** 121 (ill.), 124 (ill.)
Jackson, Mahalia, *1:* 203; *2:* **382–84,** 383 (ill.); *4:* 677

Jackson, Maynard, *5:* 253
Jackson, Michael, *1:* 93; *2:* 377, 378, **384–87,** 386 (ill.), 402, 418, 682
Jackson, Sandra, *5:* 123, 126
Jackson, Shirley Ann, *2:* **387–89,** 388 (ill.)
Jacob, John, *2:* **389–92,** 390 (ill.)
Jagger, Mick, *5:* 220, 223
James, Daniel, Jr., *2:* **392–94,** 393 (ill.)
James, Mark, *3:* 606
James, Rick, *2:* 314
Jane's Addiction, *2:* 374
Jarvis, Gregory B., *5:* 163
Jazz, 3: 543
Jazz Messengers, *3:* 496
Jefferson, Thomas, *1:* 83; *4:* 774; *5:* 1–2, 4–5, 150
Jemison, Mae C., *2:* **394–97,** 395 (ill.)
Jesse Owens National Youth Games, *5:* 102
Jesus of Nazareth, *1:* 145
Jet magazine, *2:* 405, 408
Jim Crow laws, *5:* 61
Jimmy Jam, *2:* 378
Job Corps, *5:* 82, 83, 87
Joe's Bed-Stay Barbership: We Cut Heads, 3: 468
John XXIII, Pope, *3:* 636
Johns Hopkins Hospital, *1:* 122
Johnson, Alice, *4:* 781
Johnson, Beverly, *2:* **397–99,** 399 (ill.)
Johnson, Caryn, *2:* 279
Johnson, Earletha "Cookie," *2:* 402; *5:* 127, 128
Johnson, Earvin "Magic," *1:* 5; *2:* **400–402,** 401 (ill.); *5:* **127–32,** 127 (ill.), 131 (ill.)
Johnson Gospel Singers, *2:* 383
Johnson, James P., *4:* 679
Johnson, James Weldon, *2:* **402–5,** 403 (ill.)
Johnson, John H., *2:* **405–8,** 406 (ill.)

Johnson, Lyndon B., *1:* 91, 95, 108, 203; *2:* 329, 342; *3:* 546, 634; *4:* 693, 807, 808
Johnson, Marguerite. *See* Angelou, Maya
Johnson Publishing Company, *2:* 408
Johnson, Robert, *2:* **409–11,** 410 (ill.)
Johnston, Buddy, *5:* 231
Joint Chiefs of Staff, *3:* 586, 587; *5:* 172
Jones, Bill T., *2:* **411–13,** 412 (ill.)
Jones, Cheri, *4:* 723
Jones, Emil, *5:* 125
Jones, James Earl, *2:* **413–16,** 415 (ill.); *4:* 792
Jones, LeRoi. *See* Baraka, Amiri
Jones, Quincy, *2:* 385, 386, **416–19,** 418 (ill.); *4:* 794; *5:* 122
Jones, Sissieretta, *2:* **419–21,** 420 (ill.)
Jones, Williams Augustus, *4:* 667
Joplin, Scott, *2:* **421–24,** 422 (ill.)
Jordan, Barbara, *2:* **424–27,** 425 (ill.); *5:* **133–37,** 133 (ill.)
Jordan, James, *2:* 427, 430; *5:* 139, 141
Jordan, Louis, *5:* 24
Jordan, Michael, *2:* 274, **427–30,** 429 (ill.); *5:* **139–45,** 139 (ill.), 140 (ill.), 142 (ill.)
Jordan, Vernon E., Jr., *2:* 390, **430–32,** 431 (ill.)
Journal of Black Studies, 1: 23
"Journey of reconciliation," *3:* 521, 641
Joyner, Al, *5:* 103
Joyner-Kersee, Jackie, *2:* **432–35,** 434 (ill.); *5:* 106–7, 186
Judaism, *1:* 193
Judicial Watch, *5:* 21
Judson, Andrew T., *5:* 35
Juilliard School of Music, *3:* 590
Jungle Fever, 1: 62
Junior World Golf Championship, *5:* 240
Justice, David, *1:* 62, *5:* 13, 14–15

K

Kaddafi, Muammar, *2:* 240, 241; *5:* 75, 172
Kale (slave), *5:* 31, 37
Kane, William, *4:* 685
Katleman, Harris, *4:* 770
Keats, John, *1:* 179
Keckley, Elizabeth, *3:* **441–43,** 442 (ill.)
Kellogg, Clark, *5:* 112 (ill.)
Kelly, Patrick, *3:* **443–45,** 444 (ill.)
Kelly, Sharon Pratt, *3:* **445–48,** 447 (ill.); *5:* 11
Kennedy, Edward, *2:* 224; *5:* 18
Kennedy, Flo, *3:* **448–50,** 450 (ill.)
Kennedy, John F., *1:* 20, 49, 155; *3:* 458, 528, 529, 636; *4:* 660, 693, 807; *5:* 148, 150
Kennedy, Robert, *2:* 319
Kersee, Bobby, *2:* 433–34; *5:* 103, 104, 107
Keyes, Alan, *5:* 21, **147–54,** 147 (ill.), 149 (ill.)
Khan, Chaka, *2:* 360
Kindred, 1: 111
King, B. B., *3:* **451–53,** 453 (ill.); *5:* 218, 223
King, Coretta Scott, *3:* **453–56,** 455 (ill.), 457; *4:* 661; *5:* 190, 195
King David, 2: 316
King, Edward, *4:* 706
King, Martin Luther, Jr., *1:* 5, 6, 17, 58, 61, 69, 91, 106, 118, 146, 193, 203; *2:* 260, 324, 355, 380; *3:* 454, **456–59,** 459 (ill.), 460, 482, 545, 580, 613, 641; *4:* 659, 661, 688, 711, 779, 798, 807; *5:* 61, 73, 90, 115–16, 121–22, 190, 195, 214, 249, 250–51

King of Delta Blues Singers, 2: 411
King, Yolanda, *3:* **459–62,** 460 (ill.), 459; *4:* 659, 661
Kinte clan, *2:* 302, 303
Kirchwey, George, *4:* 647
Klein, David, *2:* 306
Knight, Marion "Suge," *5:* 203
Knock on Any Door, 3: 546, 547, 548, 549
Knopfler, Mark, *5:* 222
Koch, Edward I, *1:* 199
Kochiyama, Yuri, *5:* 195
Koenigswarter, Baroness de, *3:* 535
Korean War, *2:* 393
Koslow, Pamela, *2:* 350
Kournikova, Anna, *5:* 237
Kouyomjian, Susan, *5:* 99
Kravitz, Lennie, *5:* 223
Kruger, Joanette, *5:* 233, 237
Ku Klux Klan (KKK), *1:* 178, 181, 184; *2:* 258; *5:* 166, 250
Kunstler, William, *4:* 658
Kunta Kinte, *2:* 303
Kuwait, *5:* 172

L

L'Enfant, Pierre Charles, *5:* 4
Ladies Fresh, *3:* 606
Lady Sings the Blues, 3: 598, 631
Lafontant, Jewel Stradford, *3:* **462–64,** 463 (ill.)
LaMotta, Jake, *4:* 771
Lamp, Virginia, *4:* 713
Lancaster, Abna Aggrey, *4:* 716–17
Lane, Randall, *5:* 86
Lange, Jessica, *1:* 62
The Last Days of Louisiana Red, 3: 618
Latimer, Margery, *4:* 715
Lawford, Peter, *5:* 51
Lawrence, David L., *4:* 693
Lawrence, Jacob, *3:* **464–67,** 466 (ill.)
Lay Bare the Heart, 2: 239

League for Non-Violent Civil Disobedience Against Military Segregation, *3:* 612
Lean on Me, 1: 142
Lear, Norman, *2:* 377
The Learning Tree, 3: 577
Leavitt, Joshua, *5:* 34
LeClerc, Captain-General, *4:* 720–21
Led Zeppelin, *5:* 223
Lee, Bill Lann, *5:* 175
Lee, Edward T., *4:* 647
Lee, Spike, *1:* 62; *3:* **467–70,** 468 (ill.), 490; *4:* 682, 770; *5:* 14, 142, 193
"Left," *5:* 150–51
Legion of Honor, *1:* 34
Lehmann, Lotte, *1:* 102
Lemon, Meadowlark, *2:* 320
Lenin, Vladimir, *1:* 143
Lennon, John, *2:* 301
Leno, Jay, *3:* 498; *5:* 130
A Lesson Before Dying, 2: 255
LeTang, Henry, *2:* 349
"Letter from Birmingham City Jail," *3:* 458
Letterman, David, *2:* 306; *5:* 130
Levant, Brian, *5:* 13, 15
Leventhal, Melvyn, *4:* 748, 749
Levi, Josef, *5:* 3
Levi, Primo, *4:* 687
Levin, Sander, *5:* 17
Lewis, Carl, *3:* **471–73,** 471 (ill.)
Lewis, Elma, *3:* **473–76,** 475 (ill.)
Lewis, Lennox, *1:* 77
Lewis, Terry, *2:* 378
"Liberal," *5:* 150–51
Library of Congress, *2:* 330, 332
Libya, *5:* 75, 172
Life magazine, *3:* 576, 577
Lifetime Achievement Award, *1:* 150; *3:* 453
Lilies of the Field, 3: 582
Lincoln, Abraham, *3:* 441; *4:* 730, 774; *5:* 150
Lincoln, Mary Todd, *3:* 441, 442

Lincoln University, *4:* 693–94, 695–96
Linden Hills, *3:* 559
Linkletter, Art, *5:* 44
Lister, Joseph, *4:* 779
Liszt, Franz, *4:* 766
Little, Malcolm. *See* Malcolm X
Little Richard, *3:* **476–78,** 477 (ill.); *5:* 222
"Live Aid," *3:* 497
Living Color, *5:* 223
Living Colours, *2:* 374
Locke, John, *5:* 36–37
Lollapalooza, *2:* 374
Long, Lutz, *3:* 571
Long, Vicki, *3:* 494
A Long Way from Home, *3:* 520
Lopate, Phillip, *4:* 687
Lori, William, *4:* 684
Los Angeles Lakers, *1:* 3; *2:* 400, 401–2; *5:* 127, 128, 129
Losing Isaiah, *1:* 62
Lotus Press, *3:* 486
Lou, Sweet, *2:* 320
Louis, Joe, *3:* **479–82,** 480 (ill.)
Louisiana State University, *3:* 569
Lowery, Joseph E., *3:* **482–84,** 483 (ill.); *4:* 779
"Lucille" (guitar), *3:* 451
Lyle, Ron, *5:* 84
Lyrics of Lowly Life, *1:* 214

M

Ma Rainey's Black Bottom, *4: 791*
Mabley, Jackie "Moms," *5:* 28
Macci, Ric, *5:* 234
Madgett, Naomi Long, *3:* **484–87,** 485 (ill.)
Magellan, Ferdinand, *5:* 36
Mahogany, *3:* 631
Majors and Minors, *1:* 214
Make, Vusumzi, *1:* 19
Malcolm X, *1:* 5, 12, 39, 143, 190, 193; *2:* 239, 240, 302; *3:* **487–90,** 489 (ill.), 551, 561, 609, 617; *4:* 650, 659–61, 681, 763; *5:* 72, 73, 76, 189, 190, 191–92, 195, 214
Malcolm X, *3:* 470
Malone, Annie Turnbo, *3:* **490–93,** 492 (ill.)
Mama, *3:* 523
Mama Day, *3:* 559
Manchild in the Promised Land, *1:* 88, 90
Mandela, Nelson, *1:* 58; *4:* 671
Manhattan Project, *3:* 603
Mao Zedong, *1:* 145
"Maple Leaf Rag," *2:* 423
March on Washington (1963), *3:* 458, 613, 640, 641
Marino, Eugene A., *3:* **493–95,** 494 (ill.)
Markhasev, Mikail, *5:* 44
The Marrow of Tradition, *1:* 135
Marrow, Tracey, *2:* 371
Marsalis, Branford, *3:* **495–98,** 497 (ill.)
Marsalis, Wynton, *3:* 495, **498–501,** 499 (ill.)
Marsh, Henry, *4:* 775
Marshall, James, *4:* 672
Marshall, Paule, *3:* **501–4,** 501 (ill.)
Marshall, Ray, *5:* 116
Marshall, Thurgood, *3:* **504–7,** 506 (ill.), 521, 544; *4:* 694, 710
Martel, Joyce, *5:* 154
Martin, Susan, *5:* 136
Marx, Karl, *1:* 143; *3:* 610
Maslin, Janet, *2:* 278
Mason, Biddy, *3:* **507–9,** 508 (ill.)
Mason, Bridget, *See* Mason, Biddy
Massachusetts Institute of Technology (MIT), *5:* 161–62, 163
Masters tournament, *5:* 239, 242, 244, 245
Mathabane, Mark, *4:* 795
Matthews, James Newton, *1:* 213
Matthews, Robert (Matthias), *4:* 728
Matthias, *4:* 728–29

"Maybellene," *1:* 59
Mayo, Charles, *4:* 780
Mays, Willie, *3:* **509–12,** 510 (ill.); *5:* 208
McAuliffe, Christa, *5:* 159, 162
McBride, Clara. *See* Hale, Clara
McCarthy, Eugene, *2:* 365
McCarthy, Joseph, *3:* 620
McCartney, Paul, *2:* 337
McClain, John, *2:* 378
McClellan, George Marion, *3:* **512–15,** 513 (ill.)
McCone Commission, *1:* 108
McDaniel, Hattie, *3:* **515–17,** 515 (ill.); *5:* 166, 167
McDonald, Chris, *5:* 230
McEnroe, John, *5:* 234
McKay, Claude, *1:* 74; *3:* **517–20,** 519 (ill.)
McKinley, William, *1:* 42
McKissick, Floyd B., *2:* 375; *3:* **520–22,** 521 (ill.)
McMillan, Terry, *3:* **522–25,** 524 (ill.); *5:* **155–58,** 155 (ill.), 167
McMillen, Tom, *5:* 106
McNair, Cheryl, *5:* 161 (ill.), 163–64
McNair, Ronald, *5:* **159–64,** 159 (ill.), 161 (ill.)
McQueen, Thelma "Butterfly," *3:* **525–27,** 526 (ill.); *5:* **165–70,** 165 (ill.)
McWilliams, Moses, *4:* 750
Meadman, Dhimah, *4:* 802
Media Workshop, *3:* 449
Mehta, Zubin, *4:* 768
Melanoma research, *1:* 150
Mellman, Michael, *2:* 402
Mencken, H. L., *4:* 801
Mercury Records, *2:* 417
Meredith, James, *1:* 119; *3:* **527–30,** 528 (ill.)
The Messenger, *3:* 611
Metro-Goldwyn-Mayer (MGM), *2:* 358
Metropolitan Opera, *1:* 55
Michigan State University, *2:* 400; *5:* 128

Middle East, *1:* 105; *2:* 381
Mignon, François, *2:* 366
"Migration of the Negro," *3:* 466
Mikulski, Barbara, *5:* 153
Miller, Arthur, *4:* 792
Miller, Shannon, *5:* 56
Miller, Zell, *5:* 253
Millet, Jean-François, *4:* 697
Million Man March, *5:* 71, 73, 74, 75, 194, 254
Milner, Ron, *3:* **530–33,** 531 (ill.)
Milwaukee Braves, *1:* 1
Mind of My Mind, *1:* 111
Minneapolis Millers, *3:* 511
"Minnie the Moocher," *1:* 113; *5:* 23, 24
Miss USA pageant, *5:* 14
Miss World pageant, *5:* 14
Mississippi Freedom Democratic Party (MFDP), *2:* 307
Missouri Compromise, *4:* 652, 653
Mitchell, Clarence, *4:* 669
Mitchell, Timothy, *4:* 667
Mobutu, Sese Seko, *4:* 768
Moceanu, Dominique, *5:* 56
Momyer, William, *5:* 228
Mondale, Walter, *5:* 135
Monk, Thelonious, *1:* 50, 164; *3:* **533–35,** 534 (ill.)
Monroe, Marilyn, *5:* 47
Montes, Pedro, *5:* 32, 33–34, 35
Montgomery, Alabama, *3:* 578; *5:* 250
Montgomery Improvement Association, *1:* 7; *3:* 580
Moore, Audley, *3:* **536–38,** 537 (ill.)
Moore, Emerson, *4:* 684, 686
Moore, Thomas, *4:* 735
Moorer, Michael, *5:* 82, 86
Morehouse College, *1:* 69
Morgan, Garrett, *3:* **538–41,** 539 (ill.)
Morgan, Richard, *4:* 680
Morgan State College, *1:* 197
Morgan University, *1:* 198
Morris, Stevland, *4:* 796

Morrison, Tommy, *5:* 86
Morrison, Toni, *3:* **541–43,** 543 (ill.), 558; *4:* 687, 795
Morton Thiokol, *5:* 163
Moss, Tom, *4:* 709
Mother Hale. *See* Hale, Clara
Motley, Constance Baker, *3:* **544–46,** 545 (ill.)
Motley, Willard, *3:* **546–49,** 548 (ill.)
Motown Records, *2:* 286, 287, 288; *3:* 630; *4:* 796–97
MOVE, *2:* 283
Muhammad, Elijah, *2:* 239; *3:* 488, 489, **549–52,** 550 (ill.); *5:* 72, 191, 192
Muhammad, Warith Deen, *5:* 72
Mulattoes, *4:* 719–21; *5:* 47
Multiple sclerosis, *3:* 599
Mumbo Jumbo, 3: 617
Murphy, Dwayne, *2:* 313
Murphy, Eddie, *2:* 274, 306, 362; *3:* **552–55,** 553 (ill.); *4:* 723, 769, 770; *5:* 14, 179
Murray, Albert, *5:* 68
Murray, Bill, *5:* 142 (ill.)
Murray, David, *4:* 664
Murray, Pauli, *3:* **555–57,** 556 (ill.)
Muslim Mosque, Inc., *3:* 489
Mutiny, *5:* 31–39
Mythology, *2:* 310; *3:* 541

N

Napoleon Bonaparte, *4:* 720, 721
Nation of Islam, *1:* 12; *2:* 239, 240; *3:* 488, 549, 551; *4:* 650, 660; *5:* 72, 151, 190, 191, 192
National Aeronautics and Space Administration (NASA), *2:* 396; *5:* 159, 162, 163
National AIDS Commission, *2:* 402; *5:* 128
National Alliance Against Racist and Political Repression, *1:* 180
National Amateur Athletic Union (AAU), *3:* 636
National Association for the Advancement of Colored People (NAACP), *1:* 40, 43, 50, 52, 64, 70, 106, 107, 135, 196, 211; *2:* 223, 234, 235, 249, 292, 354, 356, 402, 404, 430, 431; *3:* 504, 505, 521, 544; *4:* 668–69, 707, 712, 726, 776, 777–79; *5:* 21, 73
National Association of Black Journalists, *5:* 75
National Association of Colored Women (NACW), *1:* 43; *4:* 707, 709
National Basketball Association (NBA), *1:* 3, 127; *2:* 400–402, 427, 428–29; *5:* 127, 140–41, 143
National Black Political Assembly, *1:* 40
National Center of Afro-American Artists, *3:* 473, 475
National Collegiate Athletic Association (NCAA), *2:* 428; *5:* 128
National Convention of Gospel Choirs and Choruses, *1:* 203
National Council of Churches, *5:* 250
National Council of Negro Women (NCNW), *1:* 64; *2:* 333, 334, 335; *3:* 537; *4:* 648
National Education Association (NEA), *2:* 250, 251, 252
National Enquirer, 5: 44
National Equal Rights League, *4:* 726
National Football League (NFL), *5:* 111, 113, 208–9
National Low Income Housing Coalition, *1:* 85
National Newspaper Publishers Association/Black Press of America, *5:* 75
National Organization for Women (NOW), *2:* 341, 342; *3:* 555, 557

National Safety Device Company, *3:* 539
National Science Foundation, *1:* 150
National Security Council (NSC), *3:* 587; *5:* 172
National Sports Council, *5:* 186
National Track and Field Hall of Fame, *5:* 107
National Urban League, *1:* 96; *2:* 389, 390, 430, 431; *4:* 806, 807; *5:* 17
National Women's Hall of Fame, *5:* 186
National Youth Administration, *1:* 63, 65
Naylor, Gloria, *3:* **557–60,** 559 (ill.)
Nazism, *3:* 572
NBC Sports, *3:* 639; *5:* 112, 113, 210
NBC-TV, *1:* 153; *4:* 671
Neal, Frederic Douglas "Curly," *2:* 320
Negro American Labor Council, *3:* 611
Negro Dance Group, *1:* 216
Negro Digest, 2: 407
Negro Eastern League, *3:* 573
Negro National League, *1:* 114; *3:* 573
The Negro Soldier, 1: 185
Negro World, 2: 257
Negro World Series, *3:* 574
Neurosurgery, *1:* 122
Never Blue Productions, *2:* 276
New Jack City, 4: 682, 739
New Lafayette Theater, *1:* 100
New Orleans Philharmonic Orchestra, *3:* 498
New York Age, 1: 40
New York Giants, *3:* 511
New York Metropolitan Opera, *1:* 103
New York National Guard, *1:* 185
New York, New York, *1:* 198, 200
New York Philharmonic Orchestra, *4:* 766, 767, 768

New York Public Library, *1:* 31
New York State Assembly, *1:* 139, 199
New York State Senate, *3:* 546
Newport Jazz Festival, *1:* 187
Newton, Huey P., *1:* 120, 144; *3:* **560–62,** 561 (ill.); *4:* 657
NFL Live, 5: 210
The NFL on NBC, 5: 112
The NFL Today, 5: 112
Niagara Movement, *1:* 210, 211; *4:* 726
Nicholas, Harold, *2:* 351; *5:* 48
Nichols, John F., *4:* 804
Nicholson, Jack, *2:* 402
Nicklaus, Jack, *5:* 241–42, 244
Nike, *5:* 141, 143, 144, 244, 254
Nine Inch Nails, *2:* 374
Nixon, Richard M., *1:* 29, 193; *2:* 230, 239, 424; *3:* 463; *4:* 746, 778, 808; *5:* 94–95, 133, 135, 172
Nkrumah, Kwame, *4:* 694
No Place to Be Somebody, 2: 284, 285; *5:* 97, 98–99
No Way Out, 3: 582
Nobel Peace Prize, *1:* 104, 106; *3:* 456, 458
Nobody Knows My Name, 1: 37
Nonviolent Action Group, *1:* 91
Noriega, Manuel, *5:* 172
Norman, Jessye, *3:* **562–65,** 564 (ill.)
North Africa, *5:* 227
North American Air Defense Command (NORAD), *2:* 392, 394
North Pole, *2:* 338–41
North Star, 1: 206
Northern States Power Company, *3:* 566
Norvell, James, *3:* 529
Notorious B.I.G., *5:* 201, 203
Nucleus (theater company), *3:* 462
Nucleus Inc., *4:* 659, 661
N.W.A., *2:* 314; 371

O

O'Connor, Katie, *4:* 705
O'Jays, *2:* 312
O'Leary, Hazel, *3:* **565–67,** 566 (ill.)
O'Neal, Shaquille, *3:* **567–70,** 569 (ill.)
Oak and Ivy, 1: 214
Oakland A's, *2:* 312–13
Of Love and Dust, 2: 255
Old Greenbottom Inn and Other Stories, 3: 514
Oliver, King, *1:* 21
Olivier, Laurence, *1:* 79
Olssen, Jessie, *4:* 698
Olympic Games, Summer (1936), *3:* 570, 571
Olympic Games, Summer (1956), *3:* 638; *5:* 185–86
Olympic Games, Summer (1960), *1:* 12; *3:* 636; *5:* 185, 186
Olympic Games, Summer (1968), *5:* 83
Olympic Games, Summer (1980), *2:* 433
Olympic Games, Summer (1984), *2:* 434; *3:* 472; *5:* 103, 140
Olympic Games, Summer (1988), *1:* 77; *3:* 473; *5:* 101, 104
Olympic Games, Summer (1992), *2:* 402; *5:* 53, 55, 111, 128
Olympic Games, Summer (1996), *5:* 53, 56, 109, 112–13, 253
Olympic Games, Winter (1994), *5:* 109, 111
Once Upon a Time, 1: 30
One Church, One Child, *1:* 147
One Way Productions, *3:* 559
Onizuka, Ellison, *5:* 163
Ono, Yoko, *2:* 301
Onyx Club, *2:* 269
Operation Breadbasket, *2:* 380; *3:* 484
Operation Champion, *3:* 636
Operation Desert Shield/Storm, *3:* 588, 589; *5:* 172
Operation Equality, *2:* 390
Operation PUSH (People United to Save Humanity), *2:* 381; *5:* 123
Operation Woman Power, *2:* 335
Organization of Afro-American Unity, *3:* 489
Orlando Magic, *3:* 570
Othello, 3: 622
Our Nig, or Sketches from the Life of a Free Black, 2: 262
Owens, Dana. *See* Queen Latifah
Owens, Jesse, *3:* 471, **570–73,** 571 (ill.)
Owens, Major, *4:* 667
OyamO, *5:* 98

P

Page, Jimmy, *5:* 223
Paige, Satchel, *3:* **573–75,** 574 (ill.)
Paine, Thomas, *1:* 143
Painting, *3:* 465
Palestine Liberation Organization (PLO), *2:* 381; *5:* 252
Palmer, Henry, *4:* 780
Panella, Patricia, *2:* 350
Parents' Music Resource Center, *2:* 372
Parker, Charlie, *3:* 449; *4:* 662, 741, 783
Parks, Gordon, *3:* **575–78,** 577 (ill.)
Parks, Rosa, *1:* 6; *3:* 457, 462, 482, **578–80,** 578 (ill.); *4:* 778; *5:* 71
Parrish, Noel, *5:* 229
Partnerships for Progress Program, *1:* 45
Pasteur, Louis, *4:* 779, 780
The Path of Dreams, 3: 514
"Patternist" saga, *1:* 110
Patternmaster, 1: 111
Pay equalization, *3:* 545
Payne, Allen, *5:* 230
Payne, Billy, *5:* 253
Peace and Freedom Party, *4:* 658
Peace Corps, *1:* 56

Pearson, Pauletta, *4:* 763
Pearson's Magazine, 3: 519
Peary, Robert E., *2:* 338–40
Pendergrass, Teddy, *2:* 361
People Organized and Working for Economic Rebirth (POWER), *2:* 241
People's Political Party, *2:* 258
People's Voice, 3: 585
Perkins, Edward J., *4:* 667
Perpetual Help Mission, *4:* 744, 746
Persian Gulf War, *3:* 586
Pesci, Joe, *5:* 177
Peters, John, *4:* 773
Pharr, Pauline, *4:* 716
Philadelphia Council for Community Advancement, *2:* 282
"Philadelphia 11," *2:* 324
Philadelphia, Pennsylvania, *2:* 281, 283
Philadelphia 76ers, *1:* 128
Philadelphia Warriors, *1:* 128
Phong, Nguyen "Tiger," *5:* 240, 246
Pickett, Owen, *4:* 775
Pieh, Samuel H., *5:* 39
Pierson, Elijah, *4:* 728–29
Pierson, Sarah, *4:* 728
Pilate, Felton, *2:* 313
Pinckney, Brian, *5:* 6
Pindell, Geraldine, *4:* 725, 726
Pippen, Scottie, *5:* 142
The Pitiful and the Proud, 3: 633
The Places in the Heart, 2: 277
Plantation Club, *1:* 33
Plasma, *1:* 208
Playboy Club, *2:* 290
Plessy v. Ferguson, 4: 777
Plummer, Jonathan, *5:* 157
Poems, 3: 513
Poitier, Sidney, *3:* **580–83;** *4:* 722; *5:* 49, 167
Polio, *3:* 635
Polk, George, *1:* 80
Poole, Elijah. *See* Muhammad, Elijah
Poor People's Campaign, *3:* 459
Poor People's March, *3:* 455

Poplar, Ellen, *4:* 802
Porgy and Bess, 1: 19
Poro College, *3:* 491
Poro Company, *3:* 491, 492
Porter, Cole, *2:* 244; *5:* 78
Posse, 4: 739
"Potomac Watch," *3:* 614
Powell, Adam Clayton, Jr., *3:* **583–86,** 584 (ill.); *4:* 665
Powell, Alma, *5:* 174
Powell, Colin, *3:* **586–89,** 588 (ill.); *5:* 143, 153, **171–76,** 171 (ill.)
Powell, Shezwae, *5:* 98–99
Poyas, Peter, *4:* 743
Pozo, Chano, *2:* 270
Preminger, Otto, *5:* 49, 51
Presidential Transition Office, *5:* 118
President's Council on Physical Fitness and Sports, *5:* 101, 106
Presley, Elvis, *5:* 24, 222
Preston, Billy, *5:* 223
Price, Frank, *4:* 675
Price, Leontyne, *3:* **589–92,** 590 (ill.)
Pride, Charley, *3:* **592–94,** 593 (ill.)
Pride, Inc., *1:* 46; *5:* 9
Primettes, *3:* 630
Prince, *2:* 378; *5:* 223
Proctor & Gardner, *3:* 594, 595
Proctor, Barbara Gardner, *3:* **594–97,** 596 (ill.)
Professional Golfers' Association (PGA), *5:* 241
Project Alert, *2:* 390
Proud Shoes: The Story of an American Family, 3: 556
Prout, Mary, *4:* 753
Provincetown Players, *3:* 622
Pryor, Richard, *3:* 553, **597–99,** 598 (ill.)
Public Enemy, *3:* **599–602,** 601 (ill.); *5:* 201
Publishing Hall of Fame, *2:* 406
Purple Onion (nightclub), *1:* 18
Purvis, Robert, *4:* 654

Q

Qaddafi, Muammar Al-. *See* Kaddafi, Muammar
Quakers, *4:* 732–33; *5:* 3, 4
Quarterman, Lloyd Albert, *3:* **602–5,** 603 (ill.)
Quayle, Dan, *5:* 197
Queen, 1: 62
Queen Latifah, *3:* **605–7,** 606 (ill.)
"Queen of Soul." *See* Franklin, Aretha
"Queen of the Harlem Renaissance," *2:* 368
Qwest Records, *2:* 418

R

Rachel, 2: 293–94
Rackley, Alex, *4:* 659
Rainbow Coalition, *5:* 123
"Rainbow Tribe," *1:* 34
Rainey, Ma, *4:* 678, 680, 791
A Raisin in the Sun, 2: 317, 318
Raitt, Bonnie, *4:* 758
Ramsey, Buck, *5:* 97, 98
Randall, Dudley, *3:* **607–10,** 608 (ill.)
Randolph, A. Philip, *3:* **610–13,** 612 (ill.)
Rap music, *3:* 600, 605; *5:* 197–204
Rashad, Phylicia, *5:* 42
Raspberry, William, *3:* **613–16,** 615 (ill.)
Raw Pearl, 1: *29*
Rawls, Lou, *2:* 360
Reach the American Dream foundation, *4:* 785–86
Reading Guidance Clinic, *3:* 628
Reagan, Ronald, *2:* 301, 390; *4:* 711, 779, 805; *5:* 149–50, 163, 172, 173
Redding, Otis, *5:* 220
Reed, Ishmael, *3:* **616–18,** 617 (ill.)
Refugee, Derrick, *2:* 320
Reich, Robert B., *5:* 118

Reiser, Paul, *5:* 64
"Religious Right," *5:* 153
Remond, Charles, *4:* 654
Rendell, Edward, *5:* 75
Reno, Janet, *5:* 21, 119
Republic of New Africa, *3:* 538
Republican Party, *1:* 85; *5:* 150–51, 173–74
Resnick, Judith, *5:* 163
Revlon cosmetics, *5:* 15
Reynolds, Mel, *5:* 124
The Rhetoric of Black Revolution, 1: 24
Riccardi, Michael, *4:* 666
Rich, Frank, *2:* 350
Rickey, Branch, *3:* 625
Ride, Sally, *5:* 160
"Right," *5:* 150–51
Riley, Pat, *2:* 401
Ritchie, Lionel, *2:* 387
Rivers, Joan, *2:* 305
Robb, Charles, *4:* 775, 776
Roberts, George S., *5:* 227
Robeson, Eslanda Goode, *3:* **618–21,** 619 (ill.)
Robeson, Paul, *1:* 189; *3:* 619, **621–24,** 622 (ill.)
Robinor, Genia, *4:* 767
Robinson, Bradley, *2:* 341
Robinson, Jackie, *1:* 1; *3:* 511, 574, **624–27,** 625 (ill.)
Robinson, Ray Charles. *See* Charles, Ray
Robinson, Sugar Ray, *2:* 266; *4:* 771
Rochon, Lela, *5:* 155
"A Rock, A River, A Tree," *1:* 20
Rock, Chris, *5:* **177–84,** 177 (ill.), 182 (ill.)
Rogers, Norman, *3:* 600
Rolling Stones, *1:* 60; *5:* 220
Rollins, Charlemae Hill, *3:* **627–29,** 627 (ill.)
Roman Catholic Church, *3:* 450, 493
Rome, Italy, *5:* 36
Ronettes, *5:* 219

Roosevelt, Eleanor, *1:* 16; *2:* 407; *5:* 227
Roosevelt, Franklin D., *1:* 16, 63, 65, 185; *3:* 612, 640
Roosevelt, Theodore, *4:* 760
Roots: The Saga of an American Family, 1: 19; *2:* 301, 303
Ross, Diana, *2:* 288, 378; *3:* **629–32,** 631 (ill.); *5:* 222
Ross, Lucy, *2:* 340
Ross, Mac, *5:* 227
Rowan, Carl T., *3:* **632–34,** 633 (ill.)
Royal Garden Blues, 3: 497
Royal Roost Nightclub, *1:* 57
RPM International, *1:* 132
Rubin, Rick, *3:* 600
Rudolph, Wilma, *1:* 5; *3:* **634–37,** 635 (ill.); *4:* 762; *5:* **185–88,** 185 (ill.)
Ruffner, Viola, *4:* 759
Ruiz (*Amistad* slave owner), *5:* 32, 33–34, 35
Running a Thousand Miles for Freedom, 1: 176
Russell, Bill, *3:* **637–39,** 637 (ill.)
Russert, Tim, *5:* 75
Rustin, Bayard, *3:* **639–42,** 642 (ill.)
Ruth, Babe, *1:* 2

S

Sacramento Kings, *3:* 639
Saint Domingue, *4:* 718–21, 742–43
Sajak, Pat, *2:* 306
Sampras, Pete, *5:* 234
Sampson, Edith, *4:* **647–49,** 647 (ill.); *5:* 134
Sampson, Rufus, *4:* 648
San Francisco 49ers, *5:* 209
Sanchez, Sonia, *3:* 609; *4:* **649–52,** 651 (ill.)
Sandburg, Carl, *4:* 791
Sandler, Stanley, *5:* 230
Sanford, John, *4:* 652, 653
Saperstein, Abe, *2:* 320, 321

Sarbanes, Paul, *5:* 152
Sargent, John Singer, *4:* 698
Sartre, Jean-Paul, *4:* 803
Satchmo. *See* Armstrong, Louis
Saturday Night Live, 3: 552, 553; *5:* 179
Sawamatsu, Naoko, *5:* 235
Scat singing, *1:* 21, 112; *2:* 244; *5:* 77
Schiffer, Claudia, *5:* 15
Schmeling, Max, *3:* 480
Schomberg Center for Research, *5:* 168
School Daze, 3: 470
School dropout program, *2:* 251
Schroeder, Joyce Tanac, *5:* 55
Schwarzenegger, Arnold, *5:* 131 (ill.)
Schwarzkopf, Norman, *3:* 586
Scobee, Dick, *5:* 163
Scobee, June, *5:* 163
Scott, Dred, *4:* **652–54,** 653 (ill.)
Scott, Gloria, *4:* **654–57,** 655 (ill.)
Scott, Oz, *4:* 663–64
Scott, Will Braxton, *4:* 656
Seale, Bobby, *1:* 120, 144; *4:* **657–59,** 658 (ill.)
Seals, Frank, *4:* 756
Seattle Supersonics, *3:* 639
Seeger, Charles, *1:* 175
Seeger, Pete, *1:* 175
Seeger, Ruth, *1:* 175
Segal, George, *4:* 762
Seinfeld, Jerry, *5:* 14, 64
Sengbe Pieh, *5:* 32
Serbia, *5:* 18
Sesame Street, 5: 25
Sewing machines, *3:* 538
Sexual harassment, *2:* 344, 346
Shabazz, Attalah, *3:* 462; *4:* **659–61,** 660 (ill.)
Shabazz, Betty, *4:* 660; *5:* 73, **189–96,** 189 (ill.), 194 (ill.)
Shabazz, Qubilah, *5:* 73, 194
Shaker, Ted, *5:* 111
Shakur, Afeni, *5:* 199, 200, 202, 204

Shakur, Lumumba Abdul, *5:* 199
Shakur, Tupac, *5:* **197–205,** 197 (ill.), 198 (ill.), 222
Shange, Ntozake, *4:* **662–64,** 663 (ill.)
Shapiro, Robert, *5:* 211, 211 (ill.), 213
Sharpton, Al, *4:* **664–67,** 666 (ill.)
Shaw, George Bernard, *4:* 714
Shaw, Robert Gould, *4:* 762–63
Shepard, Alan B., *5:* 160
She's Gotta Have It, 3: 469
Shocklee, Hank, *3:* 600
Shore, Dinah, *2:* 305
Shriver, Pam, *5:* 237
Sierra Leone, *5:* 32, 37, 38, 39
Sifford, Charles, *5:* 245
"Silent March," *3:* 484
Simmons, Althea T. L., *4:* **667–70,** 668 (ill.)
Simpson, Carole, *4:* **670–72,** 671 (ill.)
Simpson, Nicole Brown, *5:* 207, 210, 212, 214
Simpson, O. J., *5:* 182, **207–16,** 207 (ill.), 209 (ill.), 211 (ill.), 244
Sims, Naomi, *4:* **672–74,** 673 (ill.)
Sims, Sandman, *2:* 349, 351
Singleton, John, *4:* **674–77,** 676 (ill.); *5:* 197
Siouxie and the Banshees, *2:* 374
Sir John's Trio, *1:* 59
Sit-ins, *1:* 46, 69; *2:* 223, 237
60 Minutes, 1: 78, 79, 163
Skelton, Red, *4:* 722
Slave insurrections, *4:* 733–36, 742–44
Slavery, *1:* 40, 63, 124, 166, 176, 204–6, 213; *2:* 225, 302–3, 317, 379, 419; *3:* 441, 504, 507–9, 518, 610, 621; *4:* 652–54, 718–21, 730–33, 733–36, 742–44; *5:* 36–37, 62, 75, 166–67
Sleeping Car Porters Union, *3:* 640

Sly & the Family Stone, *2:* 378; *5:* 220, 223
Slyde, Jimmy, *2:* 351
Smalls, Biggie, *5:* 201
Smith, Arthur Lee, Jr. *See* Asante, Molefi Kete
Smith, Bessie, *1:* 21; *4:* **677–80,** 679 (ill.), 789
Smith, Clara, *4:* 678
Smith, Dean, *5:* 112 (ill.)
Smith, Eula Mae, *4:* 692
Smith, Joe, *4:* 679
Smith, Lewis C., *5:* 228
Smith, Mamie, *4:* 678
Smith, Mike, *5:* 163
Smith, Trixie, *4:* 678
Snipes, Wesley, *4:* **680–83,** 681 (ill.); *5:* 14
Snoop Doggy Dogg, *5:* 201, 203
Song of Solomon, 3: 542, 543
Songs of Jamaica, 3: 518
Songs to a Phantom Nightingale, 3: 485
Soul City, *3:* 522
Soul on Ice, 1: 143
Soul Train, 1: 168, 169, 170
Soul Train Records, *1:* 170
"Soulja's Story," *5:* 197, 200
The Souls of Black Folk, 1: 211
South of Freedom, 3: 633
Southern Christian Leadership Conference (SCLC), *1:* 5, 19, 58, 69; *2:* 307, 380; *3:* 457, 458, 482; *4:* 665; *5:* 249, 250
Soviet Union, *3:* 623
Space Jam, 5: 142
Spector, Phil, *5:* 219
Spelling, Aaron, *1:* 62; *5:* 14
Spelman College, *1:* 150, 153, 173; *5:* 42
Spielberg, Steven, *4:* 675; *5:* 39
Spingarn Medal, *1:* 135; *2:* 236, 303, 405; *3:* 575
Spirlea, Irena, *5:* 237
Spivey, Victoria, *4:* 757
Spurlock, Charles T., *4:* 649
Spurlock, Oliver, *4:* 649
Sputnik, 5: 160

Stafford, Shaun, *5:* 235
Stallings, George A., Jr., *4:* **683–86,** 683 (ill.)
Stanford University, *5:* 242
Stapleton, Jean, *2:* 280
"State of Black America," *2:* 391
States' Laws on Race and Color, 3: 556
Steele, Shelby, *4:* **686–89,** 687 (ill.)
Steinbeck, John, *5:* 97
Steinem, Gloria, *1:* 85; *3:* 444, 449
Stepping into Tomorrow, 3: 462
Stewart, Rod, *5:* 222
Still, William Grant, *4:* **689–91,** 689 (ill.)
Sting, *3:* 497
Stir Crazy, 3: 583
Stone, Sharon, *5:* 14
Storytelling, *1:* 31; *3:* 627, 628
Stout, Charles Otis, *4:* 691–92, 693
Stout, Juanita Kidd, *4:* **691–93,** 692 (ill.)
Stowe, Harriet Beecher, *4:* 729, 802
"Strange Fruit," *2:* 353
Street Stories, 1: 80
Strone, Dan, *5:* 64
Student Nonviolent Coordinating Committee (SNCC), *1:* 45, 46, 69, 91, 92, 118, 119, 182; *2:* 272, 291, 307; *3:* 458; *5:* 254
Styron, William, *4:* 736
Sudan, *5:* 37, 75
Sudarkasa, Niara, *4:* **693–96,** 695 (ill.)
Suffrage, *1:* 206
Sula, 3: 542
Supremes, *3:* 630, 631
Survivor, 1: 111
Susan Smith McKinney-Steward Medical Society, *2:* 298

T

Taft, William Howard, *2:* 341

"Take My Hand, Precious Lord," *1:* 203
Talking to Myself, 1: 29
Talking Tree, 1: 30
Tan magazine, *2:* 408
Taney, Roger B., *4:* 653; *5:* 35
Tanner, Henry Ossawa, *4:* **696–99,** 698 (ill.)
Tappan, Lewis, *5:* 34
Tar Baby, 3: 543
Tatum, Goose, *2:* 320
Tauziat, Natalie, *5:* 235
Taylor, Clarice, *5:* 28
Taylor, Mildred, *4:* **699–702,** 701 (ill.)
Taylor, Russell L., *4:* 707
Taylor, Susan, *4:* **702–4,** 703 (ill.)
Taylor, Susie Baker King, *4:* **704–7,** 706 (ill.)
Técora, *5:* 32, 33
Teddy Hill Orchestra, *2:* 269
Temple, Edward, *5:* 186–87
Temple of Islam, *3:* 550
Tennis Hall of Fame, *1:* 26
Tereshkova, Valentina, *5:* 160
Terminator X, *3:* 600
Terrell, Jean, *3:* 631
Terrell, Mary Church, *4:* **707–9,** 708 (ill.)
Terrell, Robert, *4:* 709
Terry, Roger, *5:* 229
Texas Medley Quartette, *2:* 423
That Nigger's Crazy, 3: 598
Thicke, Alan, *2:* 305
Thomas, Beulah Belle, *4:* 755
Thomas, Bigger, *4:* 802
Thomas, Clarence, *1:* 81; *2:* 344, 345, 356; *4:* **710–13,** 712 (ill.); *5:* 153
Thomas, George, *4:* 756, 757
Thomas, Hersal, *4:* 756, 757
Thomas, Isiah, *1:* 67
"Three O'Clock Blues," *3:* 452
Thriller, 2: 416, 418
The Today Show, 2: 294, 295; *3:* 444
Tommy Boy Records, *3:* 606
Tone-Loc, *2:* 314

The Tonight Show, *1:* 171; *3:* 498
Toomer, Jean, *4:* **713–16,** 714 (ill.)
Torme, Mel, *5:* 77, 78
Torrence, Jackie, *4:* **716–18,** 717 (ill.)
Tosca, *3:* 591
Totem Press, *1:* 38
Toussaint, François-Dominique, *4:* 718
Toussaint-Louverture, *4:* **718–21,** 719 (ill.)
Towns, Edolphus, *4:* 667
Townsend, Robert, *4:* **721–24,** 724 (ill.), 770; *5:* 15
Trading Places, *3:* 554
Travis, Joseph, *4:* 735
Treadwell, George, *4:* 741
Trotter, William Monroe, *4:* **724–27,** 726 (ill.)
Trouble in the Mind, *1:* 136
Truman, Harry S, *1:* 106; *3:* 613; *4:* 648; *5:* 226, 230
Truth, Sojourner, *1:* 181; *4:* **727–30,** 728 (ill.)
Tubman, Harriet, *1:* 181; *4:* **730–33,** 732 (ill.)
Tubman, John, *4:* 731–32
Tucker, C. DeLores, *5:* 204
Tupac Amaru, *5:* 200
Turner, Ike, *5:* 217, 218, 220, 223
Turner, Mabel G., *4:* 692
Turner, Nat, *4:* **733–36,** 734 (ill.)
Turner, Tina, *5:* **217–24,** 217 (ill.), 221 (ill.)
Tuskegee Airmen, *4:* 804; *5:* **225–32,** 225 (ill.), 228 (ill.)
Tuskegee Institute, *1:* 126, 184, 185; *2:* 232; *4:* 758, 759–61
Tuskegee Machine, *1:* 211
"Tutti Frutti," *3:* 478
Tutu, *1:* 186
Tutu, Desmond, *5:* 253
2 Live Crew, *2:* 263
Tyler, John, *5:* 38
Tyson, Cicely, *2:* 255
Tyson, Mike, *2:* 273, 274, 275

U

U.S. Air Force, *2:* 325, 326, 327; *5:* 21
U.S. Amateurs, *5:* 242
U.S. House Committee on Education and Labor, *3:* 585
U.S. House Judiciary Committee, *2:* 424, 426; *5:* 135
U.S. House Un-American Activities Committee, *3:* 620; *4:* 804
U.S. Information Agency (USIA), *3:* 634
U.S. Junior Amateurs, *5:* 239, 241
U.S. Open Championship, *1:* 27; *5:* 237
U.S. Postal Service, *1:* 160; *5:* 6
U.S. Senate Judiciary Committee, *2:* 344, 345
U.S. State Department, *5:* 148–50
U.S. Supreme Court, *2:* 344; *3:* 504, 506, 507
"Uncle Remus" stories, *4:* 718
Uncle Tom's Children, *4:* 802
Underground Railroad, *4:* 730, 732–33
"Unforgettable," *1:* 155, 158
Union Missionary Society, *5:* 38
United Christian Youth Movement, *2:* 333
United Church of Christ, *5:* 250
United Nations (UN), *1:* 17, 29, 105, 106; *4:* 648; *5:* 93, 94, 131, 249, 251–52
United Nations Children's Fund, *1:* 56
United Nations Educational, Scientific, and Cultural Organization, *5:* 151
United Negro College Fund (UNCF), *2:* 431
United Negro Improvement Association (UNIA), *2:* 256
United Parcel Service (UPS), *5:* 115, 118
United Service Organization (USO), *1:* 28, 62; *3:* 536; *5:* 14
United States Lawn Tennis Association, *2:* 267

Universal Remnant Church of God, *3:* 478
University of California at Los Angeles (UCLA), *1:* 3, 182
University of Mississippi, *3:* 528, 529
University of North Carolina, *2:* 427–28; *5:* 139–40
University of Southern California (USC), *5:* 208

V

Van Buren, Martin, *5:* 34, 35, 38
Van, Lythi Bich, *5:* 246
Van Peebles, Mario, *4:* 682, **737–39,** 737 (ill.)
Van Wagener, Isaac, *4:* 728
Van Wagener, Maria, *4:* 728
Vance, Courtney B., *5:* 230
Vandross, Luther, *2:* 351
Vantage (theater), *2:* 284
Varèse, Edgard, *4:* 690
Vaudeville, *1:* 192; *2:* 421
Vaughan, Sarah, *1:* 156; *4:* **739–42,** 740 (ill.)
Vegetarianism, *2:* 291
Very Young Poets, 1: 86
Vesey, Denmark, *4:* 735, **742–44**
Vesey, Joseph, *4:* 742
Vicario, Arantxa Sanchez, *5:* 235
Victor, Don, *2:* 279
Vietnam War, *1:* 13; *2:* 393; *3:* 586; *5:* 171
Village Voice, 5: 254
Vogue magazine, *1:* 116; *2:* 397, 398; *3:* 576
A Voice from the South: By a Black Woman from the South, 1: 167
Volunteerism, *2:* 264, 265; *5:* 174
Voter Education Project, *2:* 431
Voters for Choice, *1:* 85
Voting, *2:* 307; *3:* 459

W

Waddles, Charleszetta, *4:* **744–46,** 745 (ill.)
Waddles, Payton, *4:* 746
Wagner Festival, *1:* 101
Waiting to Exhale, 3: 522, 524; *5:* 155, 156, 157, 167
Wake Forest University, *1:* 20
"Walk Against Fear," *3:* 529
Walker, Alice, *2:* 371; *4:* **747–50,** 747 (ill.)
Walker, Armstead, *4:* 753
Walker, C. J., *4:* 751
Walker, Clifford, *4:* 745
Walker, Lelia, *4:* 752
Walker, Leroy, *5:* 186
Walker, Madame C. J., *3:* 490; *4:* **750–52,** 751 (ill.)
Walker, Maggie L., *4:* **752–55,** 754 (ill.)
Wallace, Christopher, *5:* 203
Wallace, Matt, *4:* 756
Wallace, Mike, *1:* 79
Wallace, Sippie, *4:* **755–58,** 756 (ill.)
War Resisters League, *3:* 641
Warner, Malcolm-Jamal, *5:* 43, 230
Warwick, Dee Dee, *2:* 360
Warwick, Dionne, *2:* 360, 361
Washington, Booker T., *1:* 126, 211; *2:* 256; *4:* 724, 725–26, **758–61,** 759 (ill.), 781; *5:* 91
Washington Bullets, *1:* 66
Washington, D.C., *3:* 447, 448; *5:* 3, 9–12
Washington, Denzel, *4:* **761–63,** 762 (ill.)
Washington, George, *4:* 773; *5:* 4, 150
Washington Post, 3: 614
Washington Urban League, *2:* 390
Watergate scandal, *2:* 426; *5:* 135
Waters, Maxine, *5:* 21
Waters, Muddy, *1:* 59; *5:* 223
Watson, Carolyn, *5:* 253
Wattleton, Faye, *4:* **763–66,** 765 (ill.)
Watts, André, *4:* **766–68,** 767 (ill.)
Watts, J. C., Jr., *5:* 182

Wayans, Keenan Ivory, *4:* **769–71,** 770 (ill.); *5:* 144
"We Are the World," *1:* 56; *2:* 418
Webb, Chick, *2:* 243; *5:* 77
Webster, Ben, *5:* 24
Welch, Leonard, *5:* 156
Western Association of Writers, *1:* 213
Westhead, Paul, *2:* 401
Westside Preparatory School, *1:* 162
What the Wine Sellers Buy, 3: 532
Wheatley, John, *4:* 772, 773
Wheatley, Phillis, *4:* **771–73,** 772 (ill.)
Whistler, James McNeill, *4:* 698
White Citizens Council, *2:* 236
Whitefield, George, *4:* 772
Whitehead, John C., *5:* 151
"The Wife of His Youth, and Other Stories of the Color Line," *1:* 134
Wigs, *4:* 673–74
Wilberforce University, *1:* 184
Wild Seed, 1: 111
Wilder, L. Douglas, *1:* 97; *4:* **773–76,** 774 (ill.); *5:* 18
Wilkins, Roger, *4:* 688
Wilkins, Roy, *4:* 668, **776–79,** 777 (ill.), 807
Williams, Alice Faye, *5:* 199
Williams, Clarence, *4:* 678
Williams, Daniel Hale, *4:* **779–82,** 780 (ill.)
Williams, Jayson, *5:* 129
Williams, John A., *4:* **782–84,** 783 (ill.)
Williams, Maggie, *5:* 118
Williams, Montel, *4:* **784–87,** 785 (ill.)
Williams, Paulette, *4:* 662
Williams, Richard, *5:* 234
Williams, Robert, *5:* 230
Williams, Serena, *5:* 234, 235, 237, 238
Williams, Sherley Anne, *4:* **787–89,** 788 (ill.)
Williams, Venus, *5:* **233–38,** 233 (ill.), 236 (ill.)
Williams, Walter, *4:* 688
Willke, John, *4:* 765
Wilson, August, *4:* **790–92,** 790 (ill.)
Wilson, Harriet E., *2:* 262
Wilson, Martin, *4:* 688
Wilson, Mary, *3:* 630
Wilson, Nancy, *2:* 305
Wilson, Woodrow, *4:* 726–27
Wimbledon, *2:* 268
Winfrey, Oprah, *4:* 770, **792–95,** 794 (ill.); *5:* 15
Witter Bynner Poetry Contest, *1:* 179
The Wiz, 3: 631
Wofford, Chloe Anthony. *See* Morrison, Toni
The Women of Brewster Place, 3: 557, 558
Women's Bureau, *5:* 116
Women's Committee of the Baltimore Art Museum, *1:* 197
Women's Medical College of Pennsylvania, *2:* 298
Women's Political Council, *3:* 579
Women's Tennis Association (WTA), *5:* 233, 234, 235, 237
Wonder, Stevie, *2:* 286; *4:* **795–98,** 797 (ill.); *5:* 222
Wonderful Hair Grower, *3:* 491
Woodard, Lynette, *2:* 322
Woods, Earl, *5:* 240, 241, 246
Woods, Eldrick "Tiger," *5:* **239–47,** 239 (ill.), 241 (ill.), 243 (ill.)
Woodson, Carter G., *4:* **798–800,** 799 (ill.)
Woodward, Nathan, *5:* 28
World Boxing Association, *1:* 13
World Federation of African People, *3:* 538
World Town Hall Seminar, *4:* 648
World War I, *2:* 259
World War II, *1:* 183; *2:* 358; *5:* 225, 226

World's Student Christian Federation, *1:* 195
Worthy, William, *4:* 649
Wright, Orville, *1:* 213
Wright, Richard, *1:* 36; *2:* 233; *4:* 716, 788, 790, **800–803,** 802 (ill.); *5:* 68
Wright, Syreeta, *4:* 797

Y

Yancy, Marvin, *1:* 156, 157
Yeakey, Lamont H., *4:* 736
Yellow Back Radio Broke-Down, *3:* 617
Young, Andrew, *5:* **249–55,** 249 (ill.), 252 (ill.)
Young, Coleman, *4:* **803–6,** 805 (ill.); *5:* 227
Young Communist League, *3:* 640
Young Ideas, *5:* 252
Young, Jean, *5:* 252 (ill.), 253
Young, Jimmy, *5:* 84
Young Poet's Primer, *1:* 86
Young, Whitney M., Jr., *4:* **806–8,** 807 (ill.)
Young Women's Christian Association (YWCA), *1:* 193, 194
Yugen, *1:* 38
Yugoslavia, *5:* 18

Z

Zane, Arnie, *2:* 412
Zea-Daly, Errol, *4:* 701
Zeely, *2:* 310

trans to JR 8/09

$52.00

DATE			

For Reference

Not to be taken from this room

RECEIVED MAR 1 3 2002

SOUTH HUNTINGTON
PUBLIC LIBRARY
2 MELVILLE ROAD
HUNTINGTON STATION, N.Y.

BAKER & TAYLOR